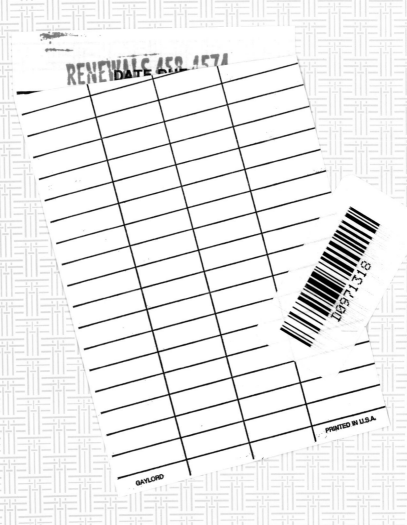

# Creating
# Do-It-Yourself
# Customers

## *How Great Customer Experiences*
## *Build Great Companies*

Peter C. Honebein

Roy F. Cammarano

Australia · Brazil · Canada · Mexico · Singapore · Spain · United Kingdom · United States

**THOMSON**
TM

Creating Do-It-Yourself Customers: How Great Customer Experiences
Build Great Companies

Peter C. Honebein and Roy F. Cammarano

Library of Congress Cataloging in Publication Number is available. See page 266 for details.

For more information about our products, contact us at:

Thomson Learning
Academic Resource
Center 1-800-423-0563

**Thomson Higher Education**
5191 Natorp Boulevard
Mason, Ohio 45040
USA

For Cassman and Our Families

# CONTENTS

# PREFACE

Customer performance is the sum of customer actions before, during, and after a sale that unlock value embedded in goods and services. Customers who can quickly find a product in a grocery store save time. Those who can use airline self-check-in systems avoid long lines and time-wasting delays, as well as reduce the need for airline agents. Those who can use all of the features found in new cell phones get the full value offered by the product. In these situations customers want to perform expertly. They want to do things themselves. Yet they are often thwarted by the products companies design, the services companies provide, and the policies companies endorse.

Technology plays a key role in enhancing customer performance, such as keyless ignition in BMW cars and direct-debit smart cards for transportation and convenience store purchases. However, we still see too much value lost due to the inability of customers to leverage the value embedded in the goods and services companies provide. Key customer outcomes, such as utility, time, accuracy, savings, and happiness, remain wasted and unused when customers don't perform well. Purchases take longer than expected, expectations aren't fully met, satisfaction decreases, and features remain idle—and that's just from the customer's perspective. Poor customer performance means that companies must absorb the costs of accommodating these customers, impacting the profitability of the company.

In today's marketplace *customer experiences* are at the forefront of how companies are framing their competitive advantage. Experiences have come to represent a company's brand. Through these experiences, more and more companies are shifting consumption-related tasks to customers through a scheme known as *coproduction*.

Simply stated, coproduction defines the work the customer does to maximize the value embedded in goods and services. One kind of coproduction, self-service, is easily seen in today's markets, where customers are doing more and more of the work that used to be done by employees. Stores such as Home Depot have self-checkout, while Southwest Airlines offers self-check-in. Dell Computer provides web-enabled tools that allow customers to configure their own systems. Banks, such as Bank of America, now ask customers to pay bills and manage their accounts online.

In a survey of 176 executives from large North American companies, Forrester Research asked executives about their outlook on customer experience practices. These executives see customers doing more work and plan to shift many of their customer interactions to self-service. The web, email, phone, and kiosk will see the largest increases. However, the executives realize that a key driver for this to happen is a fluid, usable coproduction experience.[1]

Obviously, there is a paradigm shift underway. In the past, customers expected companies to do a lot of the work for them. Now, companies are expecting customers to do more of the work themselves—and customers are responding enthusiastically.

Since customers determine the value of goods and services through usage and the service levels provided by the company, sophisticated customers have a significant advantage over unsophisticated customers. Sophisticated customers can perform more consumption-related tasks in a way that reduces company costs and achieves greater value. Companies who design experiences using human performance improvement strategies have a competitive advantage over companies that don't. These activities create do-it-yourself customers.

The next frontier for organizational efficiency is the pursuit of customer value driven by customer behavior. For the past 30 years, we have seen organizations improve their efficiency with strategies that aim to improve internal operations, such as total quality management, Six Sigma, and reengineering. The age of outward-looking, customer-focused strategies is upon us. Noted researchers and business thinkers are leading this paradigm shift with calls for greater customer coproduction/codesign/cocreation, customer experiences, treating customers like employees, and recognizing the long-term profit potential (otherwise known as *equity*) sophisticated customers offer organizations. To realize this vision, companies need rationale, know-how, and guidance to design experiences that maximize customer performance. This results in the generation of greater customer value, improved customer relationships, and the increase of customer lifetime value.[2]

## Aim of the Book

This book is for anyone who serves customers, whether those customers are individual consumers or businesses. If you lead the vision to create truly outstanding customer experiences, or are involved in evaluating, designing, delivering, and managing customer experiences, this book is especially for you.

The aim of this book is to trigger in you "ah-ha!" experiences, whereby new ideas or principles associated with designing *coproduction experiences* for your customers *in your business* become evident. To drive an "ah-ha!" reaction, we provide you with multiple ways to examine customer experiences, customer performance, and customer value.

Whether you face a problem or an opportunity in how your business delivers results-oriented customer experiences, this book can help. Using the approaches discussed in the book, you will be able to:

1. Determine the causes of poor customer performance
2. Identify, understand, and change situations where poor coproduction experiences are denying customers (and companies) the outcomes they value, such as utility, time, accuracy, savings, and happiness
3. Evaluate the need for enhanced coproduction experiences
4. Recognize situations where technological or human innovation can change the dynamics of customer involvement with a product or service
5. Assess the effectiveness of different types of coproduction experiences
6. Design or redesign a coproduction experience such that it enhances customer performance

The result? Enhanced customer experiences that enable customers to do more work, reduce costs, and unlock greater value.

## Foundations

The content for this book comes from three solid foundations: leadership, expertise, and research. As chief executives for INC. 500 and public companies, we have led organizations in the adoption of strategies that shift more work to customers. Through our successes and missteps, we clearly understand the strategic alignment associated with such initiatives and what resources must be allocated to ensure their success.

As consultants to companies, we have provided the expertise that enable companies to deliver goods and services that maximize customer performance. We have contributed to the design of some of the most technically advanced products the world has seen. We have guided companies on standardizing the way they deliver services to customers. We have created a variety of customer education solutions for improving the performance of customers. We have also created human performance systems so that employees in grocery stores, banks, and resorts can provide the support customers need for an enjoyable experience. These experiences provide us the opportunity to put our ideas into practice and learn from their effects on customers.

As researchers, we strive to ground our ideas in the work many people have done before us. This book brings together an extensive knowledge base of empirical, conceptual, and anecdotal ideas from researchers, customers, and companies worldwide. Furthermore, in preparation of this book we collected hundreds of customer stories through a method known as Critical Incident Technique. Using this technique, customers write stories describing how companies have helped or hindered their performance as they pursued various consumption goals. We have included several of these stories to help illustrate and validate the ideas we discuss in the book.

## Book Structure

This book begins with a call for action and ends with an action plan.

Chapter 1, *Rise of the Sophisticated Customer*, introduces you to the heart of the paradigm shift. Sophisticated customers, coproduction, and customer perceptions of value are driving forces for embracing customers who want to do more work themselves. This chapter looks at the trends that drive the need for do-it-yourself customers, better coproduction experiences, and what it means to be a sophisticated customer.

Chapter 2, *A New Paradigm for Customer Experiences*, introduces our view of how companies should think about customer experiences. Here we introduce the Coproduction Experience Model, which is based upon four specific performance factors—*vision, access, incentive*, and *expertise*. The model and its associated Coproduction Experience Process guide you in analyzing and designing coproduction experiences.

Chapter 3, *The Roots of Coproduction Experience Design*, explains the psychological principles behind the Coproduction Experience Model. Think of this chapter as an informal lunchtime lecture that reactivates the things you already know about people and their minds. We encourage you to pay close attention to our discussion of how these universal theories have converged to form strong, prescriptive models for customer performance. From the art of persuasion to consumer behavior, this chapter describes the psychological foundations that support the ideas found elsewhere in the book.

Chapter 4, *Discovering Where Value Hides*, is the starting point for determining the adequacy of your existing or planned coproduction experiences. Through a process we call *value mining*, you analyze the experiences, goals, tasks, and actions of customers. The results of the analysis identify where value hides. Then, using the Coproduction Experience Model, you determine whether the enhancement of the coproduction experience is worthwhile.

Chapter 5, *Improving Vision*, explores the first element of the Coproduction Experience Model. Vision means that customers know about the work a company expects of them. The chapter examines how companies can better set the customer's vision for unlocking value. We discuss the power of goals, expectations, plans, and feedback, and provide ideas for how companies can use these concepts to enhance coproduction experiences.

Chapter 6, *Facilitating Access*, explores the second element of the Coproduction Experience Model. Access describes the support structure companies offer customers to ensure customer success. Here we discuss how a hierarchy of policies, processes, people, tools, interfaces, information, and nuances form the foundation of an effective coproduction experience.

Chapter 7, *Structuring Incentives*, explores the third element of the Coproduction Experience Model. Even if customers have the right vision and the right tools, sometimes their motivation to perform effectively can wane. Therefore, companies employ several behaviorist techniques involving rewards and punishment to metaphorically provide customers the *kick-in-the-pants* they need to perform.

Chapter 8, *Enhancing Expertise*, explores the fourth and final element of the Coproduction Experience Model. Here we examine the methods companies use to enhance the expertise of customers, providing them the knowledge and skills they need to perform.

Chapter 9, *Navigating the Pathways of Learning*, discusses how the elements of the Coproduction Experience Model are communicated to customers throughout the marketplace. While you can design very effective coproduction experiences, your designs can easily be thwarted by communication you don't control. Competitors, the media, even your employees can disrupt even the most well-designed plan. We offer six key strategies for how you can better control the uncontrollable, ensuring the success of the coproduction experiences you design.

Chapter 10, *Embracing the Coproduction Revolution*, presents principles for the implementation of coproduction experiences and recommends steps companies can take to make those ideas a reality.

We know our book will help you discover the answers, insights, and ideas that enable you and your company to establish significant competitive advantages. Once read, you'll never look at customer experiences the same way again.

# ACKNOWLEDGMENTS

This book started in the Dallas/Ft. Worth airport at the TGI Friday's American Café in Terminal C. It was February 2004. We were returning home after visiting one of our clients on the east coast. Roy was talking Peter out of his midlife crisis and was wise enough to suggest a solution that didn't involve fast cars or faster women. "We need to write a book," he said. One year later, here we are. Miraculously, Peter's midlife crisis is now cured.

For me (Peter), the ideas behind this book had been fermenting for some time. Roy, as always, is a catalyst for me to achieve my goals and aspirations. Momentum was built when I was cold-called by a French doctoral student, Benoit Aubert, looking for help with his dissertation on customer education. Benoit and I formed a loose collaboration that was subsequently joined by another European academic, Thorsten Hennig-Thurau of the University of Weimar. My collaboration with these two gentlemen was the driving force in digging up research that has now formed the various foundations of this book. Vikas Mittal and Dawn Burton provided early commentary on some of the customer education pieces. Mary Jo Bitner and Steve Vargo provided encouraging suggestions based upon initial public presentations of our ideas.

Ted Mitchell and Judy Strauss of the University of Nevada, Reno, School of Business, graciously invited me to join the faculty as an adjunct professor several years ago, which provided a context for research, thinking, and reflection that went into this book. Several semesters of students in my Marketing Principles classes helped collect the stories that formed one part of our research—thanks! My teaching assistant, Ewa Buchert, is simply awesome. She and fellow MBA student Josh Crags were instrumental in analyzing the results of our research. I also want to thank my students Colin Ard, Jacob Musselman, and Jack Rhodes for their editing help, as well as writing the book's first book reports.

No acknowledgment can be complete without recognizing my good friend and mentor, Tom Duffy of Indiana University. He taught me how to think and eventually encouraged me to join IU's faculty as an adjunct professor, providing yet another context and lens by which to investigate coproduction.

For me (Roy), the initial ideas and inspiration for this book had been moving around in my head and in my heart for more than a decade. The motivation to actually complete it is fairly recent. Peter was the final push to actually take the ideas that we have been discussing and put them into writing (I thank him). My previous experiences working with entrepreneurs, visionaries, and business executives has allowed me to gain unique insights into many industries, businesses, and differing business models.

So many people have contributed so much. Bob Cowan, whose confidence inspired me. Boland Jones, who challenged me with new experiences. Stuart Wheelwright, who is not only a client but also a true friend. My wife Nicole, whose kindness, love, and support nourish and sustain me. My mom and dad for their love, compassion, understanding, and support are my heroes. The many individuals, with whom I have consulted and experimented regarding these ideas and concepts (hopefully for the best), I thank you.

Thanks to customers standing in line and lamenting the harsh reality of a process gone wrong for speaking with us and providing insights. To the frontline service people who often are asked to do their best but are not provided with the best. To the many companies that know they need to do something but are unsure of what and how. We have heard your request, we have felt your pain, and we offer you our solution.

The competitive nature of business, the change in consumer expectations, the utilization of technology, and the reality that service has a new paradigm has brought each of us here. We are focusing our attention on providing the do-it-yourself customers experiences that ensure their satisfaction and loyalty.

When Pete and I decided to write this book, we put in motion the universal law of prosperity. The simple reality is that as soon as you take on an undertaking of this magnitude the universe will provide other equally huge and prosperous opportunities. The decision to combine our insights, ideas, and experiences had been brewing for several years. The desire to provide knowledge, insight, ideas, and solutions for very real and sometimes painful problems is strong for each of us. We have worked hard to ensure that the information we are sharing with you is understandable and, more importantly, useful. Enjoy your journey!

Together, we would like to thank the following people for their efforts during the development of this book. Carl Honebein, former president of Avco Insurance, diligently critiqued and edited each chapter, providing many helpful suggestions regarding the logical structure of the book and chapters.

Susan Blohm, our experiential marketing expert and a former marketing executive with Altria, reviewed our work with her famous purple pen. She contributed the strategy linkages, several stories and examples, and the idea for the process diagrams that begin each chapter. Peter's wife and business partner, Beth Honebein, was held in reserve until the very end, helping arrange various permissions and meticulously proofreading the final composition.

This book would not have been possible without the foresight and vision of Francesca Van Gorp Cooley of the American Marketing Association. We thank her for fast-tracking this project through the AMA organization. Our editor, Steve Momper of Thomson Texere, has been a strong champion for our ideas and guided us in making this book the very best it can be. Thanks also to Elizabeth Lowry, assistant editor at Thomson Texere, who shepherded this book through the production process.

CHAPTER 1

## RISE OF THE SOPHISTICATED CUSTOMER

*To rest in the arms of perfection is the desire of any*
*man intent upon creating excellence.*

—Thomas Mann

T he rise of the sophisticated customer is a call to action for companies
intent on establishing or maintaining their competitive advantage. It
explains why companies and customers alike should strive for designing
experiences that create do-it-yourself customers and maximize customer performance. Sophisticated customers acquire the most value from products and
offer companies the highest profit, the most customer equity, and the greatest
lifetime value.

We begin this chapter by examining the attributes of sophisticated customers and why they are beneficial for business. We then introduce *coproduction*, the partnership customers have with companies in performing tasks
associated with all kinds of goods and services. This partnership reflects a
range of interactions a company can have with a customer. In some situations, customers will be passive consumers, but in others, they will be active,
do-it-yourself participants. Because of this partnership, some companies have
come to think of their customers as employees, and we examine the dimensions of the "customer as employee" paradigm. We conclude the chapter
with a discussion of the foundations for what is necessary to achieve a customer performance culture.

## CUSTOMERS DON'T WANT TO FAIL!

Ever meet a customer who had a burning desire to really screw up? You
know, just intentionally botch a product so completely that it is beyond repair or salvage, wasting every bit of value that could be wasted. From our experience, customers don't relish the thought of buying a brand new BMW
and then purposely running it into a wall. Nor do they get pleasure from microwaving the five-minute popcorn package a whopping 30 minutes to

1

totally scorch the corn kernels. It is not the customers' nature to intentionally run the morning newspaper through their lawnmower or snowblower such that they exchange the value of the morning news for the experience of a tickertape parade.

Customers pay a lot of money for the goods they buy and the services they use. They are investing time to acquire the knowledge and skill that goods and services demand. Society has conditioned customers to try to avoid failure—and customers have come to dislike failure due to its negative and embarrassing consequences. Failure does not feel good. It causes an emotion of cognitive dissonance, that tickle in the brain that triggers the "oops" or "oh, I don't think I'm liking this" feeling. Customers desperately want to avoid this feeling. To do so, they want to perform well, to achieve excellence, and to realize the value they expect from the goods and services they purchase. The cost is too great not to. The importance of customers achieving excellence is critical to the ongoing effort of organizations to create loyal customers.

Success is what customers want! As illustrated by the quote at the start of this chapter, perfection is the ultimate aim of those who pursue excellence. It is in the customers' best interest to perform well, since the value they receive from goods and services is largely dependent on their participation. Customers, not companies, are the ones who generate value. According to Walt Disney:

> "You can dream, create, design, and build the most wonderful place in the world, but it requires people to make the dream a reality."

Customers are the ones who pump the gas (in most states), take digital pictures, make calls on cell phones, and record television programs on TiVo® digital video recorders. They are not idle bystanders. Customers perform a variety of useful actions that enable the value that is contained in goods and services to become unlocked.

Customers are regularly thwarted from achieving the outcomes they so much desire. Through conditioning, customers come to expect certain outcomes and attempt to initiate behaviors to achieve those outcomes. When this doesn't happen, frustration increases and satisfaction declines. For example, we recently upgraded our cell phone. This upgrade required several do-it-yourself activities. Ordering it was quite easy, and two days later it showed up in the mail. The packaging was gorgeous, and when we opened it a poster showing the three steps to success seemingly provided the instructions we needed for success. Step 1 was easy. We charged the battery.

So far, so good. Step 2 directed us to follow the online instructions to upgrade our phone. We entered the information into the form. Error. We tried again. Another error. We abandoned the website and called the optional telephone number. Once we got a live person on the line, we found ourselves being directed to take apart our phone to locate a code number on some teeny-weeny card. We found it, gave them the number, and were then directed back to the website to finish the process. Everything now worked. Step 2 complete.

Step 3 involved setting up voicemail. Again, we followed the instructions on the poster—exactly. No luck. The feedback we received from the automated system didn't have a clue, so back to the support line. The first person we talked with had us change the voicemail access phone number. This resulted in us calling not the voicemail prompt, but a dear old lady who didn't know the first thing about voicemail. Perplexed, our service representative put us on hold—and then she was gone forever. Our call luckily was bounced back into the queue. The second person provided us with a number that worked and now we had voicemail. Before ending the call, we asked the service representative if she could inform someone in product management that the instructions that came with the phone didn't work. Sorry, she had no way of doing that. Was there someone we could talk with to let them know about this problem? No, she didn't know anyone, but we could go to the website and send an email.

Ugh! We, as customers, want to do the right thing! We want to do things ourselves! However, there is often a catch, the unset expectation, the malfunctioning technology, the flawed process, the inadequate incentive, or the piece of knowledge or bit of skill that is missing in order to have things work out just right.

## MODELS OF SOPHISTICATED CUSTOMERS

Sophisticated customers are a means to an end. Through their expertise these customers not only can do more of the work employees do now, but they are often willing to do so! Sophisticated customers can extract more value from goods and services through their ability to use more features to achieve better results. Such outcomes decrease company costs and increase the obligation of the customer to the company. It is a desirable state for a company.

Do sophisticated customers exist? Sure they do. They are the ones who have spent the time and resources to figure things out so that they get the most value from the experience. They are the ones who never seem to have problems with goods and services. They consistently generate revenue and are low maintenance. They can breeze through the supermarket checkout while the rest of us wait in the wrong line. They never are pulled aside at the airport security checkpoint. The clocks on their electronic devices throughout the house do not blink 12:00. They have developed the ability to be consumer experts, the type of customers who have figured out how to extract the most value they can from goods and services.

Most models for sophisticated customers come from the media in the form of experts, luminaries, and fictional representations. For example, Home Depot licenses video content from PBS's *This Old House* series and distributes it on its website. This show features expert craftsmen who demonstrate various home improvement techniques. This provides customers the opportunity to observe some of the most recognized experts in home improvement hanging drywall and fixing leaky plumbing.

Sophisticated customers are coveted by companies who can show the rest of us the epitome of performance and value a product offers. Luminaries such as Tiger Woods demonstrate the excellence one can achieve with Nike golf equipment through winning international golf titles. Glenn Plake, extreme skier extraordinaire, shows us how K2 skis can enable one to jump off snowy cliffs—and survive. We even had 15 minutes of sophisticated customer fame. One of our projects, a computer system that tracked the cleanup of the Exxon Valdez oil spill for the U.S. Coast Guard in 1989, found its way into an advertisement for the programming software we used to develop the system. Sophisticated customers are often the ones who are publicly recognized by the companies who provide them products.

Experts and luminaries are not the only models from which we learn about ideal performance. Flip through your favorite magazine and count the number of advertisements that feature situations where seemingly ordinary people achieve extraordinary results with products. These experts appear to make perfect cookies, brush such that they have whiter teeth, mop and dust their way to immaculate homes, and apply just the right amount of makeup to make a stunning appearance. To help potential customers understand ideal performance more easily, companies develop representational models of very sophisticated customers. Microsoft's Great Moments At Work advertising campaign features fictional sophisticated customers who are achieving world-class outcomes with Microsoft Office System products. In television, print, and web ads associated with the campaign, we are told about employees who are able to take large amounts of data and turn them into something good, or of how a team was able to quickly update a third quarter presentation overnight. By using a parody of a sports celebration Microsoft is conditioning customers to see that by using a Microsoft product they too can win the game and be a hero.

## THE COPRODUCTION REVOLUTION

In the marketplace of the future, companies need customers who are more and more sophisticated. This sophistication enables customers to do more work, reduce costs (for both them and the company), and unlock greater value from goods and services. In this section we introduce you to a new concept describing a type of do-it-yourself relationship companies can have with their customers—*a coproduction relationship.*

The first thing to understand about coproduction is the prefix "co." This means that both company and customer find a balance regarding the level of responsibility each take in how product tasks are completed. An ideal balance results in the customer being able to unlock the greatest amount of value during *production*—when the customer configures, uses, or maintains a good or service. We refer to customers who accept this role as *coproducers*, indicating their willingness to be partners with the companies that serve them.

Coproduction reflects different levels of customer involvement and engagement with a company. As shown in Figure 1.1, companies can design experiences across a range of customer involvement. Some experiences, such as a full service restaurant, find the company doing the majority of the work. As we begin to ask the customer to do more work, experiences will be shared, such as at Build-A-Bear® Workshops. In this experience children and a store employee share different tasks to create a personalized teddy bear. Quickbooks® software has customers do quite a bit of the work, but conveniently handles the messy parts of payroll and taxes. Still other experiences involve work which is performed solely by the customer, such as online banking, self-checkout, and so on.

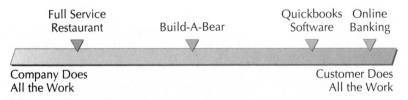

**Figure 1.1**  Coproduction experiences represent a range of customer involvement in doing work associated with goods and services.

Table 1.1   Five Levels of Customer Involvement

| Level | Customer Involvement | Example | Benefits |
|---|---|---|---|
| 1 | Emotional and physical | Using a Blackberry PDA<br>Downloading songs to your iPod<br>Shaving with a Mach 3 razor<br>Putting on perfume<br>Eating food | Primary achievement of functional goals |
| 2 | Self-service | Pumping your own gas<br>Installing your own software | Cost reduction<br>Customized solution<br>Self-determination |
| 3 | Experience participation | Disney World<br>Land Rover Ride&Drive<br>Tony n' Tina's Wedding | Belongingness<br>Self-actualization |
| 4 | Problem solving | Online Ordering<br>Technical support web sites<br>Call centers | Cost reduction |
| 5 | Codesign and cocreation | Brooks Brothers Body Scan<br>Build-A-Bear® Workshops<br>Cooking schools hosted by restaurants<br>Lego® Mindstorms<br>Levi's Original Spin™<br>M&Ms with customized messages | Customized solutions<br>Self-determination |

In most cases, it is the company who decides the level of customer involvement with respect to the level of sophistication that its customers possess. Professor C.K. Prahalad identifies five levels for involving customers, as shown in Table 1.1.[1]

The first level is emotional and physical involvement. At a very basic level, this is when customers use products as directed, such as their Blackberry personal digital assistant to send email or their iPod MP3 player to listen to music.

The second level is self-service. Here companies desire to transfer work from the company to the customer. This involves such tasks as pumping your own gas, serving your own soda, or installing your own software.

The third level is when customers become a full participant in an experience that is designed and managed by a company. This might be a visit to Disney World, or perhaps to a participatory theater. In such theaters customers become involved as participants in a murder mystery or as guests at Tony n' Tina's Wedding.

The fourth level provides customers access to internal company systems and information. Here customers themselves can process transactions and find answers to their questions. This may involve electronic systems, such as the technical support area on Cisco Systems' website, or through more traditional systems such as call centers.

The fifth level involves customers in a partnership that results in the codesign and coproduction of goods and services. Build-A-Bear® Workshops enable customers to create their own custom teddy bears. M&M's has a service that enables customers to imprint custom messages on M&M candies. Brooks Brothers is using a body scan technology that measures the customer's body and, after three weeks, delivers a suit that has a perfect fit.[2]

## Benefits of the Revolution

As customers and companies strengthen their coproduction partnerships and customer sophistication increases, benefits begin to emerge. For instance, in levels two and four, companies can realize significant cost savings by shifting work to customers, which allows companies to reduce or redirect the human resources who used to perform that task. In 2004, airlines estimated they saved $3.52 on each ticket by having customers book the ticket online themselves. Self-check-in by customers saves about $2.70. Now we find airlines charging $5 to $10 to have one of their agents book the ticket for you by phone.[3]

Consider also the shifting of work in gas stations over the past 35 years. First there was full service, where an attendant pumped the gas and collected the money. Then there was the combination of full and self-service (with self-service having the reward of a lower price), which encouraged customers to pump the gas themselves, with the attendant still showing up to collect the money. Next full service disappeared and the attendant retreated to the booth, requiring customers to pump the gas and go to a central place to pay. Now, customers pump their own gas, pay at the pump, and don't require any attendant interaction at all. In fact, some stations, using CardLock, are completely automated, requiring no employee oversight whatsoever. This shift has had a dramatic effect on the cost of labor. According to the Bureau of Labor Statistics, the number of gas station attendants declined, dropping from 308,000 in 1988 to 140,000 in 2000.[4] This decline occurred even though in the United States the number of highway vehicles increased by 12 million, the number of vehicle miles traveled increased by

500 million, and the consumption of oil for transportation uses increased by 3 million barrels per day.[5]

Another benefit that coproduction offers, as illustrated in most of the levels, is the satisfaction that comes from self-determination. After all, if a customer is not the speediest in performing a task, to whom is he or she going to complain? When the customer is in control, it feels good. John Bateson's research in the mid-1980's found that in services customers want to reduce the time the service takes and have a strong desire to control the delivery of the service.[6] Consistent with these findings is a more recent study conducted by IDC, an international research company, for NCR Corporation regarding self-checkout systems. Their findings show that customers value shorter queues, speed, greater control in checking themselves out, the privacy that self-checkout affords, and more choices about how to check themselves out.[7]

Self-determination and cost savings are driving many organizations to push more tasks to the customer. Verizon, a cell phone service provider in the United States, is betting that self-service will offer substantial cost savings and provide customers better access to account information. The purpose of its website is to provide account services to its 30 million subscribers. The "dashboard" orientation of the site provides not only a summary of customers' account information, but access to tools that enable customers to review their last six months of billing, determine unused minutes current in their account, look up a number of a person they called, change their account profile, and display charts and graphs that document their usage. The system is on track to book $2 billion in online bill payments in its first year, a critical measure that indicates a reduction in customer support costs and the increase in revenue flow. The data in Table 1.2 illustrates how companies

**Table 1.2  Customer Service Costs Through Different Technologies**

| | Forrester Research Inc., 2002 | Rayport & Jaworski, 2004 |
|---|---|---|
| Telephone | $32.74 | $9.50 |
| Live email | $9.99 | $9.00 |
| Chat | $7.80 | $5.00 |
| Email w/automated assists and macros | NA | $2.50 |
| Message board | $4.57 | NA |
| Web self-service | $1.17 | $0.50 |
| Automated emails | NA | $0.25 |

like Verizon can incur significant savings by shifting work to customers using various types of technologies.[8]

While the above examples focus on benefits associated with services, coproduction experiences offer several benefits for tangible, physical goods. First and foremost is enabling customers to use these products in such a way where they can extract as much value as possible from the product. This might be seen in the number of product features customers can use and the quality of results customers achieve with each of those features. Yet when you involve customers more fully in the codesign and cocreation of products—such as enabling customers to select ring tones and screen images on their cell phones—products have a stronger emotional effect on those customers. The products become personalized, unique to the individual, enabling customers to further differentiate themselves from the rest of the pack. This makes customers feel good.

## Yet the Revolution Is Threatened

A threat to effective coproduction partnerships, of course, is poor customer performance. If companies fail to design experiences that provide the vision, access, incentive, and expertise coproduction tasks require, customer satisfaction and ultimately customer loyalty will suffer. Jupiter Research estimates that 91 percent of customers who have a bad experience on a self-service site won't return. For example, a major financial services provider spent more than $100 million on a web-based system that aimed to shift customers away from using the telephone for various transactions. However, customers found using the website so confusing that they went back to calling the company—not just with product issues, but with issues related to the problems associated with the website.[9]

One of the sadder stories is when Coleco launched its Adam home computer in the early 1980s. Hundreds of customers returned the device because they could not figure out how to use it. Coleco blamed the user manuals—a critical element to enable customers to perform. But, from our perspective, the lack of a coordinated system of vision, access, incentive, and expertise accounted for customers' failure and the ultimate demise of the product line.[10]

We are not advocating that all goods and services require companies to delegate as many tasks to the customer as possible. As mentioned earlier, coproduction experiences are not black-and-white in terms of the work the customer provides. Instead, think of the potential experience as many shades of gray, which reflect the best mixture of company/customer work that establishes a competitive advantage.

There are risks in giving customers too much of a coproduction role, in terms of safety, theft, and desired levels of service. In some cases customers just want to talk to another human being. Over-automation can have a detrimental effect on the relationships companies build with customers. There will always be a market for customers who do not want to do it themselves, or who have become conditioned to the high level of service provided by certain establishments. For instance, when dining at a fine restaurant, customers expect to be served. Once a customer sits down, the server takes care of the rest. A napkin is placed on the lap, the correct silverware and glasses appear at the appointed times, the meal is selected (if one so desires), and every whim is arranged. The only coproduction effort in which the customer is involved is to sit back, relax, and eat. In the near future the last annoying step of what is an otherwise perfect evening, where the customer must dig into the wallet for a credit card and sign the receipt, will disappear as well. The customer's electronic money card will be scanned automatically, with the bill and the tip deducted automatically from the customer's account.

## UNLOCKING CUSTOMER VALUE

The customer's ability to unlock greater value in coproduction experiences is a significant driving force in developing strong customer relationships. In this section we take a step back to examine the nature of value and what it means to unlock it.

Recently, many public places such as shopping malls and airports have seen the installation of automated external defibrillators (AEDs). AEDs save the lives of cardiac arrest victims by electrically jump-starting the heart. When this product sits installed on the wall of a shopping mall, we say that its value is "locked up" because it is not being used. Furthermore, if a heart attack occurs and there is no one who can use the AED effectively, its value still remains locked up, in that it is not saving a life. Unlocking the value in this product, therefore, requires that (1) the product is accessible and (2) someone with the appropriate knowledge and skill can use the device to aid a person in need.

In a government-funded study involving the value of AEDs, researchers compared the effects of training two different groups of "first responders," such as merchants, doormen, and athletic trainers. One group received only CPR training, while the other group received training in both CPR and AED use. The CPR and AED-trained group achieved a survival rate among cardiac arrest victims of 23 percent, whereas the CPR only group's survival rate was 14 percent. The American Heart Association now offers classes that cover both CPR and AED use to increase the likelihood the value in AEDs will be unlocked when needed.[11]

As illustrated in this example, value is the difference between the benefits a product offers and the sacrifices a customer must make to acquire those benefits. Benefits reflect the outcomes associated with the product, such as solving customers' immediate problem or building their esteem. In the case of the AEDs, the benefit of the product is the saving of a life. To achieve such benefits customers must sacrifice something, such as money, time, effort, and psychological and emotional well-being. Customers not only acquire the product, but must invest in training and be prepared to act when the need arises.

The calculation of value has two specific states. Before a product is used customers calculate *customer value*—their expectation of the value the product holds. After using a product, customers calculate *net customer value*—the actual value delivered by the product.

## Customer Value

Customers experience the world individually. Given their culture, socioeconomic status, demographics, lifestyle, and experience, each has their own internal value calculator. This calculator enables them to determine whether the benefits of a product outweigh the sacrifices they make to acquire it. Thus, when comparing the value of one product with an alternative offering, *customer value* reflects an individual customer's perception of which option is the best deal. The customer weighs the benefits and sacrifices of each, then chooses the one that promises to satisfy the customer's need better than the other.

Up to this point, everything about the customer's determination of value regarding a product reflects not the actual outcomes associated with the product, but the *expected* outcomes. As we said earlier, in most cases a product at rest has limited value. A drill that sits on a shelf is a nonperforming asset in that it is not making holes. A computer sitting in a box is not crunching data. An apple stored in a refrigerator is not satisfying hunger. Even a work of art, such as a Van Gogh painting hanging on a wall, has limited value when it is not being observed. Because customers have to pay before they can play, they typically start their relationship with products at a disadvantage, in negative territory, realizing limited value. This is what we mean by value being locked up.

## Net Customer Value

So when does value become unlocked? It becomes unlocked when customers use the product. With the first use of a product, the benefits begin to build up. By the time the product solves the intended need (and if it met the expected benefits), the customer smiles and basks in the glory of another satisfying choice. Thus, each hole the customer drills places a tick mark in the positive column of an internal scorecard. The bite of the apple brings one closer to eliminating hunger. Viewing a real Van Gogh in Amsterdam unleashes a plethora of affective emotions. Thus the *net customer value* customers perceive is the difference between the benefits and the sacrifices they experience. The more positive the experience, the greater the customer's warm, fuzzy feeling of happiness.

However, there are many products where customers are not receiving the value to which they are entitled. A study by Ursula Hansen and Thorsten Hennig-Thurau revealed this phenomenon. The researchers surveyed shoppers in a German mall, asking questions about the customers' ability to use products they own. Sixty-five percent of video camera owners reported that they were unable to use a large proportion of features, estimating that they could not perform 26 percent of functions available in the product. Similarly, 92 percent of personal computer owners could not use all features, estimating that they could not perform 45 percent of functions available in the product.[12]

Such limited usage of product features in some respects hurts customers because they are not getting their money's worth. It also hurts the company who provides the product because customers may:

- Become dissatisfied with the performance of the product and defect to a competing solution, ending the customers' lifetime value to the company.
- Not fully utilize products that provide ongoing revenue. For example, someone who does not know how to use a razor effectively will likely buy fewer razor blades. Similarly, customers not familiar with their computers will buy fewer add-ons.
- Use products incorrectly, damaging the product and potentially causing a safety risk.
- Share negative feedback with other customers, ruining the reputation of the product.

Just as children need someone of greater skill to guide their development and capabilities, so do customers. It is a competitive advantage if companies take the leadership role in helping customers unlock the value in goods and services. In some cases such activities can save lives. But they can also encourage loyalty to a company's goods and services.

## TREATING CUSTOMERS AS EMPLOYEES

A novel concept in achieving desirable outcomes associated with coproduction and the unlocking of value is to treat customers as employees. Several researchers have been exploring this concept since 1986, and more recently the best-selling book *The Value-Profit Chain* devoted an entire chapter to the concept.[13]

In treating customers as employees, companies expect numerous outcomes:

- Customers experience greater quality and value
- Customers are more satisfied with goods or services
- Customers are more loyal to the company and its goods and services
- Customers are more willing to provide more constructive feedback to employees and the company
- Customers are more compatible with employees, other customers, and services: In other words, customers are more willing to "play nice"
- Customers are more involved with the company providing the service

As expected, the model for treating customers as employees follows a typical organizational process in terms of recruitment, job description, training, and rewards for a job well done. Ideally, companies want to recruit customers who have a level of sophistication that guarantees performance. A car dealer, for example, wants to recruit customers who possess a driver's license. Business-to-business companies typically want to recruit other businesses that have certain operating characteristics, such as the number of employees or the dollar value of sales.

For job description, the researchers found that jobs for customers are divided into three key categories. First, there are jobs that require customers to help themselves. This might be self-administering pain medication or preparing a custom hamburger at a Fuddruckers restaurant. Second, there are jobs that involve helping others. In childcare facilities, older children are often asked to "buddy up" with a younger child to provide oversight of the younger child's activities. Similarly, assisted living homes have residents that orient the new arrivals. Third, there are jobs that have customers promote the company. These customers are known as *brand ambassadors*. Apartment complexes, for example, encourage existing residents to recruit new residents and offer rewards for referrals.

Once customers are recruited and a job description is in place, the next task is training. Through booklets, videos, instructor-led courses, interactive kiosks, and experiential activities, companies take the leadership role in ensuring customers have the skills to perform. For budding home improvement customers, Home Depot offers clinics, handouts, and web-based interactive tutorials to learn key home improvement techniques. Purchasers of a new Sprint® cell phone are invited to attend a training class to learn how to use all the bells and whistles packed into the palm-sized device.

When customers perform as expected, companies should reward them. Customers in the United States have been conditioned to shift more of their payments to credit cards because of a simple reward called the airline mile. Companies can promote their most frequent fliers, as Delta Airlines does, into different silver, gold, and platinum levels of its SkyMiles loyalty program. They can upgrade customers to a better class of service, such as to the Concierge Floor of the hotel where these special guests are provided a complimentary morning breakfast and happy hour cocktails. They can provide coupons, rebates, and cash-back incentives. More simply, they can thank the customer, remember them on their birthday, or provide a small gift from time to time. These rewards aren't a replacement for bad or inconsistent service. Instead, customer rewards assist in the retention of customers by recognizing strong performance, increasing the obligation customers feel toward the company. Thus, when customers make their next purchase decision the rewards program holds their intellectual attention and drives additional purchases. If a reward program fails to do this it is a cost that does not have a benefit.

By treating customers as employees, companies can create a cadre of *brand ambassadors* whose ultimate role is to recruit other customers. After all, the word of another customer outweighs the word of virtually anyone else when it comes to driving more customers to your door. So how do you create these customer "employees"? By using the same steps you use to enable your employees to perform. As shown in Table 1.3, you need to first recruit the right customers who have the greatest likelihood of success. Then, you orient and train them so they know what to do and can experience initial success with your products and services. When they act appropriately, you recognize and reward, using the powerful effects of feedback to ensure the

**Table 1.3    Six Steps for Treating Customers as Employees**

| Step | Description |
| --- | --- |
| 1. Recruit | Select customers based on compatibility with a job description, which reflects the competence and resources they must possess to achieve success with your goods and services. |
| 2. Orient | Ensure customers know about the mission, culture, values, quality, purpose, and policies of the company, and how the company does business. Furthermore, orientation provides customers with knowledge of the full range of goods and services offered by the company. |
| 3. Train | Teach customers the skills they need to achieve success with goods and services. This includes support structures that supplement the training in real-world contexts. |
| 4. Recognize | Personally or publicly let customers know when they are performing to expectations. |
| 5. Reward | Provide tangible incentives when customers achieve specific goals. |
| 6. Retain | Have a program that salvages defections, and for those who do defect, an exit interview process to gather ideas for retaining other customers in the future. |

right behaviors stick. Finally, if they threaten to defect, you have strategies in place to retain them.

## Firing Customers

Of course, this process would not be complete without the option of firing customers. While a hotly debated topic, firing customers is useful in many contexts. Customers who are violent, abusive, or otherwise rude and unreasonable must be fired. Airlines, for example, maintain "cannot fly" lists of customers who have proved themselves unworthy of air travel. Herb Kelleher, founder of Southwest Airlines, achieved some notoriety as a no-nonsense CEO who gave customers the boot when they got out of line. Restaurants, to comply with health code requirements, can fire customers through the *No Shirt, No Shoes, No Service* policy. Customers who do not pay their bills, engage in fraudulent behavior, or have one too many run-ins with law enforcement are frequent targets for elimination, such as being denied auto insurance.

Customers sometimes just don't have what it takes to continue being one of your customers. For instance, at Best Buy, as many as 100 million of its 500 million customer visits are undesirable, according to CEO Brad Anderson. These bargain-hunting customers buy goods, return them, then buy them again at returned-goods prices. They research prices on the web and then make Best Buy honor its lowest-price guarantee. To get rid of these "devil" customers, Best Buy is changing its merchandising and promotion strategy to cater to "angels" while encouraging "devils" to shop elsewhere.[14]

Firing customers can be as undesirable as firing employees. However, it is an option companies hold as the ultimate punishment for poor customer performance when the behavior of customers is threatening the return on investment.

## CUSTOMER PERFORMANCE

Up to this point we have established that customers play a significant role in the usage of goods and services. We have shown that customers don't want to fail and that society has conditioned customers to feel that success with goods and services is the desirable outcome. Our next topic of discussion is the concept of customer performance and why it is often substandard.

To address this question, we first need to discuss the concept of performance. Performance is the execution and accomplishment of work. This work is beneficial not only to the customer, but to companies, fellow customers, and others. Performance is observable, measurable, and quantifiable. Customer performance happens when a customer performs tasks related to acquiring, preparing, consuming, and disposing of goods and services.

When customers aren't maximizing the value that exists within a good or service, the effect is a *performance gap*. A performance gap is when the customer's current performance doesn't match the potential or desired performance. You can express this gap in terms of the number of product features a customer knows how to use, the quality of results a customer extracts from a product, the savings the customer is able to achieve, or, as shown in Figure 1.2, the time it takes a customer to perform a task.

**Figure 1.2** Performance Gap. The difference between current and desired performance.

For example, customers who have adopted NCR's FastLane self-checkout technology at Home Depot stores describe their desired performance as, "get in, get out, and get on with the project." From a performance standpoint, we quantify customers' qualitative criteria into something more precise, such as, "purchase the correct one-gallon can of white primer paint at a price point that is affordable in less than five minutes." With this definition of precise performance, we can observe customers as they attempt to complete this task and objectively measure whether they achieved it. Can the customer find the correct product in the maze of competing and sometimes confusing product displays? Can the customer navigate the aisles and avoid the distractions of the other products that promise to make everything easier and better? Is the customer's expectation of five minutes even realistic?

Substandard customer performance is when there is a negative difference between the current customer performance and the desired customer performance. In stores where the FastLane technology doesn't exist, it might take customers eight minutes to buy the gallon of paint. But the customer's expectation is that it should take five minutes. We therefore have a *performance gap*, which represents a three-minute negative difference between the current and desired performance. Obviously, if customers aren't experiencing expected performance, we expect them to become dissatisfied with the experience. However, we also realize that the customers may modify their expectations, thus complicating this process even further. It is in this modification of the expectation that real customer loyalty can be won or lost. The customer who has a three-minute gap in the time expectation may be more than happy with the incredible price point or the free brush that is now part of the promotion, or the "expert" advice given during the selection process.

For many customers, time is as critical a sacrifice as cost in their calculation of *net customer value*. As this example illustrates, the three-minute gap is yet another reason the customer has to defect to an alternative solution. So it is of interest to companies to determine if there is value in closing the gap. But how? What are the options to solve this problem?

When customers perform we know there are two forces at play (Figure 1.3). Driving forces are those things that enable a customer to perform. Restraining forces, on the other hand, prevent a customer from performing. If there is an underabundance of driving forces and an overabundance of restraining forces, then we know customer performance will suffer.

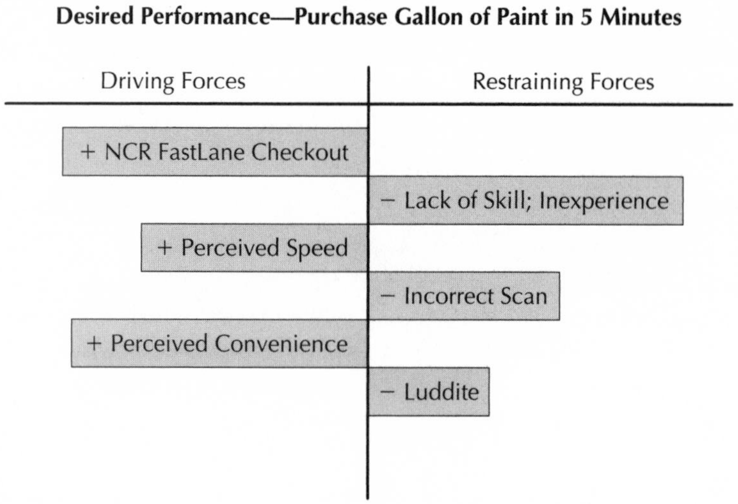

**Desired Performance—Purchase Gallon of Paint in 5 Minutes**

| Driving Forces | Restraining Forces |
|---|---|
| + NCR FastLane Checkout | |
| | − Lack of Skill; Inexperience |
| + Perceived Speed | |
| | − Incorrect Scan |
| + Perceived Convenience | |
| | − Luddite |

**Figure 1.3** Driving vs. Restraining Forces. Customer performance is enhanced when the driving forces outweigh the restraining forces.

NCR's FastLane technology is a driving force. It provides the means to check out faster, achieving the performance customers desire. The utility of such a technology is always held in balance by restraining forces. One common restraining force is skill. The first time a customer uses the FastLane technology it will probably take longer than desired to complete the transaction since the customer hasn't yet built up the skills to maximize the value the technology offers.

Another restraining force is that sometimes products do not scan, or the scan price is not the correct price. The customer might also be considered a *luddite*, or in marketing parlance, a *laggard*, one who is suspicious of new technology and refuses to adopt new technologies or methods. This behavior is a restraining force when considering desired performance, since if customers don't try it, they can't realize its value. The challenge for companies and customers alike is to provide (or demand) sufficient driving forces and eliminate the restraining forces (also known as barriers) so that desired performance can be achieved. Rewarding the customer that takes over the work historically performed by an employee is an important consideration. The customer that utilizes FastLane is rewarded with time, a valuable resource.

Research in consumer behavior and human performance demonstrates that we have a pretty good idea as to the nature of driving and restraining forces. We have already discussed some of them in the context of treating customers as employees. This leads to a process for wrangling the driving and restraining forces into a cohesive experience that enables customers to perform. We introduce this process in the next chapter.

## SUMMARY

In this chapter we set the stage for you to create do-it-yourself customers by understanding and adopting a coproduction experience orientation in your company. Customers, whether end users of consumer goods or a business, are rationale and want to succeed with the goods and services they consume. They want to realize excellence as customers who can unlock the most value from goods and services for maximum benefit. Such behaviors strengthen the relationships companies have with their customers.

Through technology, product simplification, and the evolution of consumer sophistication, companies are encouraging customers to provide more of the labor in extracting value from goods and services. In many respects, the marketplace is moving towards the need to treat customers like employees. Customers must be recruited, oriented, trained, recognized, rewarded, and retained, just as employees are. Through this strategy customers become *brand ambassadors* who have the right amount of influence to bring other customers to the company.

The heart of any coproduction experience ultimately relies upon customer performance. Customers and companies should have an idea of what defines desired performance in specific coproduction experiences. Companies must compare desired performance with current performance to discover the barriers that exist which limit or restrain the amount of work a customer can do. Removing these barriers through the design or redesign of effective coproduction experiences offers companies a significant competitive advantage—it makes them easier to do business with.

Company cases and empirical research shows that a coproduction experience orientation is an ideal strategy for creating do-it-yourself customers and enabling customers to unlock value. Through solutions that combine vision, access, incentive, and expertise, companies can enable customers to perform, to become sophisticated customers, and to experience the satisfaction they desire. The outcome of this strategy is maximizing customer equity and the lifetime value it provides to the company.

CHAPTER 2

# A NEW PARADIGM FOR CUSTOMER EXPERIENCES

*Experience is not what happens to you; it's what you
do with what happens to you.*

—Aldous Huxley

The context in which customers perform with goods and services is the *customer experience*. Designed and managed by companies, customer experiences reflect an environment in which customers feel an emotional bond. The aim of experience is to fill all 360 degrees of your sensory bandwidth. For some customers, that experience might be provided by Dunkin' Donuts, where bright pink and orange colors and fast service give customers the kick they need in the morning to get moving. However, if your morning routine involves minimizing sensory shocks to your system, then the music, lighting, laminates, wood, and the attitude of employees at a Starbucks coffee shop all come together to deliver a more relaxed experience. At Starbucks, the colors are muted, "baristas" fill your cup, and you can check your email in a comfortable chair using the store's WiFi hotspot. According to Carl Sibilski, an analyst with Morningstar, Inc., "Starbucks has spent more time working on the coffee shop experiences, and when you compare that to Dunkin' Donuts, they don't even seem to be in the same game together." But Dunkin' Donuts is trying. While the pink and orange is staying, they are adding espresso drinks and WiFi hotspots to become more competitive.[1]

Experience is the future of competitive differentiation. Authors Donald Norman and Bernd Schmitt suggest that experiences involve sensory, emotional, conceptual, participatory, and relational dimensions that "brand" a company. Companies, such as Hewlett-Packard, have executives in charge of the *total customer experience*. These people coordinate the various touchpoints of the company (a touchpoint is any interaction between the company and the customer, like an 800-number call, online help, or a store visit). A company's *brand* is now being represented by the company's *experience*. The idea is that when customers think of a brand they think of the experiences the brand provides. Customers become loyal to the company that offers them the best experiences.

We see the natural evolution of experiences going beyond that of pure sensory and emotional stimulation. These new types of experiences are *coproduction experiences*. We label them as such because companies design them to enable customers to do more work, reduce costs, and unlock greater value. To achieve the promise of coproduction experiences, companies need a tool that plots a course beyond the nuances of simple emotional experiences. This tool is the *Coproduction Experience Model*. This chapter describes the Coproduction Experience Model, the process of designing coproduction experiences, and the strategies driving its adoption.

## FOUR DIMENSIONS OF COPRODUCTION EXPERIENCES

As shown in Figure 2.1, the Coproduction Experience Model is organized around four key dimensions, or forces. These dimensions represent the wrangling of various driving and restraining forces governing customer performance. *Vision* is the starting point. Without vision, customers have no idea where they are going, making the other elements of the model useless. The next dimension is *access*. Access guides you in determining the nature of the environment and what tools you must provide to give customers the best chance of succeeding in their tasks. The final two dimensions, *incentive* and *expertise*, are relatively balanced in their function. Incentive provides

**Figure 2.1**  Coproduction Experience Model. Wrapping customer performance are experiences that provide customers vision, access, incentive, and expertise.

customers the motivation to perform, while expertise offers customers the knowledge and skill they need to develop sophistication with various goods and services.

The model serves two primary purposes. First, it acts as an analysis tool. It guides companies in the questions they should ask and the observations they should seek to determine the causes of problems and opportunities associated with new or existing coproduction experiences. Second, it acts as a design tool, suggesting an orchestration of tactics that must be in place to deliver the coproduction promise: more work, reduced costs, and unlocking greater value.

Let's take a closer look at the nature of each of the elements.

## Vision

Vision is a well-known determinant in enabling humans to achieve desired performance. Popularized by Ken Blanchard and Sheldon Bowles in *Raving Fans*, vision defines goals, objectives, and what the state of desired performance looks and feels like. It is a critical part of the customer's success and satisfaction. Marketers, through promotional channels such as advertisements and salespeople, help shape the vision for how a product performs. And through customers' abilities as problem solvers, they set their own visions for what they need to be satisfied. Once customers know what the goal looks like and receive feedback on their performance, the more effort they'll exert to achieve the goal—and the more success they'll experience.

## Access

Access describes the need customers have for the right tools, environment, and information that enables desired performance. In goods such as iPods, microwave ovens, and even socks, designers build in interfaces and nuances that support ideal performance and make products easy to use [we really do have a pair of socks that have a green/red color indicator sewn into the toe. It tells us when our socks are inside-out (red) or right-side-in (green)].

Other forms of access support efficiencies in service contexts. We remember as kids clerks in supermarkets having to key in the prices for each product in our cart. The checkout lines took forever. Then came barcode technology and electronic point-of-sale (EPOS) systems. Through these tools, checkout time decreased substantially. Now we have a change in the environment where customers are able to use EPOS systems themselves, saving even more time. When radio frequency product identification (RFID), a technology for identifying products, becomes adopted, look out! Customers will do more of the work and see checkout speeds like they've never seen before. Electronic MetroCards for accessing public transportation and EZ-Pass for tollbooths on bridges and turnpikes are already providing similar high-performance experiences for customers.

## Incentive

All the vision and access in the world is useless if customer performance is not reinforced. We know that customers don't want to fail. However, given human nature, sometimes we all need a swift kick in the pants to get us moving. This might take the form of a reward, a punishment, or both. Airlines are masters at using these techniques that trigger our desire to perform. Make your reservation through the American Airlines website and you earn a reward of bonus miles in your frequent flyer program. However, if you change your itinerary after booking your flight American Airlines extracts a punishment of $100 to make the change—reminding you to plan better the next time.

## Expertise

A quote that makes the rounds in human performance circles reads, "If you put a gun to their head and they still can't perform, then it is a skill deficiency." The lack of expertise reflects the absence of the knowledge and skill required to perform a task to a desired standard of performance. For example, many customers just don't know how to set the time on a VCR, even if threatened with their life. Thus, we can do one of two things: (1) teach customers the knowledge and skill they need or (2) make the need for knowledge and skill obsolete. Manufacturers have incorporated new technology into VCRs and DVRs, which eliminates the need for knowledge and skill since it sets the time for the customer by capturing it from an outside source. However, when technology can't save the day companies must build the expertise of their customers through user manuals, support tools, formal training classes, and assistance from knowledgeable service workers. For example, the first time customers use self-checkout technology at the grocery store they will go slow and they may become confused because they do not have expertise. However, since customers have been observing checkout clerks utilizing similar technologies for years, we expect strong performance as they gain experience. Add the help of the clerk who can provide the support and training the customer needs, and with practice, customers will develop the skills to perform well.

Individually, none of the forces described in the model can enable companies and customers to achieve the performance they desire. It requires an orchestration of these strategies to form a valuable set of solutions to maximize the driving forces and minimize the restraining forces. Through experience, customers become conditioned to the norms present in the performance environment until they ultimately reach a state of equilibrium. This enables customers to consistently perform with sophistication to unlock the value embedded in goods and services.

## THE COPRODUCTION EXPERIENCE PROCESS

The Coproduction Experience Model is not a stand-alone tool. Rather, it is the heart of a process that drives the development of optimum coproduction experiences. This process, which we call the Coproduction Experience Process, leverages the ideas behind the model into a fluid roadmap. As shown in Figure 2.2, the process outlines, at a high level, the procedure for creating

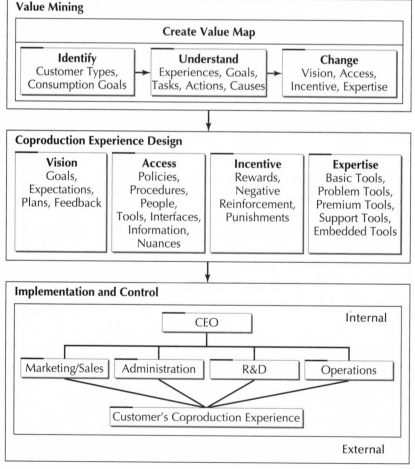

**Figure 2.2** The Coproduction Experience Process.

coproduction experiences *by design*. The following sections in this chapter describe the general flow of the Coproduction Experience Process. Subsequent chapters in the book elaborate each part of the process.

## Value Mining

The starting point in the process is the activity called *value mining*. The goal of value mining is to analyze your company's relationship with customers to determine if there are any performance gaps in the coproduction experience. For example, you might discover that customers are not able to use various features of your product, reducing their satisfaction and the likelihood that they will purchase add-ons and other consumables.

Before mining for value, you must first create a *value map* (see Chapter 4) that identifies the various customer goals. This map is essentially a matrix that pairs different customer types with different consumption goals. For example, a home computer user (customer type) might have the goal of setting up a home wireless network.

When this map is in place, you can begin surveying. For each cell in the matrix, you identify which cells indicate the greatest customer performance problems. You do this by asking eight specific questions. Depending on the answers, you label a cell green (no problems), yellow (some problems), or red (lots of problems that suggest the customer experience is not working correctly).

After problem areas are identified on the map, the next step is to start mining. This involves a drill-down process to understand what lies under the surface for a specific coproduction experience. Here you quantify customer experiences, goals, tasks, and actions, and then pinpoint the causes of any deficiencies you discover. This analysis provides sufficient data such that you can confidently recommend changes to the coproduction experience. These recommendations link us back to the Coproduction Experience Model, whereby proposed solutions involve enhancements to vision, access, incentive, or expertise.

## Coproduction Experience Design

The work done in the value mining step leads to the next task—designing the coproduction experience. This task has two parts. The first part uses the Coproduction Experience Model to guide the generation and selection of specific tactics to overcome customer performance problems. The second part involves using the model to orchestrate the different tactics into a fluid system of solutions.

Tactics for improving the customer's *vision* focus on:

- Appropriate *goals* for what customers should accomplish
- Clear customer *expectations* describing the measurable outcomes of activities
- Succinct *plans* that provide customers a script upon which they can act
- Fluid *feedback* that lets customers know how they are doing

Tactics for facilitating customer *access* focus on:

- Articulating company *policies* that establish rules for customer performance
- Specifying *procedures* that affect customer experiences
- Identifying the *people*, both employees and customers, who are best suited for the experience
- Developing *tools* that enable customers to do more work
- Designing *interfaces* that make the work customers do easy
- Creating *information* customers need to make decisions
- Coordinating *nuances* that influence the customer's natural reflexes

Tactics for structuring customer *incentive* focus on:

- Conceiving *rewards* that encourage desirable behaviors
- Crafting *punishments* that discourage undesirable behaviors

Tactics for enhancing customer *expertise* focus on:

- Creating *basic tools* to orient customers to goods and services
- Planning *problem tools* to hand-hold customers during usage
- Developing *premium tools* to teach customers high-level skills
- Publishing *support tools* to guide choice and usage
- Integrating *embedded tools* into goods and services themselves

## Implementation and Control

The implementation and control of coproduction experiences requires the participation and coordination of various stakeholders, each owning a piece of the coproduction experience puzzle. One set of stakeholders operate at a external level, beyond the direct control of the company. These include such entities as the media, other customers, and neutral third parties. Another set of stakeholders operate at a internal level. With a strategy set in place by the

CEO, executives, directors, and individual contributors throughout the organization orchestrate the execution of the coproduction experience:

- Marketing and sales promote vision
- Administration provides funding, resources, and legal guidance
- R&D develops the tools and interfaces that facilitate access
- Operations delivers the expertise and incentives

These activities ultimately create coproduction experiences for customers that enable them to do more work, reduce costs, and unlock greater value.

## STRATEGIC CONSIDERATIONS

The difference between an *experience* and a *coproduction experience* is the nature of the customer's success. Customers want to acquire as much value as possible from the goods and services they use. Anecdotal stories and empirical research show that companies play a key role in helping customers achieve valuable outcomes by orchestrating a performance environment built around vision, access, incentive, and expertise. So why is all this so critical at this time? Why should you invest in customer performance initiatives? And how should you plan their integration?

At a general level, companies establish strategic competitive advantage through cost reduction, differentiation, and product/service quality. These basic tenets still remain as the foundation for company strategy. What has changed are the tactics used to achieve these outcomes, whereby the customer has much more involvement and responsibility for unlocking the value embedded in goods and services (Table 2.1).

The critical nature of a customer performance orientation stems from a fundamental paradigm shift in the field of marketing. There is heightened awareness of the customer's role in the creation of value through the active and sophisticated consumption of goods and services. Additionally, through technology, there are many more ways for customers to become involved in the consumption process.

To avoid commoditization of goods and services, companies are establishing competitive advantages based upon the type and quality of the customer experiences they offer. Some experiences are rich and engaging, such as those at Build-A-Bear® Workshops, where kids and adults alike create personalized teddy bears. Other experiences are sparse and utilitarian, such as shopping at a Costco warehouse, where customers are expected to do almost all the work with very little help.

**Table 2.1    Competitive Strategy Has Evolved Various Coproduction Tactics**

| Strategy | Example Coproduction Tactics |
|---|---|
| Reduce costs | • Online product ordering (Dell Computer)<br>• Pay at the pump (gas stations)<br>• Self-bagging of groceries (Winco Food Stores) |
| Differentiate | • Experiential activities that involve the customer in codesign and cocreation (Build-A-Bear® Workshops, Stir Crazy Restaurants)<br>• Experiential activities that are utilitarian (Costco) |
| Goods and services quality (Making experiences easier, faster) | • Self-service kiosks (Delta Airlines)<br>• Self-checkout systems (Home Depot)<br>• Enhanced industrial design of products (Apple iPod)<br>• Streamlined service delivery scripts (Subway Sandwiches)<br>• New technologies (RFID, Internet) |

In many of these experiences companies are asking their customers to take on a larger share of the work in exchange for greater value. Customers are willing to do this if, in addition to attractive prices, it makes a company *easier to do business with* (ETDBW). We see this as a significant paradigm shift for companies. In the past, companies were expected to do the work for customers. Now, customers are doing the work for companies.

The quality of the customer's experience is dependent on increased levels of customer performance to achieve the desired outcomes. Research on customers' reactions to self-service technologies is helpful in making our point: when customers experience a dissatisfying outcome, they blame the system and not themselves. This dissatisfying experience typically triggers defection to other options. Thus companies must enable customers to perform competently and ensure that customers can generate the greatest amount of value.

As depicted in Figure 2.3, the successful usage of goods and services is the starting point in the chain of events leading to maximizing customer lifetime value.

1. Based upon the customer's goal and the customer's performance, usage of a good or service to achieve a goal results in some level of satisfaction.

2. If satisfaction is positive, then the customer's trust in the good, service, or firm is enhanced.

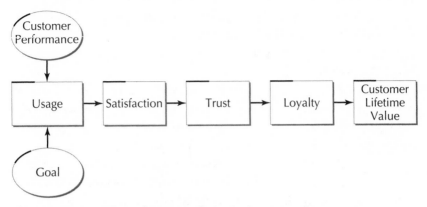

**Figure 2.3**  Customer Performance Chain. An investment in customer performance enhances the customer's experience with a good or service to ultimately influence the customer's lifetime value.

3. This trust ultimately leads to the development of loyalty behaviors, such as increased spending, more frequent purchases, and positive recommendations.

4. The net effect is the enhancement of the customer's lifetime value, the amount of revenues a customer can be counted on to provide over a period of time.

Through an investment in enhancing customer performance, companies are able to maximize the equity a customer offers to deliver (1) behaviors and actions that result in successful usage of goods and services, and (2) repeat purchases that boost the customer's lifetime value.

## A Designed Coproduction Experience

For the past eight years California World Fest has delighted the ears of world music aficionados. Held every summer in the foothills of California's Gold Country, the festival brings together musicians from around the world for four days of continuous musical events. Peace, love, and world harmony is the message that many musicians bring to the event. But the behavior of customers at this event reveals a different truth as cutthroat competition and self-centeredness infect the crowd. We relate this story to you as an example of how companies define customer value and the lengths they go to design a coproduction experience that maximizes value for all.

People pay up to $125 to attend this multi-day event. During the day musical acts perform on several stages spread throughout the Nevada County fairgrounds. This forum is very intimate, as the audience can sit close to the stage and interact with the performers when the set is complete. In the evenings, however, all the action moves to the main stage where a parade of headliners perform.

The main stage sits on the west side of a large, grassy, flat field. This field is where the problems began some years ago. As classic coproducers, customers must bring their own seats to the field, which sounds simple enough. Yet without any direction some customers would bring low-back lawnchairs, some would bring high-back lawnchairs, while others would bring large blankets and tarps. Pity the poor couple who found themselves seated in low-back chairs behind a couple in high-back chairs, as the stage would be completely obstructed. Conversely, people who brought blankets and tarps would carve out large spaces of private real estate that would ensure unobstructed views of the stage yet underutilize (in terms of bodies per square foot) the space, causing more people to sit in undesirable locations further away from the stage.

Perhaps the most annoying thing for the people who had staked out seats in prime locations front and center of the stage were the groups of "festival dancers" who bring no seating. When the music begins, these dancers converge directly in front of the stage, obscuring the view of those who have seats. Then things really get uncomfortable. The people in seats shout at those who are dancing, and the dancers don't really care about the people in seats since those sitting are not truly "participating" in the event. The inevitable altercations threaten the safety of customers, increase the complaints to festival organizers, increase defections, and reduce the value many customers expected.

Luckily the event's marketers recognized their responsibility in managing this customer performance problem. Over the years they have evolved a number of unique solutions that aim to maximize the value for all their customers. It starts with the seating policies, which are made available in virtually all festival communications, from the program to venue signage (Figure 2.4). The policy prohibits tarps, limits low-back chairs to areas in front of the sound booth, and specifically states that if a chair is unoccupied anyone may sit in it. (Of course, if the chair owner returns, the person must vacate the seat to the owner.) Furthermore, festival volunteers have a customized measuring stick by which they can objectively determine the compliance of any chair.

The next element of the festival's strategy is the process for customers to place chairs. After every evening performance, any chairs left in the field by

**Figure 2.4**  Signage informing customers about the rules for seating. Note the white line behind the sign, which delineates the seating area from the dancing area. Violators of the seating policy face having their seats removed to the "bad chair" pile. The couple shown (right) is looking for their "evicted" chairs.

6:45, line up out of range of the sprinklers...      7:00, sprinklers off, go!

7:01, stake out your turf...      7:03, first wave done!

**Figure 2.5**  The process of placing chairs at the festival.

participants are unceremoniously moved to the "bad chair" pile, resetting the field to a "clear" state. The next morning, the field becomes open for chair placement at 7:00 A.M. As shown in Figure 2.5, sophisticated customers who know the ropes begin lining up at about 6:45 A.M. To discourage cheaters from coming out earlier, the festival positions sprinklers in strategic locations on the field (negative reinforcement). As newcomers arrive, people already in line let them know in no uncertain terms where the end of the line is (social learning).

At exactly 7:00 A.M., an orange-vested festival volunteer turns off the sprinklers and indicates that seating may begin. The group then swiftly makes its move. Since many customers are carrying several chairs (for their friends who can't get out of bed), there is some scuffling as people stake their turf. The more sophisticated customers have this multiplexed task figured out. They first position the folded chairs to assure they get adequate space for all in their group. After that they unfold the chairs and put them in the final position.

As the rows of chairs begin to take shape, the orange-vested festival volunteer circulates through the rows, takes measurements when needed, and begins making adjustments to ensure appropriate aisle space that will accommodate the greatest number of chairs (without making the space too claustrophobic). Many of the customers linger for awhile, as rumors abound of overzealous festival volunteers (who evict legal chairs) and late-arriving unscrupulous customers (who put their chair in your spot and move your chair back). In fact, really sophisticated customers check their chairs from time to time during the day to ensure no one has fiddled with their chair position.

The purpose of this simple story is to illustrate some key themes we've discussed. The first theme is that of *value*. Companies undertake actions to manage coproduction experiences when value is threatened. In the case of California World Fest, the value generated by many of the sophisticated customers who arrived early and staked a seat was being undermined by a minority of customers who did not respect fairness and societal norms. This threatened customer satisfaction and loyalty to the event, which ultimately would have a bottom-line impact on the festival organizers. Thus, to preserve and enhance customer value, the festival organizers needed to act. The second theme is that of *by design*. When seating procedures were weighted more toward the control of customers, anarchy and selfishness ruled. Customers *by default* did what nature has conditioned them to do—look out for themselves. By taking control of the design, festival organizers could effectively manage a solution for the greater good of all customers.

## SUMMARY

In this chapter we introduced the idea for how well-designed coproduction experiences can enable companies to achieve their strategic aims. The backbone for coproduction experiences is the Coproduction Experience

Model, which illustrates the orchestration of four specific factors that contribute to the customer's overall performance. *Vision* helps customers know what they are doing, *access* provides the necessary tools, *incentive* offers the necessary motivation, and *expertise* develops the required knowledge and skill.

To put the Coproduction Experience Model into use, companies use the Coproduction Experience Process. The process starts with value mining, a technique that maps the landscape of customer goals. Once the goals are known, analysts can drill down to identify performance problems and understand the causes behind them. This leads to recommendations for changing the customer's coproduction experience.

The next step in the process is designing the coproduction experience. Using the Coproduction Experience Model as a guide, companies conceive of tactics that involve improving vision, facilitating access, structuring rewards, and enhancing expertise.

The final step in the process is implementation and control. This involves coordinating not only the company's resources but those of third parties and beyond to ensure that coproduction experiences are well executed and consistent throughout the marketplace.

Strategically, the Coproduction Experience Model aids companies in addressing a significant paradigm shift in the competitive landscape. In the past, companies were expected to do the work for customers. Now, customers are doing the work for companies.

# CHAPTER 3

# THE ROOTS OF COPRODUCTION EXPERIENCE DESIGN

*Accuracy of observation is the equivalent of accuracy
of thinking.*

—Wallace Stevens

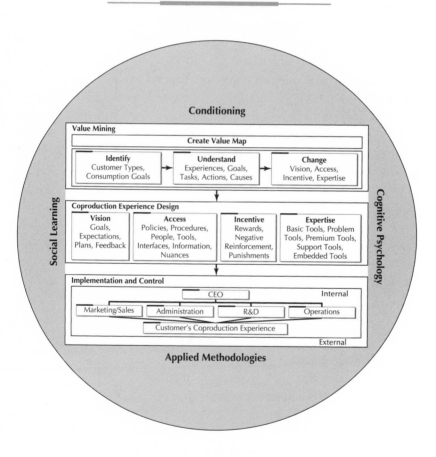

I f you want to get right to the heart of our ideas—value mining—feel free to move on and go directly to Chapter 4. If it has been a while since your last psychology course or if you feel you would benefit from a deeper understanding of the science behind coproduction experience design, read on. The content in this chapter helps you develop an *eye* for observing and understanding coproduction experiences. Our expectation is that with this *eye* you will be better able to spot problems and opportunities when you analyze or design coproduction experiences.

This chapter is about psychology. In its various forms, a general understanding of some key psychology principles will help you better understand human behavior, which is the heart of customer performance. Conditioning, social learning, and cognitive psychology—plus various applied methodologies that businesses regularly use—form the roots of coproduction experience design. In this chapter, we trace the history of consumer psychology as it weaves its way from conditioning to social learning and ultimately to cognitive psychology. We then discuss the convergence of these core psychological principles into useful, applied methodologies that impact performance: persuasion, behavior engineering, user-centered design, and consumer decision making. We'll wrap things up by discussing empirical evidence that adds life to the coproduction experience elements of vision, access, incentive, and expertise.

## CONDITIONING

Look at the two photographs in Figure 3.1. These are photos used to promote various goods and services. The first is for a boat and the second is for a beverage.

What's going on in these photographs is one of the most basic principles of human psychology: classical conditioning. The purpose of each photograph reflects customer performance at its most basic level: to trigger in you a natural, emotional reflex in response to the models used in each photograph. The children in the first photograph trigger reflexes associated with *enjoyment* and *happiness*. The woman in the second photograph, especially if you are male, triggers reflexes associated with *beauty* and *desire*.

Now that these reflexes are triggered, what happens to them? By closely associating the trigger with a product, marketers expect to slowly transfer those reflexes to the products themselves. Ivan Pavlov discovered this effect when he paired the ringing of a bell with the presentation of a meat powder to a dog (stimulus) to trigger salivation (response). Eventually, after

Boat photo courtesy of Glastron Boats. St. Pauli Girl photo courtesy of Barton Beers.

**Figure 3.1**    Attractive Models: Boat and beverage. What's your response to the different models? Since the model has a proximal connection to the products, what's your response to the products?

repeated exposures to the paired stimulus, the ringing of the bell was sufficient to trigger salivation. But as Pavlov soon learned, other stimuli, such as the tramping of the researcher's boots, could also elicit the conditioned response. In our own unintentional conditioning experiments, the donning of running shoes has conditioned our dog to respond with panting excitement. He's learned his master wearing running shoes is often followed by an enjoyable outdoor experience.

Therefore, after repeated exposures to the photographs, what responses should we expect? When shopping for a boat for the family, a Glastron should trigger emotions of enjoyment and happiness. As one strolls along the beer cases in the grocery store, the mere sight of a St. Pauli Girl beer might trigger the emotion of desire.

Conditioning is a fundamental principle of human behavior and learning. Its roots date back to the early 1900s. Many eminent psychologists have shaped what society knows about conditioning, the names of which you'll no doubt recognize: Edward L. Thorndike, Ivan Pavlov, John B. Watson, and the most famous of all, B.F. Skinner.[1] The work of these experts led to two forms of conditioning, classical conditioning and operant conditioning.

## Classical Conditioning

Early conditioning experiments focused on simple reflex behaviors, hence the name *classical conditioning*. Reflex behaviors include finger twitches, eye blinks, and changes in the skin's ability to pass an electrical current. Before long, however, psychologists were able to extend classical conditioning beyond simple motor reflexes to human attitudes. In a now classic experiment, Watson conditioned an 11-month-old child to exhibit a fear reaction when shown a white rat. Watson did this by pairing the white rat with the sound of a hammer striking a steel bar. The sound of the hammer caused the child to jump and cry, and subsequently the sight of the white rat alone caused the child to cry. So strong was the conditioning that a white rabbit elicited the fear reaction, as did other furry things, such as a dog and a fur coat.

As illustrated in the photographs that began this section, classical conditioning has seen many applications that relate to customers. The expectation is that the close association of the model with the product of interest classically conditions the viewer, to where ultimately the mere image of the product triggers the desired reflexes. But it is not just children or pretty women who can trigger influential responses. If Drew Carry, an American comedian, hosts an event, you'll likely think the event to be funny.

Sounds can also have a powerful classical conditioning effect. Victoria's Secret stores used to play romantic, classical music that triggered relaxation and fantasy reflexes, which are then associated with their products. Now Victoria's Secret stores play techno, which is supposed to trigger reflexes associated with high fashion and supermodels. During holidays, other stores play Christmas music, which trigger a different set of emotions that one associates with the shopping experience. Even ringing telephones in television advertisements have been used to trigger attention and anxiety responses.

Later in the book we'll talk about *nuances*, which you can build into coproduction experiences to enhance various kinds of customer performance. The science behind these nuances is classical conditioning.

## Operant Conditioning

The other form of conditioning, *operant conditioning*, was popularized by B.F. Skinner in the 1950s. Whereas classical conditioning focuses on reflex responses (which are not typically under the direct control of the individual), operant conditioning focuses on behaviors that are consciously controlled by the individual. Thus, operant conditioning aims to influence higher-level behaviors, such as a child's willingness to participate in games, a dog's performance of a "roll-over" trick, or a whale's exciting leap out of a pool at SeaWorld. Another difference between the two forms of conditioning is the cause of the behavior. In classical conditioning, behavior is dependent upon an individual first receiving the stimulus, which then elicits the response. Skinner recognized this key dynamic, but for complex behaviors extended it by chaining together three key elements. The first element is called the *discriminative stimulus*, which is consistently present during the behavior. This might be a verbal command or a visual cue. The second element is the *response*, which is the behavior. The third element is the *reinforcing stimulus*, which typically takes the form of a reward.

When a company gives a customer a rebate after purchasing a product or service, it is applying operant conditioning. The product and the offer are the discriminative stimuli, the purchase is the response, and the rebate is the reward. You should now begin to see how operant conditioning links to the *incentive* component of the Coproduction Experience Model.

Yet, just as the presence of a bait fish in the hand of a trainer does not naturally cause a wild killer whale to leap out of the water, eliciting desired behaviors through operant conditioning often requires a process, called *shaping*, to help develop approximate behaviors that increase the likelihood of the desired behavior.

For example, let's say we want customers to come into a store and buy something. One way to do this through operant conditioning is to stand outside the store, inform people who pass by that if they buy something in the store, they get points toward wonderful prizes. But for many people, the desired behavior is too much of a stretch—they have trouble sharing the *vision* (another link to the Coproduction Experience Model). The pure operant conditioning doesn't work. If we change our methods to shape the customer, we might experience better results. So, we redesign the experience.

First, we inform people who pass by that if they enter the store to browse, they get a reward. Second, since they are now in the store, we inform them if they sign up for a store credit card, they get a reward. Now with the approximate behaviors in place, informing customers that upon purchase they earn points toward wonderful prizes will likely result in the desired behavior, purchase. Casinos have used this shaping technique for years. Customers are lured into an establishment through the giveaway of a nominal reward, for example, a couple of rolls of nickels. Customers play the free nickels and, because of the odds, experience the thrill of winning a few times. Now, when the free nickels have run out, the casino's expectation is that the customers will keep playing—with their own money.

Another shaping example comes from the auto industry. For years, Datsun was a very well-known automobile brand from Japan made by Nissan. From 1932 to 1983 Nissan branded its vehicles using the Datsun name. People became conditioned to that name. In the late 1970s. Nissan decided to retire the Datsun brand. But it didn't do it cold turkey. Instead, it slowly shaped the new Nissan brand over a period of several years. At first, the cars were still branded as Datsun, but had the subtitle "by Nissan" added. Over time, the Nissan nameplate became more predominant on its cars, while the Datsun nameplate diminished. Once customers became familiar with the Nissan name and subconsciously associated it with Datsun's brand recognition, Nissan was able to retire the Datsun name completely and remove the Datsun nameplate from its cars.

In many situations, *incentive* plays a key role in eliciting desired behaviors. Incentive comes in three distinct flavors: positive reinforcement (rewards), negative reinforcement, and punishment. The food, prizes, points, and nickels discussed in the previous examples are best classified as positive reinforcement. They are satisfying experiences that lead to repeat behaviors. Negative reinforcement, on the other hand, is when something not satisfying is removed when the desired behavior is exhibited. Imagine the customer who must shop in a store that is too cold. As negative reinforcement, the cool air triggers an avoidance behavior, and as such the customer shops as quickly as possible in order to escape the cold. Another example is the customer who, in exasperation, informs the telemarketer who has called every night for the past two weeks that he will buy something if only the telemarketer stops calling!

Punishment, which is often confused with negative reinforcement, occurs two ways. One form of punishment is when positive reinforcement is withdrawn. For example, if a customer's AAdvantage Miles on American Airlines is below 25,000 for the year, the customer's Gold Elite status is withdrawn. The other form of punishment is when a negative reinforcer is applied, for example, the $100 fee charged when a customer changes an airline ticket. While punishment has its uses in certain cases, it can lead to undesirable side effects, which we'll discuss later in this book.

## SOCIAL LEARNING

While conditioning explains much of human behavior, it doesn't explain the wholeness of human behavior, as numerous psychologists discovered. Frustrated by the deficiencies of conditioning to explain the totality of human behavior, they sought a more robust explanation. In the 1960s psychologist Albert Bandura extended our understanding of conditioning by introducing social learning.[2] Social learning helps us understand symbolic thought, self-direction in learning, and the factors that influence imitation.

Whereas behaviorists (the label applied to devotees of operant conditioning) tend to be unidirectional on the issue of outside influences on behavior,

Bandura embraced a more dynamic perspective. He envisioned learning as a three-way relationship that linked the environment, personal factors, and behavior. The environment, of course, reflects the stimulus and reinforcement components of operant conditioning. In the Coproduction Experience Model, Bandura's concept of environment has a lot in common with *access*. Personal factors include such things as an individual's goals, choice in selecting events, and even gender and race. Behavior is the individual's response. In Bandura's model, not only do the environment and personal factors trigger changes in behavior, but behavior triggers changes in the environment and personal factors.

This dynamic relationship between environment, personal factors, and behavior gave structure to Bandura's most significant contribution, an explanation of how we learn by observation. Observational learning reflects three key parts: the model, the observed consequences, and the individual's cognitive processes.

## Modeling

The *model*, in its most identifiable form, is an individual or group who exhibits the behavior one desires to learn. Through the observation of models, we acquire social norms, strengthen or weaken our inhibitions, and learn new behaviors. Nowhere is the power of modeling more evident than when an individual is thrust into an unknown and unfamiliar environment where a different language is spoken.

For us, this experience happened to be a small, hole-in-the-wall dim sum bakery in San Francisco's Chinatown. The first time we entered this shop we found it crowded with elderly Asian women shouting their orders in Chinese. It was pandemonium, and we were perplexed by how we would ever get service. So we hung back and watched the next customer enter the store. She calmly walked to the back of the store, selected a number from a number dispensing machine, and waded into the crowd. We followed her lead, got a number, and entered the fray as well.

The next thing we learned was that the clerks were calling out the numbers in Chinese. Because we didn't speak Chinese, our number was virtually meaningless because if called, we wouldn't know to respond. Thus, we quickly located the woman who had taught us about getting the number, and waited until she was called. We then knew we would be next. Sure enough, moments later the clerk yelled something meaningless to our ears and the woman pushed her way to the counter. No one seemed offended by her pushing, so when the next clerk called out, we knew our number was up and gleefully pushed our way to the counter, as we had learned.

Unfortunately, our teacher had taught us so well the behaviors, gestures, and actions associated with the consumption culture of that store that the clerk, who no doubt observed our flawless behavior, now expected us to speak Chinese. Much to her surprise we didn't, and thus with much smiling, finger pointing, and mispronounced names of several dim sum treats, we finally acquired our fresh dim sum lunch.

Modeling is not limited to the observance of individuals or groups. Models can just as easily be portrayed in virtually any type of media, from text to symbolic media such as drawings or photographs. Models are most effective when they appear to be trustworthy, have high status, are competent, and effuse power.

## Consequences

As with conditioning, reinforcement plays a strong role in Bandura's conception of social learning. In addition to the reinforcement component associated with operant conditioning (which Bandura calls *direct reinforcement*), Bandura introduced three other reinforcement techniques. *Vicarious reinforcement* describes one's observation of a model being rewarded, and as such imitates the behavior of the model. *Vicarious punishment* describes the opposite. Here, our observation of a model being punished for a specific behavior restrains us from imitating the model. Advertisers have used vicarious punishment in many situations to shape customer behaviors. One example is the Wisk laundry detergent commercials from the 1970s and 1980s. In these commercials various hapless men were punished by their coworkers, children, and wives for having "ring around the collar" on their shirts. From these commercials, the rest of us learned that "ring around the collar" was a bad thing, and that your friends would ridicule you if your shirts had it.

Consider also that the absence of punishment also has an effect, in terms of strengthening imitation. For example, in the dim sum bakery the pushing behavior was neither rewarded nor punished, thus we determined it was acceptable. In a different context, such as a Starbucks store, we likely would have experienced a different outcome.

Bandura's third reinforcement technique, *self-reinforcement*, opened the door to what is now known as intrinsic rewards. With self-reinforcement, individuals reward or punish themselves according to their own internal performance standards. For example, after successfully purchasing their first home, new homeowners might reward themselves with a bottle of champagne.

## Cognitive Processes

The dynamics of Bandura's ideas ultimately led to speculation about a person's cognitive processes in terms of collecting information from the environment and processing it in the context of one's personal factors, with the result being an appropriate response. Bandura eventually settled upon four key mechanisms that describe cognitive processes, *attention, retention, motivation,* and *motor reproduction.* The observation of a model describes attention, whereby the relevance of the model and what is being modeled affects the level of attention exhibited. As the learner observes the model perform, the behavior is symbolically coded by the learner and stored in memory. Through motivation, the learner is induced to perform the behavior, which triggers the motor reproduction and ultimately the learner's observable performance.

# COGNITIVE PSYCHOLOGY

Cognitive psychology aims to explain human behavior from the perspective of mental processes, such as awareness, reasoning, perception, and judgment. Now a dominant force in psychological circles, cognitive psychology evolved from Gestalt psychology. During the rise of conditioning and behaviorism, Gestalt psychology was a competing theory that advocated a holistic, systems-oriented view of the mind that focused on the whole rather than the sum of the parts. Through the work of Ulrich Neisser, Jerome Bruner, David Ausubel, and George Miller, cognitive psychology rose in prominence through the later half of the 20th century. It is now a mainstream science.

While cognitive psychology has many forms and branches, there are some key principles that enhance our understanding of human performance. First, cognitive psychology sees individuals as self-directed, whereby specific goals and tasks drive the development of behaviors. This concept contributes to the *vision* component of the Coproduction Experience Model. Second, cognitive psychology views the mind as an information processor, whereby information (stimulus) enters the body through the various senses, is first processed by short-term memory, then if deemed important enough by working memory, is further processed and transferred to long-term memory as knowledge. When the knowledge is needed to achieve a goal or perform a task, it is subsequently retrieved and applied to the task. Perception, memory, encoding, and retrieval are all processes commonly associated with this information processing perspective. This reflects the Coproduction Experience Model concept of *expertise*. Third, cognitive psychology places a significant emphasis on context, that is, the environment in which knowledge is acquired and tasks are performed. Meaning and structure of knowledge are indelibly tied to the task context. This further reinforces the Coproduction Experience Model concept of *access*.

As work in cognitive psychology progressed, several key innovations associated with improving expertise and performance began to appear. Benjamin Bloom and his colleagues introduced learning domains (cognitive, affective, and psychomotor) and learning taxonomies within each domain, which offered a pragmatic guide to human behavior.[3] For instance, in the cognitive domain, simple behaviors, such as knowledge, comprehension, and application, were differentiated from more complex behaviors, such as analysis, synthesis, and evaluation (which are more commonly referred to as problem-solving skills). Robert Gagne introduced his own version of Bloom's taxonomy, called the conditions of learning, as well as techniques for sequencing and structuring learning. One of his key contributions was to distinguish between expository learning (which is associated with lecture-style teaching methods) and discovery learning (which is associated with case study or experiential learning activities).[4]

## APPLIED METHODOLOGIES

As practitioners, we don't worry too much about the academic distinctions between conditioning, social learning, and cognitive psychology. In the day-to-day activity of analyzing performance problems, resolving customer performance issues, and building support for our tactics, we have found it useful to blend and converge these ideas into workable tools and solutions. More often than not, we find ourselves borrowing liberally from other practitioners who have learned how to apply these psychological principles to bring about change in everyday situations.

Therefore, in the sections that follow we would like to introduce you to what we feel are the key applied methodologies for designing coproduction experiences. They include the power of persuasion, behavioral engineering, user-centered design, and consumer choice.

### Persuasion

Robert Cialdini, in his best-selling book *Influence: The Psychology of Persuasion*, provides an insightful, if not humorous, tour of what it is like to be a *patsy*, otherwise known as an *easy mark*. Patsies, of course, are those of us in society who get tricked, taken, or otherwise persuaded to exchange our hard-earned cash for something of little or dubious value. Sometimes we are the target of dishonesty, but for the most part we are paired with people of the best intentions who thrive on doing whatever it takes to close the deal.[5]

Cialdini refers to his convergence of various psychological principles as *weapons of influence*, painting them primarily as evil tools that drive one to seek a means of defense. While this is true, we also think you can effectively leverage his ideas to encourage desired customer performance. Most of Cialdini's principles have a strong link to classical conditioning, which Cialdini affectionately, and more appropriately, terms *click, whirr*. Let's look at his six principles and how they work in various contexts.

## 1. Reciprocation

Reciprocation leverages our conditioned response associated with fairness. That is, if I give you something, you give me something. If I say hello, you say hello back. If I give you a present on your birthday, then you give me a present on my birthday. If I give you peanuts and a drink, then you'll sit in your seat quietly and not bother other passengers. In marketing, this frequently takes the form of a small gift (keychain, pen, golf ball) given to a client by a salesperson. The expectation, of course, is now that I've given you something, it is your turn to give me something.

## 2. Commitment and Consistency

A true double-whammy. Here the persuader gets the victim to verbally agree to a statement or make a statement favorable to the persuader's position. The persuader then uses that statement to leverage the victim's desire for internal consistency. This tactic is a common manipulative sales technique. In our experience, a car salesperson will say something like, "If I can find you this car in blue and set up a monthly payment for which you are qualified, would you buy the car?" As soon as you say "yes" you are trapped, because you have made the commitment and if the salesperson returns with such a deal, your desire for consistency leaves no choice but to sign the papers.

## 3. Social Proof

Consistent with the principles of social learning, social proof triggers the rationalization of, "If everyone is doing it, then it must be okay!" As such, marketers have not been beneath such tactics as paying people to form lines outside nightclubs. Others have been known to purchase copies of their own books to get them put on a bestseller list. Cialdini makes use of his own principle by listing a whopping 11 favorable testimonials on the back jacket of his book. *Click, whirr.* Must be a good book!

## 4. Liking

Liking is also known as the friendship principle. People are more apt to be persuaded by a friend, or someone who claims to be referred by a friend. Physical attractiveness, similarity, compliments, contact, and cooperation are all determinants of liking. In the movie about manipulative salesmen, Glengarry Glen Ross, Jack Lemmon's character, Sheldon Levine, uses all the tricks to ingratiate himself with a prospect—but to no avail. Upon entering the prospect's home he notes how nice the home is (compliment). He spots a fishing pole and begins talking about fishing (similarity). He also asks the prospect to call him by his first name, Sheldon (contact). However, the prospect is not tricked and eventually asks Sheldon to leave.

## 5. Authority

Recognized authority or expertise is a sure path to persuasion. Through titles (General, Ph.D.), clothes (police uniform, three-piece suit), and trappings (expensive cars, Rolex watches), people will defer their decision or choice to the one who is perceived to have greater authority. Now you know why bankers dress so nice and why so many of them are vice presidents.

## 6. Scarcity

Absence makes the heart grow fonder, which is the general principle behind scarcity. If people think something is in short supply, they will be more apt to get their share, and hence more easily persuaded to do so. Airlines, with their yield management systems, perpetuate the scarcity of reasonably priced tickets. This persuades travelers to buy months in advance.

While Cialdini's principles help us defend ourselves against telephone solicitations, door-to-door salespeople hawking free water test services, and our golf buddy's latest investment scheme, it would be negligent to shuffle these principles away as being purely evil. They can be useful, convergent strategies in the context of customer performance if used correctly and appropriately. Consider the task of the nurse educator who must persuade a 13-year-old boy to adopt a rigid regimen of insulin, diet, and exercise to manage his diabetes. Wouldn't it be negligent of the nurse educator to not leverage his authority (uniform, title), manipulate commitment to the regimen ("You know, if you don't follow this regimen you can become seriously ill, even die. You don't want to die, right?), and use the patient's affirmative response to help shape compliance?

Your answer to the question is, of course, "yes." Congratulations, you've just committed to using Cialdini's strategies for the purposes of good.

## Behavioral Engineering

Another source of convergence comes in the form of a lesser known book by Thomas Gilbert called *Human Competence*. Trained as a behavioral scientist, Gilbert left the academy and worked diligently in applied practice to converge not only principles of psychology, but complementary principles from fields such as engineering, economics, and sociology, into what he called, "a common single assumption." In short, to borrow phrasing popularized by the Democratic party in the 1990s, Gilbert recognized it is not about behavior, it's about performance, stupid.[6]

Gilbert's engineering and economic influences set the context for implementing behavioral change. He was adamant about the need for clear goals, measurable accomplishments, standards of performance, and recognizing when and where change was worthwhile. Once these issues were satisfactorily addressed, then the process of behavioral change could begin, as represented by Gilbert's behavioral engineering model.

Gilbert's model has six key elements that reflect causal explanations for various performance problems. Through *information*, you aim to understand whether people know what they are expected to accomplish, what the standards of accomplishment are, and whether they are informed quickly and frequently. *Instruments* uncovers whether the tools and materials people use to perform tasks are available and usable. *Incentives* examine WIIFM—What's In It For Me—from the perspective of incentives for good performance as well as poor performance. *Knowledge* investigates whether people have the requisite knowledge and skill to perform tasks. *Capacity* determines whether people have the mental and physical capacity to perform tasks, such as having a high IQ, being able to speak a foreign language, not being color blind, having 20/20 vision, and so on. *Motives* assess the relative excitement or dullness of the task, and whether the task is rewarding or punishing.

## User-Centered Design

In the late 1980s cognitive psychologist Donald Norman published *The Psychology of Everyday Things*, a provocative and solidly grounded work that explored the frustrations people have in their attempt to use various everyday objects. Light switches, doorknobs, faucets, VCRs, and stoves, just to name a few, were rigorously analyzed to uncover why they inhibited people's performance. Goals, perception, information processing, and context were the primary lenses Norman used to discover successes and flaws. The key results from Norman's work are seven principles that describe what it takes to make difficult tasks simple (hence improving customer performance).[7]

## 1. Use Both the Knowledge in the World and Knowledge in the Head.

Knowledge in the world describes the artifacts and cues about the function of an object, such as a doorbell button. Knowledge in the head is knowing what happens when the button is pressed. When there is consistency between both, performance is enhanced.

## 2. Simplify the Structure of Tasks.

Tasks become complex when there are numerous steps or elements; if the timing, frequency, or location of acts is varied; or if there is a state-change during the performance of the task. If none of these conditions can be simplified, for example, reducing the number of steps or automating a procedure, then job aids or reference cards may provide some relief. It used to be that to call a friend you had to remember the friend's phone number. Now phones simplify the task by remembering the number for you—you just need to remember which speed-dial button to press.

## 3. Make Things Visible.

People need to see a connection between their actions and the effects. Thus, if you turn on a light switch, you expect to experience a light turning on. If you don't, you wonder if something is wrong, or take an extra step to confirm your expectation—such as opening your front door to confirm the illumination of the porch light.

## 4. Get the Mappings Right.

Objects we interact with must reflect our mental models and structures. For example, consider a fancy front door that has the doorknob right in the center. The door looks great, but do you really know which side will open?

## 5. Exploit the Power of Constraints.

Constraints help people stay out of trouble. Guardrails on a twisty mountain road are an example of a constraint. The retractable barriers in airports that indicate where one should line up also illustrates this principle.

## 6. Design for Error.

People will fail. They will make mistakes. Be kind; allow them to recover from their mistakes without too much pain. The Undo button in software programs is a great example. Now if only life had an Undo button.

## 7. When All Else Fails, Standardize.

People will adapt to most any annoying task. Respect the learning curve they've experienced by making sure other things they will interact with allow them to apply what they've learned. For example, the DVORAK keyboard is proven to increase typing performance. However, since legions of people are conditioned to the QWERTY keyboard and have no clue how to use a DVORAK keyboard, computer makers have standardized on the QWERTY design.

## Consumer Choice

Consumers are rational decision makers. At least that's what professor James Bettman believes. In the late 1970s Bettman introduced what he called an *information processing approach for understanding consumer choice*. Strongly associated with the tenets of cognitive psychology, Bettman sees the customer as an information processor. In order to achieve goals, customers collect information that is relevant to a goal they are pursuing, process that information, make choices based upon the result of the processing, and then adapt their processes based on actual experience with a good or service. From a coproduction experience standpoint, customers who can process information more efficiently and effectively are more likely to unlock greater value.[8]

Because consumers spend much of their time acquiring information and responding to information, Bettman's ideas are well accepted. His work provides a model for consumer choice structured around six key foundations: goal hierarchy, attention, information acquisition and evaluation, decision processes, and consumption and learning processes.

### Goal Hierarchy

The driver of consumer motivation is the hierarchy of goals and subgoals consumers aim to attain. For example, *acquire a digital camera, determine the differences between brands,* and *select payment method* are all goals that initiate subsequent behavior.

## Attention

There are two kinds of attention. Voluntary attention is the consumer's allocation of processing effort to complete activities related to current goals. For instance, if the goal involves finding information, then attention is focused on product data. Involuntary attention is the automatic response to events not associated with the goal, such as a loud noise or a novel situation. This leads to interruption of the consumer's attention toward the goal.

## Information Acquisition and Evaluation

Consumers acquire information from internal sources (memory) and external sources (advertisements, product labels, salespeople, other customers). External information is sought when internal information is insufficient. For instance, reading the nutrition information on the label of a cereal box helps make a purchase decision.

## Decision Processes

Decision processes involve the comparison and selection of alternatives. For example, when deciding what kind of car to buy, a consumer may narrow the choices to a Honda Accord, Toyota Camry, and Nissan Altima. The consumer then applies rules or heuristics to compare key features, such as fuel economy, comfort, and power. The model that offers the highest "score" becomes the consumer's choice.

## Consumption and Learning Processes

This is the stage after the purchase has been made. The outcomes the consumer experiences become a source of information for future choices. This experience affects information acquisition (more information stored in memory) and decision processes (new heuristics are adopted). For example, after purchasing a Honda Accord, the customer experiences the lack of utility the single fold-down rear seat offers. This feature then becomes a rule for future car purchases.

## LINKAGES TO COPRODUCTION EXPERIENCES

The Coproduction Experience Model is yet another convergence of the aforementioned principles. The model focuses specifically on customers and their coproduction role in the consumption process. Through the lenses of vision, access, incentive, and expertise, one can use psychological principles in customer contexts to diagnose unsatisfactory customer experiences and design ideal coproduction experiences. This enables customers to unlock as much value as they can from goods and services.

What follows are summaries of several customer-oriented research studies. These studies clearly show the effect vision, access, incentive, and expertise has on customer performance, whether that performance be conserving energy, using self-service technologies, losing weight, or searching an information database.

## Conserving Energy

The trinity of conditioning, social learning, and cognitive psychology suggest that consumers who have *vision* (that is, they are aware of performance goals and receive feedback related to the achievement of goals) deliver overall better performance than consumers who do not. In 1989, Jeannet Van Houwelingen and W. Fred Van Raaij conducted a study that examined the effects of goal setting and feedback on home energy usage in the Netherlands. The researchers established a goal that they expected all homes in the study to achieve a 10 percent reduction in energy usage. However, the feedback homes received varied four ways.

- In the first group of homes the researchers installed a real-time energy-consumption indicator. Homeowners could observe the information provided by the device at any time.
- In the second group of homes the researchers provided homeowners monthly statements reporting their energy usage.
- In the third group of homes homeowners were asked to self-monitor their energy usage by recording meter readings on a piece of paper.
- The fourth group of homes was the control group. These homes received no feedback regarding their energy use.

Results from the study show that the goal and feedback schemes associated with the coproduction experience drove stronger performance (Figure 3.2).

Homeowners in groups 1, 2, and 3 experienced a significant reduction in energy use when compared to group 4, the control group. Homes that had the real-time indicator experienced the greatest reduction, 12.3 percent, surpassing the researcher's goal by 2.3 percent. The monthly statement group experienced a 7.7 percent reduction, the self-monitoring group experienced a 5.1 percent reduction, and the control group experienced a 4.3 percent reduction. These results show that *vision*, in the form of clear goals and

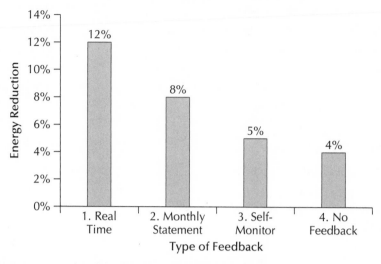

**Figure 3.2**  Results of the energy usage reduction study.

active, real-time feedback devices, contributes to a coproduction experience that enables customers to deliver sophisticated performance. Customers are able to unlock greater value in the form of reduced energy costs.[9]

## Using Self-Service Technologies

Shifting to the science of behavioral engineering, Tom Gilbert suggests that instruments and tools have a strong influence on performance. From a coproduction experience standpoint, instruments and tools are forms of *access*. One kind of tool, self-service technologies (SSTs), such as automated tellers, pay-at-the-pump terminals, and package tracking systems, enhance coproduction experiences a number of different ways. In 2000, Mark Meuter and his colleagues conducted a survey to investigate customer satisfaction with SSTs. The survey asked consumers to describe their usage of SSTs, as well as discuss "critical incidents" associated with usage. A critical incident is a story describing memorable positive or negative experience a consumer has with an SST. Meuter found that SSTs strongly contributed to customers being able to unlock more value from experiences. Specifically, they:

- Were better than alternatives, in terms of ease-of-use, time savings, cost savings, and greater control (68%)
- Did their job, such as fully completing a pay-at-the-pump transaction (21%)
- Enabled consumers to solve intensified needs, such as acquiring cash in emergency situations (11%)

Additionally, the results show that positive experiences with SSTs have a significant effect on the future behaviors of consumers, such as positive recommendations to other consumers and continued use of the SST. It is also interesting to note that when SSTs deliver a satisfying experience, consumers take the credit for success, whereas for dissatisfying experiences they assign the blame elsewhere.[10]

## Losing Weight

While vision and access are key factors that drive customer performance, the direct or vicarious inclusion of rewards and punishment in a customer setting can have a significant impact on coproduction experiences. There are a number of studies that examine this effect, especially in the area of monetary reinforcement related to behavior modification services. In 1994, Brian Mavis and Bertram Stoffelmayr compared the effects of five monetary incentive strategies on the performance of customers in a weight management program. The study randomly assigned 101 people to different experimental groups, representing different incentive strategies (monetary vs. lottery). One group received monetary rewards for achieving weekly goals (up to $8 per week over a 10-week period), while another group had money subtracted from their "bank account" when they did not meet weekly goals (a punishment). A similar scheme was used for lottery tickets, where people received lottery tickets or had lottery tickets taken away. The lottery tickets enabled people at the end of the 10-week program to win a significant share of a bonus pool (for example, a $1,000 first prize).

Results from the study show the monetary incentive as either a reward or punishment was a key factor in achieving weight loss, evidenced by an average weight loss of 12.01 pounds. This result was consistent with previous studies of rewards in the weight loss context. While a greater number of people favored the monetary award over the lottery award, the researchers found there was no difference between the various monetary incentive schemes on weight loss.[11]

## Searching an Information Database

We now turn our focus to the last element of the Coproduction Experience Model: *expertise*. Social learning and cognitive psychology have a direct impact on the methods we use to develop expertise in customers. One line of research in this area examines customer's usage of products and the effects of training on usage. Usage is believed to be a strong determinant in developing customer loyalty, in that if customers can successfully use products they are more likely to be loyal.

In 2001, Vikas Mittal and Mohanbir Sawhney conducted a study in collaboration with the Gartner Group. This study investigated the effects of content and process training on customer usage of Gartner Interactive's electronic information website, which provides fee-based access to research reports and documents covering the information technology (IT) marketplace. The desired customer performance is efficient usage, which results in renewed subscriptions to the site and incremental income generated from the purchase of affiliated products.

In their experiment, the researchers manipulated two kinds of training, content-oriented training and process-oriented training. Content training helped customers learn what was available on the site. Process training helped customers learn how to access the content. The results show that customers receiving training on both content and process had triple the usage of any of the other three treatment conditions (no training, content-only training, and process-only training). Hence, the development of expertise contributes to the creation of expert, high-performing customers. However, building expertise is costly in terms of time and money for both customers and companies.[12]

## SUMMARY

In this chapter we discussed the psychological foundations that drive customer performance. Consciously or unconsciously, companies leverage these principles to influence the behavior customers exhibit while consuming goods and services. Understanding these principles helps one observe customer performance with a renewed appreciation, in terms of the dynamics and complexity of human behavior. Additionally, the principles can help diagnose performance problems and drive solutions to improve the customer's experience.

The core psychological theories that drive the design of coproduction experiences are conditioning, social learning, and cognitive psychology. Each represents a slightly different view of the mind, but through their integration we come to understand human behavior through some combination of goals, inputs, processing, outputs, and feedback. Since humans are always seeking the path of least resistance (or the least effort), we become conditioned to repeating the experiences that we have learned, proudly wearing the label, "creature of habit." While this is desirable in some cases to preserve social order and maximize the value for all concerned, it can be a barrier to innovation and evolution, especially if we expect our customers to play a stronger role in unlocking value from goods and services.

Our examples of convergence, *persuasion, behavioral engineering, user-centered design*, and *consumer choice* are only a subset of the applied psychological principles dealing with performance that exist in the world. Yet they rise to the top of our list in terms of relevance since (1) most are strongly tied to customer behavior, and (2) they represent the leading thinking on what it takes to be a high-level performer. As an introductory collection, they provide a good foundation for understanding the ways we can design effective coproduction experiences.

Now that we have a common understanding of the psychological foundations behind customer performance, the remainder of the book provides a more pragmatic and practical look at how vision, access, incentive, and expertise contribute to the design of effective coproduction experiences.

# CHAPTER 4

# DISCOVERING WHERE VALUE HIDES

*Value is the most invincible and impalpable of ghosts,*
*and comes and goes unthought of while the visible and*
*dense matter remains as it was.*

—W. Stanley Jevons

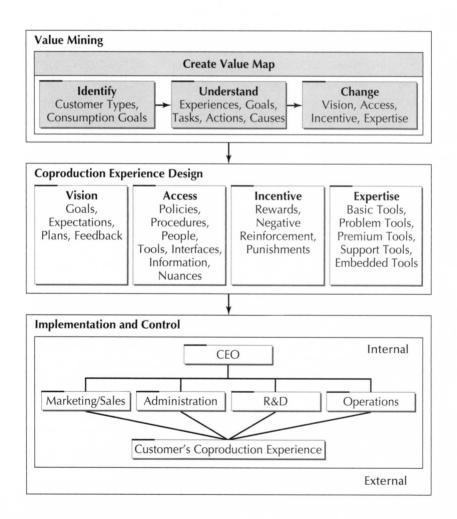

**Value Mining**

**Create Value Map**

| **Identify** | **Understand** | **Change** |
|---|---|---|
| Customer Types, Consumption Goals | Experiences, Goals, Tasks, Actions, Causes | Vision, Access, Incentive, Expertise |

**Coproduction Experience Design**

| **Vision** | **Access** | **Incentive** | **Expertise** |
|---|---|---|---|
| Goals, Expectations, Plans, Feedback | Policies, Procedures, People, Tools, Interfaces, Information, Nuances | Rewards, Negative Reinforcement, Punishments | Basic Tools, Problem Tools, Premium Tools, Support Tools, Embedded Tools |

**Implementation and Control**

Internal

CEO

Marketing/Sales · Administration · R&D · Operations

Customer's Coproduction Experience

External

In this chapter, we introduce you to a marketing research technique we call *value mining*. The purpose of this technique is to help you analyze where value hides in various customer experiences. To mine this value, we start by showing you how to construct a *value map*. A value map enables you to examine the interactions between customer types and customer goals throughout the experience process. The chapter continues with sections that discuss how you:

- Identify customer goals that have performance gaps
- Understand the nature and causes of the performance gaps
- Change customer experiences in order to close the performance gaps

## VALUE MINING

Earlier in the book we introduced the concept of value, describing it as the difference between the benefits a customer receives and the investments a customer must make to acquire those benefits. Value in a good or service remains "locked-up" until a customer uses the good or service, at which point the value is "unlocked." As rational entities, customers want to be successful in their use of goods and services, they want to avoid failure, and they want to realize the value that is embedded in the goods and services they consume. You must help customers realize these aims.

To find hidden value, you must examine two key dimensions of your business, *customer type* and *customer goal*. The model you use to analyze these two factors is called *value mapping*. As illustrated in Figure 4.1, value mapping enables a company to visualize the interactions between its customers (customer types) and the goals customers are attempting to accomplish (customer goals). An interaction between customer type and customer goal (represented by a cell in the matrix) identifies a point where value may be locked up. Once you identify the *customer types* and *customer goals* and the matrix takes shape, you now know where to start looking. You can use research techniques such as field visits, critical incident reviews, focus groups, intercepts, and internal data analysis to drill down into each box and discover whether the goal or its associated tasks and actions possess hidden value.

### Customer Type

The first part of value mapping focuses on identifying customers. The rows in the value mapping matrix represent the various customer segments that can unlock value. The example in Figure 4.1 shows three generic customer

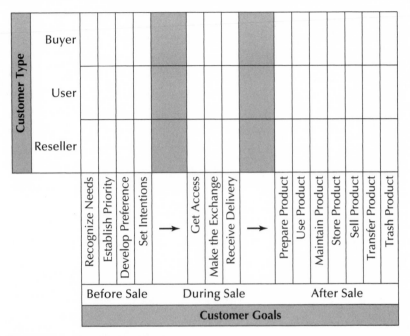

**Figure 4.1**   Value Mining Matrix.

segments, buyer, user, and reseller. This represents, at a high level, the range of customers any company can have. A *buyer* is a customer who buys a product, but does not use it (such as a dog owner buying dog food), a *user* is a customer who uses a product, and a *reseller* is a customer who buys a product with the intention of reselling it at a profit, such as a retailer.

These high-level segments, however, must be elaborated to match your company's context. The matrix is most effective when you replace the generic segments listed in Figure 4.1 with ones that are more meaningful and specific to your company's business. You can do this through generally accepted segmentation characteristics—geographic, demographic, psychographic, and behavioral. For example, buyers can be extended to distinguish between infrequent and frequent buyers. Users can be extended demographically, by age and gender. Resellers can be extended by their sales volume, such as under $250,000, $250,001 to $1 million, and over $1 million.

## Customer Goals

The second part of value mapping focuses on what customers and the company want to achieve. The columns in the value mapping matrix represent specific customer goals, structured in a timeline that follows a typical consumption process. These goals reflect a specific state or outcome the company and customer want to attain. For example, *Establish Priority*, the second goal listed under the category *Before Sale*, describes an outcome whereby a customer has recognized various needs and wants those needs prioritized in order of importance. At this phase the customer might recognize needs for a new car, a home improvement project, and a college education for children. The goal is to put these needs in order, from most important to least important, such that the customer can allocate his or her limited resources appropriately.

We find that orienting goals on a timeline similar to the one represented in Figure 4.1 is an easily understood means of representing goals. It also forces you to think about the customer's experience as a process. What is important to note here is that customers can unlock value at any time during the consumption process, before, during, and after a sale. Before the sale, customers have goals associated with acquiring information about a product so that they can make a choice. By using the company's website to obtain product information they are unlocking any value that service offers. During the sale they have goals associated with accessing products. By visiting a store or visiting an e-commerce site they are unlocking the value the channel offers. After the sale they have goals tied to using products. Knowing the full functionality of their cell phone enables them to more fully unlock the value embedded in that product.

As with customer segments, the generic consumption goals that we've listed should be elaborated to match the company's context. For example, a software company might take the generic goal of *Prepare Product* and elaborate it to reflect more relevant goals such as *Install Software*, *Register Software*, and *Configure Software*.

Figure 4.2 shows an example of a value matrix for a client of ours. The map was generated during the development of a system (chemistry, software, and detection instrument) that analyzes genes. In our analysis, we identified three specific types of customers: principal investigators (the folks who oversee the research), lab scientists (the folks to run the experiments), and biostatisticians (the folks to analyze the data for the principal investigator). Customer goals reflected goals that occurred before, during, and after the experiment. These included such goals as *Order Gene Kit*, *Collect Data*, and *Analyze Results*.

## Interactions in the Model

After you define the customer types and customer goals in the value mapping matrix, the resulting cells in the matrix provide a map of where value

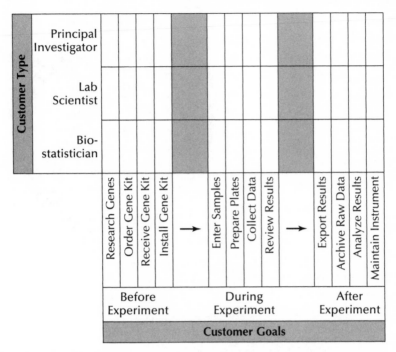

**Figure 4.2**    Value Mapping Matrix for a product that analyzes genes.

might be hidden. The next step in value mapping is to take a deep dive into each cell to discover its nature. Some interactions might be empty, which means that a goal is not meaningful to a specific customer segment. Other interactions are full of life, consisting of actions, tasks, goals, and experiences (Figure 4.3).

There are two primary forces at play in each cell, the customer and the company. The customer, represented by the diamond in Figure 4.3, owns the goal and must perform specific tasks and actions to achieve the goal. The company, represented by the Coproduction Experience Model, wraps the goal, tasks, and actions with a set of experiences that facilitate the customer's achievement of the goal in a satisfactory way.

It is within such an experiential context that customers unlock value by achieving goals. A goal represents the top of a hierarchy, below which are tasks and actions. In order to achieve goals, customers must perform tasks, which are measurable units of work. Each task is comprised of specific actions, such as steps in a procedure that must be performed in a certain way. For example, using the example from Figure 4.3, a hierarchy of goal, tasks,

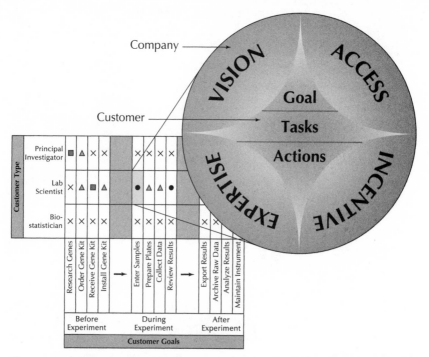

**Figure 4.3**  The DNA of Hidden Value: Experiences, Goal, Tasks, and Actions.

and actions is represented in Figure 4.4. At the top of the hierarchy a customer has the goal of *Enter Samples*. Within the experiential context afforded by the gene analysis system, the customer must perform several tasks that contribute to entering samples and subsequently unlocking value. The customer must determine which samples to include in the experiment (Task 1), format the selected samples into a sample file (Task 2), and import the sample file into the system (Task 3).

Value mapping enables you to visually depict the coproduction experiences afforded to your customers. Once you define the dimensions of customer type and customer goal, you can begin looking for areas where value is locked up. The process you lay on top of the value mapping model is a method of root cause analysis featuring the steps of *identify, understand,* and *change.* If one desires to create solutions *by design* rather than *by default,* one must first *identify* where problems exist, then *understand* the nature of those problems before effective and efficient *changes* can be made. The aim is to treat the causes, not the symptoms. The next three sections explore these concepts.

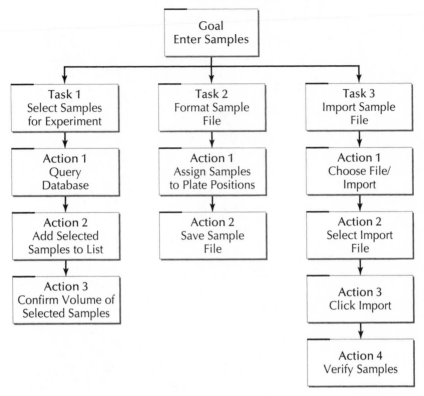

**Figure 4.4** Hierarchy of customer goal, tasks, and actions.

## IDENTIFY—EIGHT QUESTIONS FOR DISCOVERY

Imagine the value mapping matrix as a status board, where each cell in the matrix is colored green, yellow, or red (Figure 4.5). Green (square) indicates that customers are accomplishing goals and are satisfied with the experience. Yellow (triangle) indicates that while customers are accomplishing goals, their performance is not as good as it could be—they are not unlocking value efficiently or value is being threatened. Red (circle) indicates serious problems, such as customers not being able to accomplish goals and being dissatisfied with the experience. For our client's gene analysis product, the filled-out value mapping matrix ended up looking like the one in Figure 4.5.

The purpose of identification is to figure out whether a cell in the value mapping matrix should be colored green, yellow, or red. This is done by asking eight specific questions:

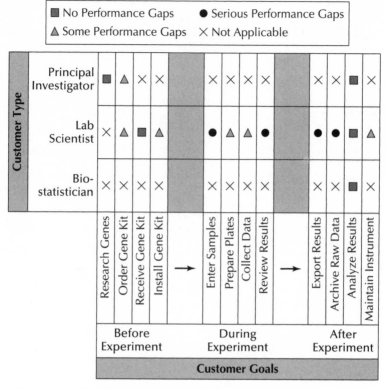

**Figure 4.5**  Completed value mapping matrix.

1. Are customers accomplishing goals?
2. Is the customer's experience a nuisance?
3. Is the experience that wraps the customer's goal by design or by default?
4. Is unconscious competence limiting customer performance?
5. Is employee job satisfaction low?
6. Are the tasks employees perform simple?
7. Is competition threatening how customers accomplish the goal?
8. Will significant forces affect how customers accomplish the goal?

## 1. Are Customers Accomplishing Goals?

When customers are not accomplishing goals tied to the consumption of goods and services, the color of a cell shifts to red. Goal attainment is critically important since it is correlated with repeat usage and customer satisfaction. The bottom line is that if customers are not accomplishing goals, they are not unlocking the value embedded in goods and services.

We know customers are not accomplishing goals by looking at one key indicator, *abandonment*. Abandonment is when customers quit, give up, or leave an experience because they find it impossible to achieve whatever goal they are attempting to accomplish. This indicator is a critical measure for one of our clients in the retail food industry. When customers become frustrated with the shopping experience they abandon their shopping carts and walk out of the store. This causes lost revenue, clutter in an already crowded store, and the extra expense of having to restock the goods, many of which are perishable. In another situation, a storyteller from one of our studies recounts an experience where she abandoned a company twice.

> Last year I was in the market for a digital camera, but I didn't know anything about them. So I went to Big Box Retailer A and looked at the variety they had. With all of the different functions on the camera it is real easy to get lost with those things. So I talked with a sales rep. For the most part the rep could tell me about everything that is labeled on the camera, what it means, and what is best for the different style of pictures one takes. However, when it came to operating the different functions the rep didn't know anything about it. I left and went to other stores and asked questions about the different functions of the camera. After going to three camera stores I finally figured out what I wanted. Big Box A had it so I went to go buy it on a Saturday afternoon. It was pretty crowded, but the guy in the camera department had seen me in there a couple of times looking at the cameras so he knew I was there to buy. He said to me, "I'll be right with you." I stood there for ten minutes while he waited on another customer—which was no problem. Time passed and numerous times he came to me and said, "Couple more minutes." I ended waiting a total of 25 minutes before I left, going instead to Big Box Retailer B, where what I wanted ended up being a good fifty dollars cheaper, including an extended warranty, for which Big Box Retailer A wanted to charge an extra $50.

In this situation the customer could not achieve her goal of acquiring product information, thus abandoning Big Box Retailer A to visit three other stores. When the customer decided to buy, Big Box Retailer A had a second chance to help the customer attain her goal. Unfortunately the customer could not achieve the goal (which at this point was time-limited), resulting in a second abandonment.

## 2. Is the Customer's Experience a Nuisance?

Customers will go to great lengths to achieve goals, but sometimes the experience is so horrible that they would abandon and switch if another option becomes available. Other options, however, aren't available so cus-tomers muddle through, dissatisfied and hoping for something better. We call this the *PITA factor*. PITA stands for Pain In The Ass, the colorful, subjective standard by which customers label experiences that offer little or no value, coloring a cell in the matrix red.

Webster defines PITA as, "something or someone that causes trouble; a source of unhappiness; e.g., washing dishes was a nuisance before we got a dish washer." We think of the PITA factor in similar terms, but try to make it more meaningful by describing it as a scale from 1 to 10, where 10 equals a major nuisance. As customers assess various consumption activities, they assign a value to the activity. Standing in line, waiting on hold, and assem-bling vast amounts of paperwork (for instance, a mortgage application) typ-ically have high PITA factors. Traveling using EZ Pass (an automatic device for paying bridge tolls), renting cars through National Car Rental's Emerald Club (which eliminates stops at the car rental counter), and ordering home pizza delivery typically have low PITA factors. In other words, a low PITA factor means that a company is easier to do business with.

PITA experiences are driven primarily by complexity, which reflects a cus-tomer's difficulty in using goods and services. Complex goals are sometimes seen as a challenge for some customers, who revel in the intellectual challenge of figuring out the bounds and limitations of a new product, such as a 3D graphics and animation software package. However, for the most part com-plexity is something that customers and companies wish to avoid. Several research studies suggest that complex goods and services result in negative word-of-mouth, avoidance, steep learning curves, and higher switching costs.

## 3. Is the Experience That Wraps the Customer's Goal by Design or by Default?

Default experiences are risky, and as such shift the color to yellow. Although a default experience might be working, it warrants investigation to deter-mine if the experience can be optimized.

Default experiences are relatively easy to identify through one or more of the following tests. If the experience is not written down in the form of a script, plan, or process, it's by default. If the experience hasn't been tested, then it's by default. If employee tasks associated with the experience are not covered in training, it's by default. If you ask the question, "Who decided that this should work this way?" and the response is, "He did," "She did," or "I don't know. It just happens," then it's by default (designs are typically cre-ated by a committee of stakeholders, not individuals).

Consider this fiasco that occurred in a well-known express fast-food out-let occupying space within a larger convenience store. Both the fast-food outlet and the convenience store shared a self-service soft drink machine. When the fast-food outlet sold a drink, the clerk would hand a cup and a lid to the customer. If the convenience store sold a drink, the customer would pick up a different type of cup and lid from next to the soda machine, and pay for it at the convenience store cashier. That was the design. Odd, but it seemed to work okay for customers and the store.

One day, the fast-food outlet manager independently decided it would be more efficient for his workers if customers took soft drink cups and lids off the counter. This would eliminate the task of the fast-food outlet clerk reaching under the counter and handing the customer the cup and lid (which was the "by design" scheme for this unique setting). He made the change, had employees place the cups and lids on the counter, and explained the new procedure. The new scheme wasn't tested. Stakeholders from the convenience store weren't consulted.

Over the next week or two, the problems began to compound. Cus-tomers would forget to take the cup. Knowing they had paid for a drink they would then use the convenience store's cup for their drink. The convenience store would then try to charge the customer for something the customer had already paid for at the fast-food outlet counter. This caused confusion and complaints. Another more frequent situation was when customers took the cup but forgot to take the lid. After filling their cup they tried to place a convenience store lid on the cup (a stack of which were right next to the soda machine). Since the cups were different, the lids weren't compatible. This caused a big mess of damaged lids being discarded around the soda ma-chine and complaints to the convenience store cashiers about the lack of correctly sized lids.

Did these failures cause the fast-food outlet manager to return to the old way of doing things? Not likely. The last we heard was that a handwritten sign was being installed that read, "The only lids that work with the [fast-food outlet] cups are right here [arrow points to the lids]." Handwritten signs are another dead give-away that the process is by default rather than by design.

## 4. Is Unconscious Competence Limiting Customer Performance?

Unconscious competence is a state customers enter when they have done a task so many times that it becomes rote. This equates to very high levels of expertise. However, with high levels of expertise customers can become conditioned to the status quo and no longer think about how a task could be done better, faster, easier, and so on. When customers enter this state, their ability to unlock value may diminish as they become creatures of habit to the "one way." This can shift the color of a cell to yellow.

For example, when we have evaluated the usability of software applications we often have test subjects who perform all tasks using the toolbar menus, never using the shortcut keys on the keyboard. Obviously, using the toolbar menus slows the performance substantially since the user must shift between keyboard and mouse constantly. Yet when we ask why they aren't using the more efficient shortcut keys the subjects react in surprise that such a feature exists—because the toolbars worked, they never thought to investigate if there was a better way.

## 5. Is Employee Job Satisfaction Low?

The dissatisfaction of employees, especially frontline employees, can indicate problem areas in a company's operations. In our experience much employee dissatisfaction comes from the inability of employees to help customers accomplish goals, and the subsequent customer complaints employees must endure. Identifying this kind of dissatisfaction in relationship to a customer goal shifts the color of a cell to yellow.

An experience that illustrates this point occurred in one of the businesses we managed. When we came into the business, we immediately noticed that the morale of call center employees was very low. The employees were responsible for providing services to customers, such as helping customers get information about their account, changing service levels, and resolving customer problems. Due to other issues in the business one of the frequent problems customers had was tied to the goal of resolving billing errors.

When customers discovered an error on their monthly bill, they would call to get it resolved. Unfortunately, the call center employees did not have access to customer billing records on their computers. They could not answer the customer's questions nor resolve the issue on the spot, which usually involved issuing a credit card refund. They would tell the customer that they would forward the issue to the billing department, who would contact the customer in three to five days (this added complexity and invariably things would get lost, prompting a more irate customer call). Of course, customers would scoff at this since they had become conditioned by other service providers in other industries who could resolve billing issues on the spot. Invariably, customers would insult the employees by telling them, "If the phone company can resolve these kinds of problems instantly, why can't you?" Nonetheless, this vicious cycle had continued unchecked, dragging down the morale of employees who weren't able to help customers achieve what was perceived as a simple goal.

Another dimension of low employee job satisfaction is that of tedium and redundancy. If tasks are extraordinarily simple employees will become bored. They will subsequently communicate their boredom verbally or nonverbally to customers, diminishing the customer's experience. In such situations companies might be better off shifting the work to the customer, since the customer won't be doing the task eight hours a day.

## 6. Are the Tasks Employees Perform Simple?

When customers pursue certain goals, employees provide assistance to help the customer accomplish the goal. Whether the goal is grocery shopping, buying clothes, or setting up a computer, a knowledgeable employee can do most of the work or assist the customer with completing the task. However, in some cases an employee does nothing more than slow down the process and perhaps makes the customer feel a bit awkward. These are ideal situations where work might be better performed by customers themselves.

Bellhops in today's modern hotels are an example of such inefficiency. A carryover from the times when travelers overpacked in steamer trunks and hotel signage was limited, bellhops used to perform a useful function. They'd put your baggage on a wheeled trolley so you didn't have to carry it. Then they'd show you the location of your room. In today' atmosphere of well-conditioned travelers who, with their wheeled luggage, can easily follow hotel signage to their room, what purpose does the bellhop serve? Yes, they do humanize the hotel experience, assist with overweight bags, and make the lowliest of customers feel like big shots. But for us, get these guys out of our way! They slow us down, make us feel awkward, reduce our control, and expect to be compensated to boot.

Moving luggage, operating a barcode scanner, carrying plates from a counter to a table, and filling one's gas tank are simple tasks. We know they are simple because they involve simple motor behaviors and basic cognitive processing. There really isn't any complex problem solving or domain-specific knowledge required for these tasks. In most cases, customers have probably had a job at some point in time where the elementary skills were developed, or they perform the task at home. We also know these tasks are simple because the money companies pay people to perform theses tasks hovers around minimum wage.

Simple tasks of this sort are always candidates for shifting work to the customer. The customer can probably perform the task better, faster, cheaper, and with a more positive attitude than the employee. There will always be contexts where the service provided by employees is expected and appreciated. For example, we don't think customers will be making their own sandwiches at Subway shops anytime soon. But these days companies are giving us the choice of whether we want to perform the task or not. Self-checkout at grocery stores and Home Depot is a clear example. However, as customers gain more skills and companies develop new systems that improve their trust in customers, customers should expect more work coming their way.

## 7. Is Competition Threatening How Customers Accomplish the Goal?

One of Michael Porter's key competitive strategies is differentiation, and many companies are differentiating themselves with claims of being *easier to do business with (ETDBW)*. ETDBW means that customers can accomplish goals associated with the company's goods and services better, faster, and with less effort than competitors. Robert Johnson, in his research on Service Excellence, describes ETDBW as something that "... simply requires organizations to do what they promise and if and when things go wrong have a good system in place to deal with them."[1] If competitors threaten a company's ETDBW advantages associated with a customer goal, the appropriate cell in the matrix shifts to yellow or even red.

ETDBW is a competitive advantage that is being leveraged in virtually all industries. Technology researcher IDC lists ETDBW as one of the top six criteria companies use to choose an information technology supplier. Tyco Electronics recognized Arrow Electronics as its "Distributor of the Year" based on Arrow's ETDBW characteristics. Chuck Stephens and Gloria Green, consumer lending specialists with the Credit Union National Association (CUNA), advocate ETDBW principles and suggest that credit unions are easier to do business with when they:

- Grant loan approvals quickly
- Have a 24/7 call center
- Provide website services such as approval tracking, payment calculators, and product information
- Use technology that eliminates repetitive actions and frees staff from routine roles

- Acquire the same or better tools than competitors
- Have regular reviews of customer processes
- Strengthen processes at which they excel, and outsource the rest
- Synchronize technology, processes, organization, and lending systems[2]

## 8. Will Significant Forces Affect How Customers Accomplish the Goal?

A *significant force* is one that has a macro effect on a company's business. These forces are typically technological, social, political, or environmental in nature. They have the power to shift a cell in the matrix to yellow over time or to red overnight. For example, in the 1970s the barcode was a significant technological force that changed how customers shopped. In the 1980s legislation deregulating the telecommunications industry was a significant political force that changed how customers acquired their telephone services and hardware. In the 1990s curbside pickup of recyclable waste was an environmental force that changed how customers dispose of products. In the 2000s, air travel was forever redefined through the terrorist acts of September 11, 2001.

Recognizing significant forces and their effects on customer goals takes a bit of gazing into a crystal ball to envision what the future might hold. As we write this book we know that the web and similar computing technologies will make it easier for customers to do more work in their relationships with companies. We used to go to a video store to rent videos; now we have Netflix deliver our movies by mail. Soon we can expect video-on-demand systems to deliver videos right to our televisions. In fact, such systems are being tested now.

It doesn't take a rocket scientist to envision the day when we walk into a hotel, go to a pre-designated room listed on our Blackberry, and use our thumbprint to check in and gain access to our room. This completely bypasses the laborious check-in process hotels now use. If radio frequency identification (RFID), a technology that tracks products using radio chips, should come to replace product barcodes, we can envision a shopping experience in which customers bag their own groceries as they shop and check out by wheeling their cart through a scanning device that will not only scan the products they are buying but their electronic payment card as well.

Two decades ago trend-spotter Faith Popcorn coined the term *cocooning* to describe the social trend of people spending more time in and about their homes. This trend saw the shift of many customer goals. Rather than going out to do their shopping, customers went in, first using mail-order catalogs and the telephone, then web-based e-commerce systems to buy everything from clothes to home accessories. Even though many delivery-based companies such as Pets.com and WebVan failed to find success following this trend, being at a disadvantage with heavy, low-margin products, companies such as Costco enabled customers to stock up on bulk food inventories so that visits to the local grocery store would be less frequent.

A force that offers a quantum change in how customers accomplish goals and unlock greater value is the concept of the *trusted customer*. Customers, as viewed by many businesses, are untrustworthy. Banks require collateral for loans. Deception, theft, cheating, delinquency, and sabotage by customers force companies to adopt procedures and policies that limit the unlocking of value for all customers. Businesses have to endure the hassle of a credit check when establishing an account with a vendor. Shoppers must have their goods inspected and security tags removed before being allowed to leave a store. During a visit to a CompUSA store for a repair estimate, we were carrying our laptop computer, Palm Pilot, and other technology associated with our "mobile office." All of this had to be inspected and tagged before going into the store, then inspected and detagged upon our leaving the store.

For those of us who are trustworthy, the label of a trusted customer is empowering and full of value. Our first experience with such a label came on the Berlin subway. There were no turnstiles, ticket checkers, or other inconveniences that hindered our access to the trains. Rather, we were trusted to have purchased a ticket. If a random check by a conductor revealed we didn't, then we suffered the consequence of a hefty fine. Such policies have been mimicked in the United States, specifically on the San Jose Light Rail System (where 2 to 3 percent of riders are found not to have purchased tickets).

National Car Rental, like many car rental companies, has a great scheme for trusting customers. It is called Emerald Club. In exchange for giving National lots of information about yourself as well as unfettered access to your credit card, you receive easy access to their cars. Need to rent a car? Make a reservation, show up at the lot, select your car, and drive away, showing your Emerald Club card and driver's license to the attendant at the gate. Our trustworthiness and collateral excuses us from having to wait in line at the counter.

The latest trusted customer effort underway is in air travel. In July 2004, the Transportation Security Agency (TSA) began testing its voluntary Registered Traveler Program (otherwise known as "trusted traveler"—a great name but unfortunately it assumes all other travelers are not trustworthy). In exchange for personal information, including fingerprints and iris patterns, travelers who are accepted into the program benefit from an expedited security check process. Several schemes for verifying trusted travelers are being tested, from biometric (eye) scans to card-based systems. Members of airline frequent flier programs and airline crews were the first to be invited into the program, and the Minneapolis test quickly accepted 2,400 travelers into the program.

Similar systems are already in place for passport control in high-risk airports such as Tel Aviv's Ben Gurion Airport. The value these systems offer travelers is impressive. A traveler can complete what would be a two-hour process in less than 20 minutes. To date, over 100,000 travelers have enrolled in the program and they pay a $25 annual fee for the privilege.[3]

## UNDERSTAND

Once a customer goal in the value mapping matrix is identified as having problems, the next step is to understand the nature of the problems. A problem means that there is a gap between what customers expect to experience and what they are experiencing. Recall the story earlier in the chapter in which a customer wanted to buy a digital camera. She expected a wait of no more than 10 minutes to buy the camera, but after 25 minutes she was no further toward accomplishing her goal.

When we want to understand a customer performance problem our aim is to (1) quantify what the customer is going through, and (2) determine what is causing the problem. With regards to quantification, Figure 4.6 illustrates how we analyze the problem by working from left to right. We begin by investigating specific customer actions and end by analyzing the experience. Actions and tasks tend to be more objective, meaning that measures such as quality, quantity, and time are ideal for understanding their nature. Goals and experiences, on the other hand, tend to be more subjective. This means that we must investigate customer attitudes regarding the degree of satisfaction a goal or experience provides.

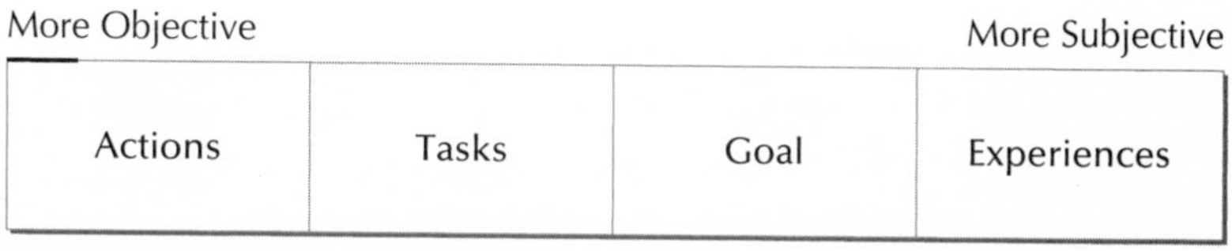

More Objective                                           More Subjective

| Actions | Tasks | Goal | Experiences |
|---------|-------|------|-------------|

**Figure 4.6**   Levels of Understanding.

## Understanding Actions

Actions are specific steps customers take to accomplish tasks. For example, if the task is to check out of a supermarket using a self-checkout system, then actions would include such steps as removing an item from the cart, scanning it, bagging the item, processing the payment, and exiting the process. The measurement of actions is objective since the measures must be observable. We can easily determine if customers perform the action (yes/no), how fast an action takes (less than two seconds), and the number of errors experienced (less than one error per ten items). The measures, which are known as *standards of performance*, define a level that is comfortable and acceptable to customers. If customers can accomplish actions within a standard of performance then they are on their way toward being satisfied customers.

Desired standards of performance may be defined numerous ways. The easiest way is to define a standard that maximizes a company's efficiency. Electronic point-of-sale systems can, for example, track the number of rings (items) per minute. One of our clients knows that 18 rings per minute is an acceptable standard. Anything slower means customers are getting irritated (due to inefficiency) and anything faster means that more mistakes occur. Other companies ask a sample of customers to perform the actions and measure their performance. These customers can also provide feedback as to whether the standards are acceptable in the given context. An extension of this is customer councils, a technique used by Hewlett-Packard. Important customers are invited to participate in the council to help define product performance and service measures. Companies can also benchmark performance by examining the standards of competitors or other industries for similar actions.

Companies also think about standards in the context of easier to do business with (ETDBW). ETDBW essentially means that customers are meeting the standards of performance expected in an experience. Service experts Ron Zemke and Chip Bell quantify ETDBW in services through seven specific measures, gleaned from their research:[4]

1. The number of times a customer is put on hold
2. The number of times a customer is transferred
3. The number of employees who say "I'm not sure we can do that" or some variation
4. The number of employees who complain about their day or why your request is a bother

5. The number of employees who tell you "No, you can't have that" or some variation
6. The number of times a customer asks to speak to someone in charge
7. The number of times a customer has to repeat himself

In this analysis, the lower the aggregate number, the easier a company is to do business with.

So, to understand actions one must ensure that actions are:

- Observable
- Measurable
- Compared to a standard of performance

Actions that do not meet the standards of performance are candidates for change.

## Understanding Tasks

Tasks are measurable units of work. Like actions, they are observable, measurable, and compared to a standard of performance. The measurable components of a task, therefore, aren't the specific actions a customer performs but the result of those actions. For example, assemble product, make reservation, compose letter, change profile, retrieve messages, and analyze data are all tasks since the output is an observable, measurable work product. To carry forward the previous checkout example, self-checkout is a task in which the work product (the state of being *checked out*) is assessed with the following measures:

- All items scanned
- Correct prices for all items recorded
- Correct payment tendered
- Correct change remitted
- Within five minutes for up to 50 items

To understand tasks we analyze them *systemically*—in their entirety. One of the more popular techniques is that of process mapping, where the actions associated with a task are mapped in relationship to time (when the action occurs) and place (who performs the action). Through process mapping, complexity, inefficiency, bottlenecks, feedback, and other deficiencies become visible. This enables people to understand the nature of a problem and its causes, and begin to conceive of alternative solutions.

Customers describe tasks that are free of problems as *simple*, while tasks that are problematic are *complicated* or *complex*. Thus, when we observe customers performing tasks, or when we analyze a process map, we look for specific attributes that help us understand the relative complexity of tasks. We know tasks are complex when:[5]

1. Customers must perform many actions to achieve a task
2. Customers must process many information cues while performing actions
3. Customers perform actions infrequently
4. Customers perform actions in different locations or contexts
5. Customers perform actions in environments or contexts that are dynamic or distracting

Thus to understand tasks one must look first at the measures and standards associated with the task, then to the nature of the task itself. If one finds that customers are not meeting standards, and/or that the structure of the task is complex, the task is a candidate for change.

## Understanding Goals

Like tasks, goals represent a desired customer outcome. For example, customer goals could be an enjoyable vacation, a quick shopping trip, a romantic evening, or buying a car with straight talk and no run-around. The nature of goals is that they represent a significant outcome and that their attainment is more subjective than objective. Notice the qualifying words in the above examples: *enjoyable, quick, romantic, straight-talk, no run-around.* These qualities are typically unique to an individual and evaluated on a case-by-case basis. Plus they are affective in nature, meaning they reflect the feelings of an individual rather than an objective, clinical standard.

To understand goals we need to use techniques that enable us to observe the unobservable, that is, what is going on inside the customer's head. The most common technique is the attitudinal survey, where customers rate on a scale of five, seven, or nine their agreement/disagreement with a qualitative statement. When IBM tests new products with customers, not only do they assess the objective components associated with goals, such as time, errors, and completion rate, but also the affective components associated with the goal, which include:[6]

- Ease of Use—Satisfaction associated with the ease of applying a product to achieve a goal
- Function—Satisfaction associated with a product's ability to perform tasks associated with a goal
- Information—Satisfaction associated with the information that is available to acquire, use, or support a product

- Initial Experience—Satisfaction of the initial experience provided by a product
- Integration—Satisfaction with a product's ability to communicate with other goods and services
- Overall—Satisfaction with the entire experience associated with a product
- Performance—Satisfaction with the speed or response time exhibited by a product to achieve a goal
- Reliability—Satisfaction with the reliability of a product in achieving a goal

Other methods of understanding customer goals include focus groups, one-on-one interviews, story completion, picture completion, and so on. Gerald Zaltman of the Harvard Business School has pioneered a technique that uses magnetic resonance imaging (MRI) to peek into customers' brains. He calls this technique "*interviewing the brain.*" Coca-Cola, Ford, and other companies have used this technology to investigate when products trigger in customers feelings of happiness and joy, as well as thought and memory.[7]

Thus to understand goals one looks primarily at the affective responses customers have toward their completion of goals. If one finds that customers are dissatisfied, the factors surrounding the goal are candidates for change.

## Understanding Experiences

In order to differentiate themselves from competitors, appeal to customers' aesthetic preferences, and facilitate the satisfying attainment of goals, companies wrap the customers' actions, tasks, and goals in experiences. As described earlier in this chapter, experiences manifest themselves as levels, ranging from the experience a product offers (such as the customized ringing tones on a cell phone) to the sociocultural context an experience affords. Think of Starbuck's, where its "third place" positioning offers customers a destination other than home (the first place) and work (the second place) that affords the feeling and camaraderie often found in an English pub.

In many regards experiences are the environments Albert Bandura describes in his social learning theory. When combined with one's personal factors, these experiences trigger the release of certain kinds of behavior.

Understanding experiences is akin to taking an inventory of sights, sounds, smells, and touches associated with goods and services. One must adopt the role of a connoisseur, with eyes, ears, and a nose to notice not only the big picture but the foggy nuances as well. From the pressure of a salesperson's grip to the color of paint on the wall, experiences are perceived by all of our senses. Experiences can communicate *competence*, such as the "wall of diplomas" found in many doctors' offices, or *control*, such as the presence of TensaBarrier® retractable tape system (the retractable devices that form lines), line monitors, and armed guards in airports. Soft lighting and classical music can enhance a romantic mood, while bright lights and a pulsating beat can energize!

In Costco warehouses, oversize shopping carts, wide aisles, and pallet racks stacked four high communicate that customers are expected to buy lots of goods, in volume, while the dim lighting reinforces the sense of frugality. We wonder if the real reason why Costco provides free food samples and a hot dog bar is that pushing a 100-, 500-, or even 1,000-pound trolley loaded with goods takes energy! With services we know that modern-looking equipment and visually appealing facilities, employees, and signs are desirable features that increase a customer's confidence in the service. With goods, visibility of functions, simplified tasks, clear mappings, constraints, forgiveness, and standardization make them easier to use.

Thus to understand experiences one must examine a company's contributions to customers' actions, tasks, and goals. Does the company let customers fend for themselves? Or does the company take a leadership role by ensuring customers have what they need to unlock value from goods and services? The analysis of experiences helps a company confirm causes and uncover deficiencies. It is also in this context where solutions become apparent, which usually means that the experience is a candidate for a change.

## Making Connections to Causes

As you develop an understanding of the performance problems associated with actions, tasks, goals, and experiences, causes become evident. Customers might claim that no one told them what they were supposed to do. Customers might also complain about the absence of a key tool, or that they didn't know how to perform a task. Using the Coproduction Experience Model as a guide, you can begin to classify each cause as being associated with one of the four forces: vision, access, incentive, and expertise (Figure 4.7).

Once the causes are correctly classified, you can explore possible solution areas. As shown in Table 4.1, each cause is correlated with a set of possible solutions. This ultimately helps you to determine what changes you must make.

The story of Procter & Gamble's Pur water-purifying powder illustrates the connection between cause and solution. Acquired from another company in 1999, Pur was thought to be a solution for cleaning the world's water supplies—especially in developing countries lacking water treatment infrastructure. The product, however, had lackluster success due to cost and

**Figure 4.7**   Vision, Access, Incentive, and Expertise categorize the causes of customer performance problems and suggest appropriate changes to the coproduction experience.

**Table 4.1    Correlation Between Causes and Solutions**

| Cause | Possible Solution Areas |
|---|---|
| **Lack of Vision**<br>Customer doesn't know what to do. | • Goals<br>• Expectations<br>• Plans<br>• Feedback |
| **Diminished Access**<br>Something in the coproduction environment prevents the customer from performing. | • Policies<br>• Processes/Procedures<br>• People<br>• Tools<br>• Interfaces<br>• Information<br>• Nuances |
| **Inappropriate or Missing Incentives**<br>Customer is not performing as desired or is performing in an incorrect way. | • Rewards<br>• Punishment<br>• Negative Reinforcement<br>• Removal of punishing conditions |
| **Absence of Expertise**<br>Customer does not have the competency to perform actions or tasks. | • Basic tools<br>• Embedded tools<br>• Premium tools<br>• Problem tools<br>• Support tools |

complexity. Treatment takes about 30 minutes and involves transferring the treated water between different containers. Through this process, the powder turns muddy water laden with bacteria and viruses into pure, uncontaminated drinking water.

When the 2004 tsunami struck southern Asia, Pur had its opportunity to shine. Relief agencies were calling for the product, and P&G sent its expert, Dr. Greg Allgood, to oversee the diffusion and adoption of the product in the region. Because of the complex purification procedure and lack of customer expertise, the Pur process requires a hands-on demonstration—a basic tool that Dr. Allgood provided to villages. Customers also needed vision. People were skeptical of the product's ability to turn muddy well water into safe drinking water. After Dr. Allgood demonstrated the purification procedure, he'd drink the purified water, and then encourage others to do the same. They did.

However, there was one last catch. For most people in the region, most of their belongings had been washed away. From a coproduction standpoint, it was a case of diminished access; people didn't have the buckets to perform the purification task. One villager, Mohamed Irshad, attended Dr. Allgood's demonstration and wanted to use the product if it became available at the local store (and was sold for a reasonable price). However, he lacked the buckets that were required for mixing. This situation was the opposite of what P&G experienced when selling Pur in Central America and Pakistan. P&G developed a Pur kit that included the buckets. In those countries they sold 2 million packets of Pur, but only a very small number of bucket kits. Customers already had the buckets.[8]

This story demonstrates the need for orchestrating all four elements of the Coproduction Experience Model. By linking causes to the model, you can quickly develop the tactics that will enable customers to perform.

# CHANGE

Value mining assists you in identifying and understanding where customers are experiencing difficulties unlocking value from goods and services. Through the process, you develop the knowledge that enables you to answer these questions:

1. Is this happening in our business?
2. How much is the problem costing?
3. What are the causes?
4. What are the solutions?

The focus of this section (and the remainder of the book) is on linking the last two questions—what are the causes and what are the solutions? That is, what should you change about the customer's process or the customer's experience to realize bottom-line benefits? The old paradigm was that companies did the work for customers. Now, the paradigm has shifted to where companies and customers expect customers to do more things for themselves.

Change, therefore, must reflect this paradigm shift. It must bridge the gap between customers' current level of performance and the performance they should be exhibiting in the future. Unlocking value is a partnership between the company and the customer. Customers provide the labor and the company provides an orchestration of vision, access, incentive, and expertise in the form of a coproduction experience. This enables customers to be peak performers.

As you begin to understand the driving and restraining forces involved in coproduction experiences, causes and their associated solutions, in hindsight, become apparent.

- If customers aren't aware of what they're supposed to do, *tell them.*
- If there is a simpler way for them to do tasks, *change it.*
- If they're having trouble getting motivated, *reward them.*
- If they don't have the knowledge and skills, *teach them.*

As you gain experience with such concepts, you'll recognize that it is not just a single action that closes the gap. Rather, it is an orchestration of remedies in varying doses.

For example, if you want customers to conserve energy in their homes, telling them to cut their electrical consumption by 10 percent is a good start. But we can already hear the questions. How am I going to do that? How do I know if I am anywhere near that goal? What happens if I don't reduce my consumption? What happens if I exceed the goal? Isn't there some fancy device you can install in my home that turns things off automatically so achieving this goal won't be such a nuisance?

We have talked much about the importance these strategies offer customers in terms of time and the PITA factor. However, the decision to adopt and implement changes is dependent upon whether the solution increases the customer's lifetime value (CLV). CLV is expressed as the value of all purchases a customer makes during his or her lifetime as a customer. Changes that improve customer performance will not have a direct, observable effect on CLV. Instead, changes are the first domino in a chain reaction that ultimately leads to enhanced CLV, as depicted in Figure 4.8.

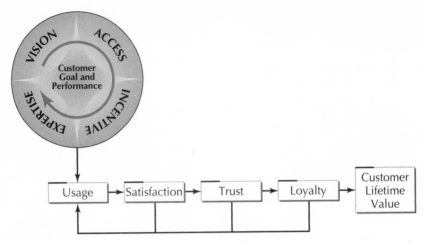

**Figure 4.8**  The chain of effects associated with an enhanced coproduction experience.

When you implement an enhanced coproduction experience two things happen. First, the customer's goal is modified. Ideally, this new goal is more effectively aligned with the nature of the coproduction experience. The shaping of goals is critical if a company is shifting more work to customers, for example, making customers responsible for maintaining their own account information.

Second, the customer's performance improves. The result is that customers are better able to perform do-it-yourself tasks and actions. A company might make tasks simpler or increase customer expertise in efficiently completing tasks.

The goal and the customer's performance influence usage. Usage involves how much a customer uses a good or service. This is evidenced by such measures as the number of minutes per month (cell phone), the number of consumables purchased (filters for a Brita water filter), or the number of visits to a store or website. If the customer uses a good or service in such a way that it achieves the customer's goal, the result is satisfaction. The greater the satisfaction, the more likely the customer increases usage.

Over time and based upon the level of satisfaction achieved through usage, the customer slowly begins to develop trust. When a customer trusts a company, the customer holds the belief that the company can and will deliver the experiences that result in the achievement of goals.

Consider a cell phone services customer. Every time he presses the talk button on his cell phone he gets a clear, crisp connection. He's experienced this for nine months, and the cell phone company has reinforced it by teaching him where and how to use the cell phone to ensure a clear, crisp connection. You can expect that through these experiences the customer comes to trust the cell phone company since it has delivered consistent performance and it has been benevolent—evidenced by its teaching the customer key phone usage techniques. This pays off when the cell phone company introduces a broadcast television service that enables the customer to watch television on his cell phone. Based upon the prior experience, the cell phone customer is more likely to believe that this new service will have similar qualities as the standard voice service. We expect the customer will adopt the new service from the same cell phone company if he has a need for the service.

This level of trust leads to loyalty. A loyal customer is one who is willing to recommend a good or service to another person. Why does this action reflect loyalty more than usage and repeat purchases? Because by making a recommendation the customer is taking a risk. In the eyes of the customer (and in the eyes of others), the customer's reputation may suffer if the recommendation proves faulty. Loyal customers, therefore, are *brand ambassadors* who support a company's efforts to acquire new customers, even if those loyal customers are no longer customers themselves.[9]

Increased usage, the trust to adopt other goods and service offerings, and the recruitment of other customers through recommendations all contribute to the customer's lifetime value. This magic number should guide a company's investment in improving coproduction experiences. By comparing these expected outcomes with the magnitude of the problem and the cost of the solution, companies can decide how and when they want to invest. The magnitude of the problem may be expressed in terms of cost or opportunity. Costs involve such things as too many customers calling the company for help, customers returning the company's products, customer demands stretching the company's resources too thin, and customers defecting to competitors. Opportunities involve customers not utilizing fee-based services, customers not recommending the company's products, or customers not defecting to the company. Solution costs include not only the direct costs of employees, consultants, materials, and capital to make it happen, but also intangibles such as time and the psychological impact of pushing change through an organization. To synthesize the right course of action we liberally borrow a handy little formula from Tom Gilbert that expresses the most important factors as:

$$\text{Worth} = \text{Value} - \text{Cost}$$

Companies make changes to the coproduction experience when the worth-whileness of a solution is positive. The value a solution provides must outweigh the cost of implementing the solution.

## SUMMARY

In this chapter, we discussed an approach for discovering where value hides. We call the approach value mining and it is based upon two dimensions. First, you segment customers to determine who can unlock value. Second, you uncover customer goals that exist throughout the consumption process. When you link customer types with customer goals, you map the landscape, creating a value map of possible spots where value might hide (it might also be worthwhile at this point to map competitors as well). Once this map is in place you can begin looking for gold.

Each cell in the value mapping matrix represents four specific compo-nents. From the customer's perspective, the cell represents not only the goal, but the tasks and actions the customer must perform to unlock value. From the company's perspective, the goal, tasks, and actions are wrapped with experiences—which the company provides. The intention of these experi-ences is to enable the customer to achieve the goal in an efficient, effective, and appealing manner.

When using the value mapping matrix, your first step is to identify where problems exist. This is done by investigating the cells in the matrix, asking questions such as "Are customers achieving the goal here?" or "Is achieving the goal a nuisance for the customer?" Depending on the ques-tion and the intensity of the response, cells are marked as green, yellow, or red, with red representing a goal in which the customer is unlocking little or no value.

When the triage is complete, you can then address the high-priority goals to understand their causes and impacts. You first look at the actions and tasks associated with a goal quantitatively to uncover the gap between existing customer performance and desired customer performance. You then assess the customer goal, with close attention to the subjective components of satisfaction. This is then followed by an analysis of the experience, from which possible causes, deficiencies, and solutions arise.

So now the analysis is complete. Problem areas are identified, causes are understood, and you're ready to change the customer's experience with innovative solutions. Solutions, however, require an investment, and subsequently some kind of return. The business case for improving customer performance should rest upon the increase in customer lifetime value, evidenced by customers' increased usage, adoption of other company goods and services, and willingness to recommend the company to others. The following chapters explore how companies determine the worthwhileness of solutions and manage the implementation of vision, access, incentive, and expertise to deliver results.

# CHAPTER 5

## IMPROVING VISION

*When my expectations are exactly fulfilled, I feel that
something uncanny has happened.*

—Mason Cooley

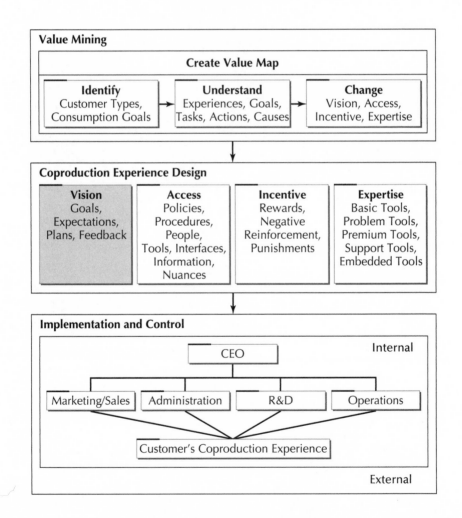

In this chapter, we examine the first element of the Coproduction Experience Model, *vision*. By enhancing the company's and customer's vision, many customer performance gaps can be eliminated. Why? Because customers are self-regulating. When you provide customers clear goals and appropriate feedback, they can often figure things out on their own. We start this chapter with a discussion of the situations in which vision is an appropriate solution. The chapter continues with sections that show you how you design vision into coproduction experiences by:

- Establishing goals that trigger performance
- Setting expectations for how customers will perform
- Forming plans that guide performance
- Providing feedback that lets customers know their performance is on the right track

## SITUATIONS CALLING FOR IMPROVED VISION

Coproduction experiences must help customers acquire vision. Through clear goals, objective expectations, a suitable plan, and appropriate feedback, vision is enhanced. Goals, expectations, and plans let customers know what they are supposed to do, while feedback lets them know how they are doing. For optimum performance one cannot be without the other.

In 1983, Albert Bandura and Daniel Cervone ran a simple experiment to prove this. They were interested in the effects of goals and feedback on performance. Using a stationary exercise device as the means to measure performance, they designed an experiment that varied goals and feedback. Using a sample of 45 men and 45 women, the researchers assigned subjects to one of four treatment groups. One group, the control group, received no goal or feedback. The second group received just feedback, the third group just a goal, and the fourth group received both a goal and feedback.

The results are persuasive. As shown in Figure 5.1, goals and feedback increased performance nearly 60 percent, while the other conditions, including the control group, increased in the 20 percent range. Neither goals alone nor feedback alone improve performance. Only in combination do goals and feedback enable people to perform better.[1]

The guidance we offer on how to incorporate goals, expectations, plans, and feedback into coproduction experiences contributes to maximizing customer performance. Goals and expectations must be specific so that customers can objectively assess their own performance. Plans must be accurate

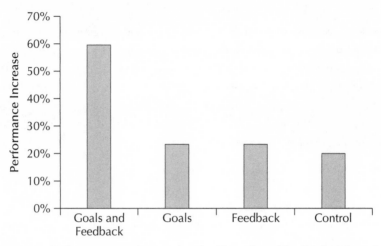

**Figure 5.1**    Performance results associated with goals and feedback. Adapted from Bandura and Cervone, 1983.

so that customers have a clear course of action such that they experience fewer distractions and avoid dead ends. Feedback must be timely, helpful, and communicated so it informs and persuades.

Because companies own the coproduction experience, they can increase their competitive advantage by having customers perform tasks. However, when customers don't have *vision*, even the best-laid plans go astray. What does it mean to not have vision? Consider the following situations.

### Customers Don't Know What They Are Supposed to Do

These are frequent and often embarrassing occurrences. We remember a situation when Palm Pilots were just hitting the market. A colleague had purchased one and it piqued our interest. We asked to give it a try. He handed it to us. We held it in our hand. We looked at the front. We looked at the back. We were clueless. We finally swallowed our pride and asked, "How do you turn it on?" We had been looking for a clearly marked on/off button—which wasn't apparent. It turned out that any button turns it on.

### Customers Don't Know When to Do It

Several years ago we needed to stain the siding on our house. We bought the stain, read the directions, prepped the siding, then picked a pleasant sunny day to start the project. We merrily went about our business, spraying, brushing, and rolling, till the entire house had a new coat of stain. Then we noticed something that wasn't quite right—a two-tone paint job. Seems that shadows cast by the roofline eaves caused the stain to dry at different speeds, resulting in the top of the walls being a darker color than the bottom of the walls. Painting on an overcast day or when the sun wasn't shining on the wall would have been a better choice.

## Customers Don't Know When to Stop Doing It

We were doing a bit of motorcycle maintenance, replacing the oil filter. We successfully removed the retaining bolts on the oil filter cover. We removed the old filter and replaced it with a new filter. We then installed the oil filter cover and proceeded to tighten the bolts. We tightened and tightened until the head of one of the bolts snapped off. Whoops! Luckily a neighbor had the right tools to extract the shank of the bolt from the engine block. He then proceeded to explain to us the concept of "proper torque."

## Customers Don't Know What the End Result Is Supposed to Look Like, Feel Like, Sound Like, and so on

We had just purchased a brand new Dodge RAM 2500 with the Cummins turbo diesel engine. After driving it around every day for a week to break it in, we parked it in the driveway and then went on vacation for a week. Upon our return we hopped into the truck, started it up, threw it into reverse, stepped on the accelerator, and ... NOTHING. The engine raced but the truck didn't move. We put it into drive. Same result. No movement. We put it into park, thinking about our options. Just to make sure we weren't doing something wrong, we put it into reverse again—and it worked! Not trusting this possible lemon, we hurried down to the dealer and explained the problem. No problem, says the service manager. Turns out the Dodge transmission operates on pressure. If the vehicle sits idle for a time, or if it gets really cold, the transmission pressure drops. Rebuilding the pressure takes 10–15 seconds.

"If only we would have known, things would have been much different," is a popular lament of customers who lack vision.

The starting point for designing coproduction experiences is ensuring customers have a *vision* of their performance. People for the most part are self-regulating. They perform tasks to accomplish the goals they have. As they perform tasks, they are constantly looking for information that lets them know they are heading in the right direction.

For instance, when driving down the freeway, *lines* define the lanes in which people are supposed to drive. Speed limit signs indicate what their rate of travel should be. This information helps them and our fellow motorists travel in a relatively safe and orderly fashion. However, in our neighborhood when the snow falls and the lines are no longer visible, confusion reigns. Vision is obscured, and as such we (and everyone else who is out there driving), make up our own lanes. Some are too far to the right, some are too far to the left, and others are content driving right down the middle of the road.

Vision, therefore, is when customers know:

- Where they are going
- The status of their progress
- When they have succeeded

Good vision relies upon two key components. The first component involves knowing where you are going and what it should be like when you get there. Goals, expectations, and plans are the usual terms that describe your future journey. The second component is feedback, which tells you how your journey is going and whether you have reached the destination. Feedback helps customers make adjustments to their actions and maximizes performance. Coproduction experiences must include a consistent linkage between goals, expectations, plans, and feedback.

## DEFINING GOALS

As mentioned in the previous chapter, goals describe a state or outcome a customer desires. Goals enable customers to be self-evaluative and self-regulating, resulting in stronger performance. Weak performance in coproduction experiences stems from goals that are absent or ill-defined. Thus, to enhance coproduction experiences companies should help customers develop appropriate goals (Table 5.1).

### Goal Is Absent

You can expect customers who have no goal to deliver the worst performance. The absence of a goal frequently occurs when customers encounter goods or services in which they have no prior experience. For instance, new technologies and innovations can trigger a response of "Now what am I going to do with that?" In the 1970s when the first home computers started appearing, many people could not conceive of what they would do with such a device. Goals such as *communicate with friends* or *manage your home finances* were, at the time, unknown. Now they are second nature.

**Table 5.1    Goal States and the Enhancement of Coproduction Experiences**

| Situation | Probable Result | To Enhance the Coproduction Experience |
|---|---|---|
| Goal is absent | Low or no performance | • Help customers formulate goals<br>• Elevate customer need |
| Goal is inconsistent | Annoying performance | • Realign the customer's goal<br>• Accommodate the customer's goal<br>• End the relationship with the customer |
| Goal lacks specificity | Uncertain performance | • Increase the objectivity of the goal<br>• Ensure subordinate tasks and actions are objectively defined |
| Goal lacks challenge | Under performance | • Ensure customers are challenged<br>• Tighten the specificity of goals<br>• Introduce alternative goals<br>• Make the conditions more challenging |
| Goal is too far in the future | Undirected performance | • Reframe and shape the goal |

Goals can also be absent if the product or service addresses a need not shared by the customer. A simple home experiment proves the point. Go to the kitchen and open the drawer that contains all the secondary kitchen tools and appliances friends and relatives have given for gifts. Rummage around and select one that's never been used (or hasn't been used for quite some time). In our drawer we found a thing called a Spaghetti Measuring Stick (Figure 5.2). It is a piece of plastic with different size holes in it. Each hole is marked with measures like "man or teenager." The need driving this device is precise portions. The goal is to precisely measure spaghetti. We don't care about either so the device remains idle in the kitchen drawer. However, for people who must know exactly the quantity of food they need to consume, such as those with diabetes, such devices offer the help they need to achieve the goal.

To enhance the experience you can do two things. First, you can obviously help customers formulate goals. When Intel introduced the microprocessor they flooded the market with advertisements and other marketing communication that described what one could do with a microprocessor.

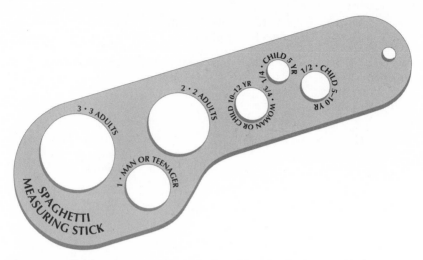

**Figure 5.2**    The Spaghetti Measuring Stick. This kitchen tool goes unused because we don't share the goal—precise measurement—for which the product was designed.

They created booklets that described various microprocessor applications. Through this awareness campaign Intel was able to motivate a legion of engineers who now had a vision of what this new technology could offer.

Second, you can elevate a customer's need. At any one time customers may be juggling many different needs. Some needs have a high priority, while other needs have a low priority. Those with low priority mean that goals are likely absent. In the insurance industry, the need for life insurance among young people is typically a low priority. If a customer is without a family then the goal of financial security for loved ones is probably off the radar. Yet if the insurance company can elevate the need by framing it in the context of the customer's future family and the value of reduced quarterly payments if the customer acts now, it becomes easier for the customer to formulate goals.

## Goal Is Inconsistent

An inconsistent goal is when the customer's goal does not match those deemed "acceptable" by the company. The result is annoying performance, where the customer's actions cause trouble for the company, its employees, or other customers.

When companies design goods and services, the designs typically accommodate a range of acceptable customer goals. Customers, on the other hand, have goals that may or may not fall within the *box* companies have established. Some customer goals may reflect antisocial behavior, such as theft, which is unacceptable. Other customer goals involve outcomes that the company is not able to deliver. Such is the case with our favorite mechanic. Several years ago when we first met him he came up with an innovative solution to a persistent starting problem with one of our vehicles. His level of service, honesty, integrity, and success were such that we wanted to bring all our vehicle problems to him. However, his specialty is fuel systems. If the problem doesn't involve the vehicle's fuel system, he won't touch it—no matter how much we annoy him.

The ideal approach to enhance a customer's experience is to change the customer's goal. This is where the company helps the customer realign the goal so it fits within the company's box. A friend of ours was thinning the sagebrush in his yard, creating a giant pile over eight feet tall. Being environmentally conscious, he formulated a goal to chip the sagebrush, turning it into mulch that he could compost. He called the local equipment rental service to inquire about the rental of a chipper. The clerk asked what he needed the chipper for and our friend explained how he needed to chip a load of sagebrush. "Not possible," said the clerk. It turns out that sagebrush is so stringy that when it is run through a chipper the wood fibers wrap around the blade spindle and jam up the works. This is the point of inconsistency. The customer's goal is to chip the sagebrush, but the chipper only accommodates goals related to chipping branches of trees. The poorly run rental company simply says no and hangs up—ending the possible relationship with the customer. The well-run rental company salvages the experience by helping the customer reframe the goal.

"You need to clear the sagebrush off your land, right?" asks the clerk.

"Yep," responds our friend."

"Have you looked into getting a burn permit?" asks the clerk.

"Yes, but our lot is too small so the fire department won't give us one. Plus, there really isn't a good space on our lot to burn safely," responds our friend.

"Do you have a truck to haul it away?" asks the clerk.

"Nope. And I really wanted to use the sagebrush for mulch," responds our friend.

The clerk thinks for a moment and says, "Tell you what. We have a truck we could rent you for a couple hours. Shouldn't take you too long to load up all the sagebrush you have—it's light. Then you can bring it to the county yard where they have a yard waste recycling program. Drop it off and they'll compost it and use the soil for various county programs."

With the goal reframed in an acceptable way the customer can continue the coproduction experience that maximizes value for both him and the rental service. Had the customer been able to rent the chipper, the result would have been annoying performance, resulting in a damaged machine.

Another solution is to accommodate the customer's goal. This means that the company modifies its goods or services in such a way that the customer can accomplish his goal. In one of the businesses we managed, our experience with initial customers led to invoices that summarized customers' use of services. As the business grew and attracted other customer segments, we found new customers having the goal of allocating charges to various departments that used our services. To accommodate this goal we had to customize the company's billing system. Invoices were reformatted to provide these customers the information they needed to allocate charges accurately. This added complexity to our operations but in the long run it enabled us to acquire more customers and accommodate other various customer goals.

## Goal Lacks Specificity

When goals are not specific, customer performance becomes more uncertain, variable, and inconsistent. Customers have trouble figuring out the best course of action. Because the end state is not well defined customers take more time, exert more effort, and encounter more dead ends, false starts, and backtracking. This does nothing more than increase the PITA factor. Since goals paint a picture of a future state, it is more desirable to have a picture that is painted by a realist, such as Rembrandt, rather than an impressionist, such as Van Gogh.

As we discussed in Chapter 4, the natural hierarchy of goals, tasks, and actions represent the specificity of goals. Specificity is enhanced when standards of quality, quantity, time, and money are incorporated into the descriptions of goals, tasks, and actions. However, customer goals tend to be represented more subjectively than task and actions due to the customer's feelings about the goal.

Thus to enhance customer experience, you must help customers make their goals more specific. For example, consider the customer goal, *a romantic experience*. For some, such a goal might be just the right specificity. For others, perhaps those inexperienced with romance, the goal is vague. They ask, "What is romantic? How do I know whether I am feeling romantic?" We can increase specificity by taking the clinical approach—*a romantic experience in which your heart rate increases 15 percent, respiration increases 10 percent, and galvanic skin response indicates more conductivity*. But who thinks in those terms on Valentine's Day (and thinking in those terms is certainly *unromantic*)? Perhaps a better goal might be one toned down a bit—*a romantic evening where your heart will go pitter-patter*. Describing this bit of easily recognizable, culturally conditioned biofeedback helps one know when they are on the right track.

If such specificity in a goal is uncomfortable or not logical within a goal hierarchy, then the alternative is to ensure that tasks and actions are objectively defined.

## Goal Lacks Challenge

One of the interesting effects of goals is that customer performance is diminished if goals are too easy. Research shows that difficult goals, ones that are challenging but not beyond the ability of the customer, lead to better performance than easy or moderate goals. In management circles, these goals are called *stretch goals*. These goals push people to accomplish things outside of their comfort zone. Since people want to be successful, they try harder and are more focused on success.

Why do goals with no or low challenge result in diminished performance? Customers become bored, complacent, and sloppy when goals aren't sufficiently challenging. Customers make more mistakes because their attention is diverted to things that are more interesting in their environment. Linus Pauling was asked, after winning the Nobel Prize in Chemistry, what he was going to do next. He announced that he "was changing fields," illustrating human desire to move on to other things when goals are accomplished and thus no longer challenging. He subsequently won the Nobel Peace Prize.

While a goal might be initially challenging, the challenge is diminished over time as the customer gains experience. According to professor Stephen J. Hoch, product experience is seductive. While we often think experience makes us better performers, it often leads to diminished performance and unwise choices. Experience causes customers to "let down their guard." Experience seduces customers into a level of comfort that dulls their attention. We'd rather have customers who stay sharp—hence the need for enhancing goals from time to time so they challenge customers appropriately.

To ensure goals are challenging, companies can help customers choose appropriate experiences. We've had friends in the whitewater rafting business who do this very well. They know that customers are more excited about the experience when the challenge is greater. For a customer who has already done time on class 1 and 2 rapids, another similar experience results in the customer being bored. Instead, our friends bump up the challenge, suggesting instead a trip that involves rafting rivers in the class 3, 4, or 5 range. With the increased difficulty the trip becomes a stretch goal for customers. There is some anxiety, which is always the case when one tries something new. But customers pay more attention to safety talks, and when they are on the river their senses are heightened and their actions are quicker. Adrenalin has them pumped up, and they are able to paddle harder and withstand more discomforts, such as cold water. When the day is done, everyone feels great because they have accomplished something beyond their initial comfort level.

Another strategy is tightening the specificity of a goal. The goal remains the same. It is just the standard that changes. Perhaps the customer is encouraged to be neater in painting, faster in checking in for a flight, or more accurate when completing a home improvement project. The stretch of a higher standard motivates more precise performances.

Companies can also guide customers to more challenging conditions in which to accomplish goals. For example, consider a novice skier whose goal is to *ski safely on my own*. The skier can only spend so much time on the bunny hill until becoming bored out of his skull. Thus as the skier progresses in ability the ski instructor starts changing the conditions. The goal is still the same, but now the goal must be accomplished on faster lifts, steeper hills, imperfect terrain, deeper snow, and so on. The changing conditions make the goal more challenging and hence stimulate greater effort to perform.

## Goal Is Too Far in the Future

If a goal is not timely, it is difficult for customers to value the goal. Consider the investment company who encourages people in their 20s to accumulate X number of dollars by the time they are 65 to ensure a well-funded, happy retirement. That's 40 years in the future! For most people that goal is just too far off to warrant their attention. Additionally, with something so distant it is difficult for people to have a good sense of whether they are on track to achieve the goal. So they do what most of us would do: ignore it, avoid it, and worry about something else.

An alternative is to help customers form goals that are more immediate. Rather than setting a goal that is 40 years in the future, reframe the goal. Change the timing to this year, this month, or even this week. For example, if the customer is paid weekly, a timelier goal might be *put $100 a week into* *your investment account.* Now this is something the customer can see doing! The likelihood the customer will pursue the goal is increased.

The retirement planning advice offered by Charles Schwab & Co., Inc. is a great example of how a goal is reframed. In Schwab's example situation it sets the goal that one needs $1 million at age 65 to generate $40,000 in income. It then proceeds to localize the goal to four age ranges: people in their 20s, 30s, 40s, and those over 45. Within these ranges Schwab suggests appropriate yearly savings goals as a percentage of salary. For example, if you start saving when you are 22, you need to save 10 percent of your yearly salary. If you are 28, then the percentage jumps to 14 percent. Age 36? You should be socking away 23 percent. For ages 45 and better you fall into the "OUCH!" category, where your savings rate can be as high as 58 percent or more.[2]

So, what is the more realistic goal for young people? $1 million in savings by the time you are 65? Or, saving 10 percent of your salary each month? Divide and conquer! Research says the latter will drive greater effort and performance.

## SETTING EXPECTATIONS

Expectations help customers determine whether experiences are appropriate or inappropriate, pleasant or unpleasant, tolerable or intolerable. Expectations stimulate interest and arousal. They clarify outcomes and reduce uncertainty. They also reduce ambiguity and ignorance. From our perspective, expectations reflect the standards customers associate with tasks and actions.

Like goals, expectations predict a future state for the customer. However, while goals stimulate general motivation, expectations are localized to specific goods and services. Expectations name who or what is going to have primary accountability for accomplishing the goal. For example, "I want to look young again" is a goal. "I want Botox to make me look young again," is an expectation—where Botox has the accountability.

Accountability is an important topic when thinking about coproduction experiences. By its very nature coproduction assumes the customer is doing some kind of work. Thus, who is accountable for the expectation being achieved? The customer or the company? Keep this thought in the back of your mind as you continue reading.

We all know the phrase, *setting customer expectations.* The phrase illustrates the active role companies have in ensuring customers know what to do and what they are getting. From the customer's perspective, the creation of expectations is dependent upon:

- Direct observation and experience
- Previous learned relationships or rules
- Information from the environment

Setting expectations requires a delicate balance. When customer expectations are too high and the performance of the goods or services too low, then customers are *dissatisfied*. However, high expectations often translate into stronger evaluations of the goods or services when performance is proved. If the expectations and performance match, then customers are *satisfied*. But when performance exceeds expectations customers experience *delight*, which, from a marketing perspective, is a desirable emotion. The classic story for setting expectations goes something like this.

> A customer walks into a car showroom with the intention to buy a new, expensive sports car. The dealer explains the features of the car, discusses its precise engineering, and takes the customer on a test drive. The customer is impressed. The car is powerful, sleek, and he looks good driving it. Thoroughly smitten, the customer buys the car.
>
> As the customer gains more experience with the car he notices something odd. When downshifting into second gear there is a noticeable "thunk" coming from the rear axle. $60,000 sports cars shouldn't be "thunking," thinks the customer. Something must be wrong. So he returns the car to the dealer to check things out. Turns out nothing is wrong, the noise is just one of the engineering quirks of this particular car. The customer is devastated. For 60 grand, he expected perfection. That's what the dealer led him to believe. Now there is this flaw that he didn't notice before. The experience is not as perfect as he thought it should be.

Overpromise and underdeliver. When the dealer discussed precise engineering it set an expectation in the customer's mind. This also communicated that the car has accountability for being precise. Precise engineering means that things work smoothly. There are no thunks, rattles, bangs, smoke, or other artifacts of a poorly engineered machine. Since there is the mismatch between the customer's expectation and the performance of the car, satisfaction is not at a desirable level.

Yet customers are rational beings. The marketplace has conditioned them to accept that everything has some kind of flaw. If we don't tell them up front about the flaw, then we fall into the trap of overpromising and under-delivering. If the car dealer in the story had explained the downshift *thunk*, bringing attention to this slight flaw, which does not affect performance or maintenance, the situation would be different. If the customer buys the car the flaw is accepted and doesn't become part of the customer's subsequent calculation of satisfaction.

Expectations can also paint a picture of how goods and services are used, and the role customers have in using them. To help customers experience consistent results, companies model *expected performance*. For years Alka-Seltzer ran advertisements featuring people solving stomach problems by dropping a single Alka-Seltzer into a glass. These were great product demon-strations and set the expectation of how to use the product and what would happen when the product hit water (the fizz). Through the 1960s consump-tion of Alka-Seltzer dropped and the company was hunting for ways to re-verse the trend. As part of their research, the advertising agency employees happened to visit a doctor to learn more about how medicines worked. The doctor explained that for some medicines, such as aspirin, two doses were necessary to break through and relieve pain. Eureka! The Alka-Seltzer pack-aging was changed to contain two tablets. The instructions were changed to direct using two tablets. And from then on all advertising featured two tablets dropped into a glass, while the merry jingle in the background, *plop-plop, fizz-fizz*, reinforced the expectation that two tablets, not one, be used to re-lieve digestive pain. It also shifted the accountability to the user, who must choose to use two tablets instead of one to achieve the desired results.[3]

To enhance experiences through expectations, several questions arise. What are the types of expectations? Where do they come from? Who has ac-countability? And how do we best manage them to create experiences that maximize customer performance? Several researchers have put us on track to answer these questions through the hierarchy of expectations (Table 5.2). They have defined the various types of expectations and how customers form expectations. We build upon their model by providing ideas for en-hancing a coproduction experience.[4]

## Ideal Expectations

The highest level of expectations customers have is that of the *ideal*. An ideal is what the customer wishes will happen. Typically, these wishes reflect a per-fect standard, that of the highest customer expectation available. Ideals are based upon the enduring wants and needs customers have and may not have a relationship to reality. For example, the ideal "I wish ThighMaster will give

Table 5.2    Hierarchy of Expectations

| Expectation | How Formed | To Enhance a Coproduction Experience |
|---|---|---|
| Ideal | What the customer wishes should happen | • Ensure the person, place, or thing is identified<br>• Make expectation more objective |
| Should | What the market says should happen | • Tell the customers what work they must do<br>• Tell the customer the standards associated with the work<br>• For physical actions, model expectations<br>• Incorporate passive visual cues |
| Desired | What the customer wants to happen | • Ensure the customer knows the conditional task or action<br>• Give customers a choice in how they solve the task |
| Predicted | What past experience says will happen | • Ensure consistency in previous experiences<br>• Simplify the customer's next experience (chase the *ideal*) |
| Deserved | What the return should be on the customer's investment | • Make the benefit of doing more work visible |
| Minimum Tolerable | What does the job<br>What the customer will accept | • Offer multiple service options that reflect different work effort |
| Intolerable | What the customer won't accept | • Ensure customers know what they won't be doing |
| Worst Imaginable | What screws everything up | • Have reliable contingencies |

me beautifully toned thighs" is a pretty good stretch. Maybe it will, but it ignores the fact that beautifully toned thighs require more than an exercise contraption—namely a willing participant and a good diet. In the context of coproduction, for ideals to work they must be framed to indicate the person, place, or thing that has the responsibility for doing the work. In this case, ThighMaster isn't doing the work. You are! Hence, a more appropriate ideal would be "With my ThighMaster I will develop beautifully toned thighs."

Don't get us wrong. Expectations based on ideals are good. But if ideals are too far off in never-never land you'll never have the opportunity to delight the customer. However, if the ideal is properly framed and the company helps the customer achieve the ideal, the customer's response is delight! Customers are happier, more loyal, and more apt to tell their friends of their happiness. This contributes to increasing the customer lifetime value.

## Should Expectations

For some coproduction experiences, expectations based upon ideals are beyond what a company can achieve. Therefore, companies spend significant effort shaping *should* expectations. These expectations are what the market says should happen. Companies, through products, advertisements, and sales calls, set expectations. Competitors, through their alternative offerings, set expectations. Even neutral third parties such as Consumer Reports set expectations. Expectations in this context tend to define the bar of generally accepted performance and establish points of differentiation between competitors.

In the context of coproduction, there are some basic expectations that customers need to know about.

- They should know what work they are expected to do.
- They should know the standards associated with that work, such as the amount of time the work will take.

An area on the Fidelity Investments website contains retirement planning tools. The expectation set here is that the customer does the work of entering data, and Fidelity does the work of crunching the numbers. What enhances the experience is that Fidelity lets the customer know how long the analysis will take: for a Quick Check, two minutes; for an Income Estimator, five minutes; or for the full-blown Retirement Income Planner, up to 30 minutes. Just excellent![5]

For tasks that involve more significant physical actions beyond hammering away on a keyboard, companies should consider modeling the expectations. Examples include hiring actors to be customers in fast-food restaurants who make an attention-getting performance of clearing their trash off the table, and Alka-Seltzer demonstrating in advertisements two tablets being dropped into a glass. The key principle here is that if you want customers to do something, then show them how to do it!

Another means of setting *should* expectations are visual cues in the coproduction environment, such as lines on the road, trash cans in fast-food restaurants that have a place to put trays, buttons with clearly marked functions, and colored markers on the floors in hospitals that lead you to specific departments. All these cues help tell you what you should do.

## Desired Expectations

As we continue down through the expectations hierarchy we shift back to expectations that are internally generated by the customer. *Desired* expectations are what the customer wants to happen. For example, customers *want* their car to start on the first turn of the key. They *want* Fedex to deliver their packages by 8:30 the next morning. They *want* Hilton Hotels to accept their web-submitted hotel reservation the first time. These expectations are a blend of what *should be* and what *can be*.

In a coproduction experience the *want* is dependent on tasks or actions the customer *must* perform. To have the car start on the first try, the customer *must* fill it with gas, or *must* make sure lights are turned off so the battery doesn't run down. To have a package delivered by 8:30 the next morning, the customer *must* have the address right and *must* have the package ready by 5:00 P.M. To make sure the hotel reservation goes through the first time the customer *must* enter their credit card number correctly. The conditional task or action must be known by the customer.

Another strategy for accommodating want expectations is to give customers greater choice in how they solve a task—and let them know they have that choice. Salad bars have worked this way for years. You have your choice of what you want in your salad. Now we see the same thing in other industries. National Car Rental enables Emerald Club customers to choose whatever car they want from an available selection. Home Depot allows customers to choose self-checkout or checkout with a clerk. Giving customers a choice enhances the self-determination (and accountability) of the outcomes they want.

## Predicted Expectations

Although experiences are seductive, they do teach us what to expect. This is the nature of *predicted* expectations. These kinds of expectations give the customer justification, as in, "The last time I was in this hotel I was able to make calls without being charged an access fee." Or better yet, "At the Oakland Airport they don't make me take my shoes off to pass through security. Why here?"

As customers we spend so much time learning, accommodating, and changing just to do something the first time. So don't make us have to learn something all over again the next time! When things aren't the same it frustrates us. After a week-long backpacking trip we found ourselves at our favorite diner in Lee Vining, California—the eastern gateway to Yosemite

Park. We ordered a beer. It came in a frosty mug. Mmmm. It was so good we ordered a second one. When it came it was half-full of foam and in a warm glass. Excuse me, Miss...

Imagine this experience collected in one of our studies:

> I had been working at a fine dining restaurant for two-and-a-half years when the head chef decided to change the menu. For the past ten years the restaurant served a la carte meals. The menu consisted of salads, soups, steaks, chicken, fish, and pasta dishes. When the restaurant began having money problems, the chef decided to make the menu all inclusive. This meant that for a fixed price of $35 the customer would receive a small appetizer, a cup of soup or a salad, one entree, and the chosen dessert of the night.
>
> But after this change was made the restaurant still kept two different menus. There was the bar menu, which consisted of a la carte appetizers, and the dinner menu, which consisted of the fixed price menu. When the hostess would seat the people at their table she would simply hand them a menu and walk away. As a server it was my job to explain how the fixed price menu worked. But since many of the customers had been in the bar having a pre-dinner cocktail, they had seen the a la carte menu. People were confused to say the least. They would ask why we changed it and then ask if they could order things off the bar menu. To keep the guests happy, we let them order off the bar menu. This caused many dilemmas. People that had not been in the restaurant before or had not entered the bar did not know about the separate bar menu. If they saw a server walking by with an a la carte item, they would rant and rave and complain that no one had told them about this separate menu. It was a huge mess. People were complaining left and right and many would leave after seeing the fixed price menu. The menu change was a complete failure.
>
> When the people came to the restaurant they expected a la carte because that's the way the business had operated for many years. The fixed price menu ended up causing frustration amongst the customers, especially the elderly. They did not want all of the food that the fixed price menu came with. The menu was not user friendly, and in fact, when the customers saw the $35 price on the dinner they thought they were spending more (when in actuality they were spending less). The whole plan backfired. Not only did people complain, but many never returned because they did not want to have to

order from this menu. Six months later the restaurant closed and to this day I still hear people complain to me about that horrible menu that the restaurant adopted. For a business that relies primarily on regular customers, it was a huge mistake to create this type menu that no one was accustomed to.

The time to mess with a customer's experience-based expectations is when you are *improving* the next experience. We call this *chasing the ideal*. When web-based ordering was new we came to expect that for whatever technology reason we would have to enter our name and address each time we wanted to order something. No problem. That was our coproduction contribution, but of course we wished for something simpler. Then one day something miraculous occurred. We opened the page and ... all the information we entered last time was there! Similarly, to us there is no sweeter sound than a hotel clerk, reservation agent, or other service professional telling us that, no, they don't need our information because they already have it. We can envision the day when we walk into a grocery store, grab a loaf of bread, and walk out, just as we do in our own home when we raid the pantry. The only difference is that somehow we paid the store in the process, and we didn't even have to reach into our pockets. How is that for an ideal?

Some people are frightened by this vision, citing invasion of privacy, identity theft concerns, or a Big Brother conspiracy. There is no doubt there is risk in such transactions, but with risk comes rewards—namely a reduction in the PITA factor. We're confident that through new technologies, such as biometric identification, and progressive legislation, criminal and ethical threats to simplification will disappear.

## Deserved Expectations

When customers ask, "Am I getting the most for my money?" they are articulating a *deserved* expectation. Here the customers are concerned about getting a return on their investment. In other words, the customers are expecting value from their efforts. In the case of coproduction experiences, customers are looking to see how they will be compensated for doing more of the work.

Earlier in the book we discussed the principle of value sharing, whereby when customers do more of the work in a coproduction experience they expect to share in the savings. Some companies, such as WinCo Foods, a discount supermarket chain, complete the bargain by offering overall lower prices than their full-service competitors. At WinCo, customers must package bulk foods, pay in cash, and bag their own groceries. In exchange they receive lower costs for bulk foods and packaged goods that come in sizes somewhere between those offered by Costco and the full-service supermarket. Airlines "promise" that lower fares may be available when you do the work to book online, but typically supplement the exchange with some other value-enhancing reward, such as frequent flyer miles.

## Minimum Tolerable Expectations

Every customer has a walk-away point. *Minimum tolerable* expectations are right at the border. These expectations define the bare minimum of what the customer expects to be doing. We all have our minimum tolerable expectations for various tasks and actions and the level of that tolerance is dependent on context. In some cases when we are feeling leisurely, waiting an hour for a table at a restaurant is tolerable. However, if we are feeling impatient, our tolerance might last only ten minutes.

In terms of coproduction experiences, minimum tolerable expectations describe the least amount of work customers need to do in order to get a positive result with goods or services. For example, when customers buy a gas grill at Home Depot they have two coproduction options. The first is that they can bring the grill home in its original box and assemble it themselves. The second is that they can pay an extra $20 and take home a fully assembled grill. Home Depot supports this second option by renting customers a truck if their car isn't big enough to hold the assembled grill. Both options lead to a positive result. Depending on their minimum tolerable expectations in terms of work effort, customers can choose the option that best suits their needs.

Similar option designs can be seen in other businesses. Airlines have three options in terms of checking in for a flight. Customers can print boarding passes from home using the company's website. They can print boarding passes from self-service kiosks at the airport. Or they can wait for a ticket agent to serve them in person and have the ticket agent print the boarding passes. Customers may choose which option is right for them at the time of consumption.

Just outside Grass Valley, California, is a roadside restaurant called The Willo. The restaurant is rustic, to say the least, but what makes it unique is the giant grill that sits in the middle of the dining area. The Willo serves meat. Steaks are its specialty. In terms of getting dinner, guests have two options. Guests can cook their own steaks on the grill, or for $0.50 extra the grill master will cook the steaks for them. When we last visited The Willo we splurged, shelling out the $0.50 for the service. That evening the only co-production we wanted to be doing was eating. Cooking was just intolerable.

## Intolerable Expectations

*Intolerable* expectations describe outcomes or performances a customer just can't accept. Customers might not want to cook their own steaks or assemble a complicated gas grill. They might not want to set up the home network and DSL connections for their computers. They might not want the responsibility of making complex travel arrangements for a round-the-world trip.

To address customer intolerance in coproduction experiences it is critical to let customers know what they won't be doing. A package whose labeling shouts "No Assembly Required" makes the product acceptable to those who don't want to spend time assembling. "Guaranteed Availability" at the local movie rental store makes it known that you won't be making the trip for nothing.

## Worst Imaginable Expectations

*Worst imaginable* expectations are nightmare scenarios for customers. When using goods and services, especially in critical situations, customers can dream up what they don't want to happen. For example, for someone who has the most important job interview of their career, having the car break down on the way to the interview would be a worst imaginable expectation. Similarly, for a person who is presenting to 600 people at a conference, having the computer, projector, or other piece of presentation technology crash during the presentation is a worst imaginable expectation.

Certain coproduction experiences may need some kind of insurance policy that protects customers (or allows them to recover) when the worst imaginable outcome comes true. Service guarantees, travel insurance, money-back guarantees, product warranties, and extended warranties are some of the common contingencies.

A creative coproduction contingency is OnStar, the customer assistance system developed in collaboration with General Motors. The service is comprehensive, providing a solution for the worst imaginable experiences one might encounter while driving. Lock the keys in the car? Call OnStar, and they'll unlock the door. The vehicle is stolen? Call OnStar, and they'll activate the stolen vehicle tracking service. Get lost? Call OnStar, and they'll give you driving directions. Lose your vehicle in the Disneyland parking lot?

Call OnStar, and they'll toot the horn and flash the lights for you. In some cases you don't even have to call. If you are in an accident and the airbag deploys, OnStar is notified automatically by the vehicle. OnStar will attempt to contact you to see if you need help.[6]

## DEVELOPING PLANS

With goals and expectations in place, customers are at the point where they can begin to visualize what they need to do to accomplish the goal. These visualizations are called *plans*. Plans represent the sequence of tasks and actions customers envision themselves performing to achieve a goal. Successful performance and greater value is greatly enhanced when customers have a plan.

A plan is like a computer program. It contains a hierarchical series of steps that, when executed, yield a desired result. The original model that describes this is *test-operate-test-exit*. This describes the algorithmic process in which a person first gets information from the situation (test). Based on that information the customer forms and then activates a plan (operate). After performing the operation the result is tested (test). A positive result exits the routine, while a negative result loops back and repeats, with adjustments to the plan. Obviously, this model suggests that customers who form better plans experience better results (and get to exit quicker).

The marketplace recognizes that planning ahead offers customers greater value in coproduction experiences. Customers who plan weekly menus and shopping lists are more efficient in their grocery shopping. Their plan enables them to shop faster and eliminate return trips for forgotten goods. Other examples include customers who plan ahead to:

- Arrive early (first choice)
- Make reservations (less wait time, assurance of a spot)
- Buy in advance (discounts, availability)
- Use services at non-peak hours (lower cost, availability, less time)
- Perform maintenance (fewer breakdowns, less expensive repairs, avoidance of catastrophic failures)

In order for customers to maximize value in a coproduction experience, you need to help them form a plan. Where do plans come from? How are they formed? Psychologists suggest that customers rarely create these plans from scratch. Instead the most common source of new plans are old plans. Old plans are a kind of template that customers copy, then modify as needed.

Customers generate plans from three primary sources:

- Inheritance. Customers (and other living things) come genetically pre-wired with plans that do not need to be learned or discovered. A gosling is encoded with the instinct to follow the first thing it sees. That thing can be its true mother, the farmer, or a dog. Customers come wired the same way, with plans for dealing with opportunity (be first), fear (run away), hunger (eat), and exhaustion (sleep).
- Learning. Through the observation of others, training, and reflection about their own experiences, customers develop skills. Skills represent a plan. For example, before being allowed to land an airplane pilots must first be able to recite the steps for landing a plane—which is their plan.
- Socialization. As part of a social group, customers will collectively negotiate and form plans. These plans, called *shared plans*, describe the collective and coordinated actions the group will take to achieve a desired goal. A family visiting an amusement park will, for example, collectively develop a plan for choosing the rides, allocating preferred seats, and scheduling other activities, such as eating.

You can enhance coproduction experiences by helping customers recall existing plans, learn new plans, and facilitate the development of shared plans. The subsequent chapters on access and expertise provide guidance on how you design experiences that aid the formation of effective plans. For example, using principles discussed in the *access* chapter, an amusement park might provide a map or worksheet to help a family plan a day's worth of activities. Similarly, a company such as Home Depot might offer a weekend workshop on how to install tile—which helps customers form a plan for how they'll complete the task in their own home.[7]

## PROVIDING FEEDBACK

When customers perform they want to know if they are on the right track. They want to know that the plan is working, expectations are being met, and the goal is being achieved. To acquire this knowledge customers rely on feedback, also known as the *knowledge of results*, from both themselves and outside sources.

As a process, feedback involves three key stages (Figure 5.3). First, there is an action, which causes an event to occur. From that event, our first experience is *internal feedback*. Internal feedback is feedback we generate ourselves. It includes such physiological responses as the stomach reporting it is full, the

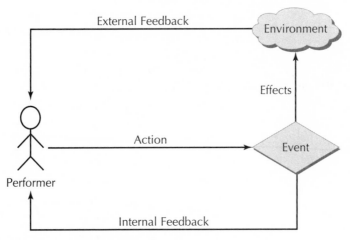

**Figure 5.3**   The Process of Feedback.

tongue sensing something nasty has entered the mouth, the pain of a loud noise in the ears, or the touch of fingertips on a keyboard. It can also include psychological responses such as happiness and satisfaction based upon the self-evaluation of performance.

Following internal feedback is *external feedback*. The effects of the event impact the surrounding environment. This is feedback the environment provides you, which influences internal feedback of your performance. By environment we mean people, machines, and other devices. A colleague might say "good job" when you do something right. A computer might emit an annoying beep when you do something wrong. The grooves on the shoulder of the highway might cause your tires to buzz loudly, alerting you to get your car back on the road.

To illustrate the relationship between action, internal feedback, and external feedback, consider this story collected in one of our studies:

> I wanted to try out the new self-checkouts. I had seen them before but believed they would be too much of a hassle to learn how to use. One day at the grocery store I had only one item to buy. The lines in the regular checkouts were pretty long, especially for someone like me only purchasing one quart of ice cream.
>
> There were four self-checkout machines and all were occupied. There was also a "line" to use them, which was just one guy. The people using them looked like they knew what they were doing. Only one asked for help from the clerk watching the four machines. I decided to give it a try. When it was my turn, I walked over to the

machine and followed the instructions. They were very simple and
easy to follow. I was surprised that you could pay with cash. I had
expected credit or debit card only.

I was laughing a little as I used the machine. I was doing the work
that the paid employees usually did and the machine was telling me
(it even had a voice) what to do every step of the way—including
telling me what the item was and its price. It was kind of funny.
When I was ready to pay I selected cash and inserted a $20 bill. It
gave me the right coin change but I didn't see where my paper
money change was put. I turned around to ask the clerk—perhaps
she gave us the paper change (since she had a cash register). She told
me where it was (it was kind of out of sight). When I turned around,
some little kid was taking my money. His mother scolded him and I
got my change and left.

In this story the customer's first task was scanning the item. When he
scanned the item (action, event) he visually confirmed the scan (internal
feedback), followed by the voice from the machine (external feedback). This
went well. The second task was paying. Here the customer presented his payment, then confirmed the receipt of change (internal feedback). But there
was a problem—the change was incorrect (due to the paper change tray
being out of sight). The customer solicited help from the clerk (external
feedback), which enabled him to learn the location of the additional change.
What about the little kid? He briefly experienced happiness by possessing a
few illicit dollars (internal feedback) until his mother discovered what he
was doing (external feedback).

For customers to be successful, coproduction experiences must provide
feedback. It is the final component of vision that guides the successful completion of plans, expectations, and goals. To enhance coproduction experiences, the question is not whether to provide feedback. Rather, it is how to
provide feedback. There are three principles that enhance coproduction
experiences:

- Timing of feedback
- Type of feedback
- Format of feedback

## Timing of Feedback

The first principle guiding feedback is *timing of feedback*. Feedback is most
effective when it is provided immediately. The passage of time between

action and feedback can cause a person to lose track of the connection between action and result. This increases uncertainty over whether the action was done correctly. It can also cause frustration on the part of the performer. There is evidence that longer durations between action and feedback still enhance performance. However, the choice of duration seems dependent upon the person's expertise. Novices must get feedback immediately.

Nowhere is this more apparent than in computing systems. The response times of computers and software reinforce the importance of immediacy. For example, usability researcher Jakob Nielsen suggests the following limits for timing feedback:

- 0.1 seconds = limit for the customer perceiving a system is responding instantaneously. An example is pressing a key (action) and having a character appear on the screen (feedback).
- 1.0 seconds = limit for the customer's thought process to remain uninterrupted. Here, the absence of feedback exceeding this limit, such as characters appearing on screen, lists scrolling, and so on, causes the customer to wonder if things are working correctly (hence shifting the customer's attention away from the task).
- 10 seconds = limit for keeping the customer involved in the task. For instance, when a customer saves a document, a wait time of 10 seconds might result in the customer wanting to use the time to do a different task.[8]

## Type of Feedback

The second principle guiding feedback is the *type of feedback*. Depending on the situation, feedback can include a variety of information, from operational status to corrective teaching, that is additive (Figure 5.4).

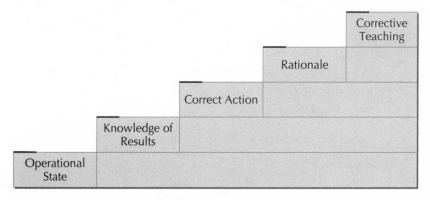

**Figure 5.4**    The types of feedback and their additive structure.

As illustrated in the diagram and in Table 5.3, an effective structure of feedback builds upon each of the preceding levels. The lowest level of feedback customers need to know is the *operational state* of any device or system. This enables them to know if they can perform the action. Immediately

Table 5.3   **When to Use Different Levels of Feedback**

| Type of Feedback | Use | Examples |
|---|---|---|
| Operational State | To indicate whether a person, tool, or system is ready for action | • Another person says, "Hello, may I help you?"<br>• Green light indicating a device is turned on<br>• Noise emanates from a device<br>• Fuel gauge reads full |
| + Knowledge of Results | When the customer performs the action | • Another person says, "Nice job" or "That's not the way to do it."<br>• A speedometer displays the speed of a car<br>• Characters appear on the computer screen<br>• A part you are assembling "clicks" into place |
| + Correct Action | When the action is performed incorrectly | • Another person says, "Here, let me show you the right way."<br>• The auto-spell feature in Microsoft Word automatically fixes a misspelled word you just typed |
| + Rationale | When the customers are frustrated or unmotivated to improve on their own | • Another person says, "Well, it's not working because you forgot to plug it in."<br>• An error dialog box displayed on a computer screen reads, "Could not save the file because the name you entered already exists." |
| + Corrective Teaching | The customer is totally off track due to significantly flawed actions, plans, expectations, or goals | • Another person says, "Let's go look in the instruction manual. You see, it says right here you need to deactivate the safety lock-out."<br>• An error dialog box has a button labeled "Help." This button displays a help document that provides a description of the task and a step-by-step procedure for the task. |

after performing an action customers want to *know the result* of the action. Did it work or didn't it? If it didn't work customers might need to see the *correct action*. If the task is complex and the customers become frustrated, feedback might include *rationale* (why the task needs to be done a certain way). Finally, if the customers' actions, plans, expectations, or goals are significantly flawed, then the feedback must include *corrective teaching*.

## Format of Feedback

The third principle is the *format of feedback*. Format describes the different ways you can package and communicate feedback. As shown in Table 5.4, the most basic formats involve *proximity, obviousness,* and *richness*. These formats are concerned with ensuring that customers receive the feedback message. Richness, for example, suggests that feedback should involve at least two of the senses. This provides redundancy, increasing the chance that the person notices the message.

The next set of formats, *focus* and *persistence*, guide us in determining how much information to include in a feedback message. Focus, for example, suggests that if one overloads a feedback message with too much information, the feedback becomes meaningless. Persistence, on the other hand, guides us in determining how long feedback should be given. Some actions require low persistence, such as removing the feedback when the customer takes action. Filling a gas tank to cause the low fuel light to turn off is an example. Other situations require high persistence, which means the feedback remains active to indicate a particular state. This might include an indication that a device is in an "on" state or the display of oil pressure and engine temperature while driving.

The remaining set of formats actively aims to change behavior. Feedback that is *persuasive* must convince a customer that an action must be taken. This action aims to avoid an undesired state, such as a car breaking down or situations impacting the safety of the customers or people around them. *Formative* feedback aims to help customers change their plans, expectations, or goals by providing some form of instruction. Additionally, formative feedback is seen as being positive in its language (rather than negative feedback, whereby admonishments such as, "no," "don't do it that way," or "you stupid idiot" are not productive in helping customers perform better). An example is in computer user interfaces. A design principle for software is that the user is never at fault. Computers should never blame the user. Given this principle, error messages now take a different tone. They are written in a format of

## Table 5.4 Feedback Formats

| Format | Definition | Examples |
| --- | --- | --- |
| Proximal | Feedback is part of or close to the action. | • Press an on/off button, and it lights up (on) or goes dark (off)<br>• Spray Round Up® weed killer and it foams up when it hits a surface (clearly indicating where you sprayed)<br>• Audible "clicks" are heard when a Cuisinart® Food Processor's safety lock-outs are engaged |
| Obvious | Person doesn't have to search for the feedback. | • Paper change is provided next to where coin change is provided on a self-checkout system<br>• Car chirps and blinks its lights when locked using the keyless entry device<br>• Mechanical counter device on a Brita® water filter that indicates when to change the filter is located on the filter |
| Rich | Feedback provides a lot of information and activates multiple senses. | • A beep and a dialog box are displayed when there is a computer input error<br>• Color and aroma of a well-preserved Bordeaux<br>• A tactile "give," a mechanical "click," a digital "tone," slightly different tone frequencies (do, re, mi), and a number appearing on a display when a number is pressed on a cell phone keypad |
| Focused | Just the right amount of feedback is provided. There is no ambiguity or overload. | • Microwave oven chimes three times when a meal is cooked (beeping constantly would be overload) |
| Persistent | Feedback remains in effect until person changes behavior, action, or acknowledges feedback. | • Laser printer out-of-paper light illuminates when the last sheet of paper is printed<br>• Seatbelt light on a car's dashboard remains lit while your seatbelt remains unfastened<br>• All Caps mode indicator on a computer remains lit when the computer is in that mode |
| Persuasive | Feedback convinces the person to change or strengthen behavior. | • Different types of computer messages, for example, Information, Warning, and Critical<br>• Siren sounds, horn beeps, and lights flash when a car alarm is activated<br>• Feedback comes from a person of authority |
| Formative | Feedback guides and instructs when performance is unacceptable rather than criticizes. | • A person says, "That is not quite right. Let me show you how to do it."<br>• Wording of computer message reads, *"There is not enough disk space to save this file. Free additional space on this disk, or save the file to a different disk."* |

*problem, cause,* and *solution.* In the old days, a message read, "File save error." This message can imply that the user is the source of the problem. These days, the message reads, "Could not save the file because the disk is full. Delete some files from your hard disk and try saving again."

## SUMMARY

In this chapter we discussed ideas that use vision to enhance coproduction experiences. Vision enables customers to know what they are trying to achieve. Not having vision means customers do not know what to do, do not know when to do it, do not know when to stop doing it, and do not know when it is done right.

Vision within a coproduction experience has four primary parts: goals, expectations, plans, and feedback. Goals define the primary accomplishments customers (and companies) expect to achieve. For goals to have the appropriate effect in motivating customer performance, they must be present, consistent, specific, challenging, and short term.

Expectations help qualify experiences in terms of those that are satisfying and not satisfying. Expectations can range from what customers think is ideal to what would be the worst thing they could imagine. Ideally, expectations should describe the performance companies expect from customers, from how to use products to the standards of performance associated with co-design, cocreation, and coproduction tasks.

Plans provide customers the script they need to perform. They enable customers to visualize the steps they need to perform in order to successfully complete tasks. Some plans are genetically inherited, such as eating, while other plans are learned through training and direct experience.

As illustrated in the Bandura and Cervone research that started this chapter, goals, expectations, and plans alone do not have a substantial impact on performance. In a coproduction experience, these elements must be combined with feedback to truly enhance customer performance. Feedback gives customers the information they need to regulate performance and make the necessary adjustments that result in peak performance.

## CHAPTER 6

# FACILITATING ACCESS

*We shall not fail or falter; we shall not weaken or tire ...*
*Give us the tools and we will finish the job.*

—Sir Winston Churchill

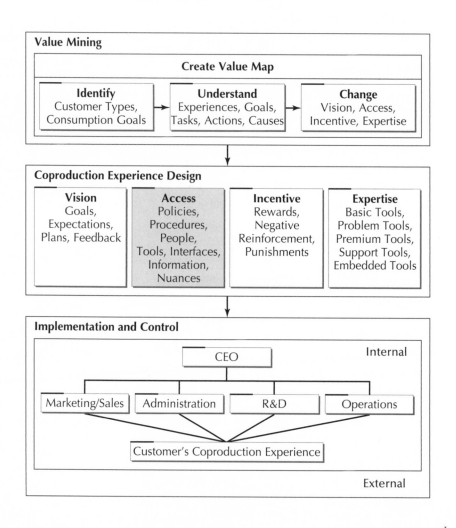

In this chapter, we examine the second element of the Coproduction Experience Model, *access*. Access defines the physical elements of the experience that enable customers to access the value embedded in goods and services. We start this chapter with a discussion of the situations for which access reduces customer performance gaps. The chapter continues with sections that show you how you design access into coproduction experiences by:

- Articulating company policies that establish rules for customer performance
- Specifying procedures that affect customer experiences
- Identifying the people, both employees and customers, who are best suited for the experience
- Developing tools that enable customers to do more work
- Designing interfaces that make the work customers do easy
- Creating information customers need to make decisions
- Coordinating nuances that influence the customers' natural reflexes

## SITUATIONS CALLING FOR IMPROVED ACCESS

Access helps guide the design of coproduction experiences so that you provide customers the resources they need to perform. Because humans are self-regulating and desire to perform well, shaping customers' *vision* sets customers on the path to accomplishing tasks and obtaining desired outcomes. Yet there are factors that are often beyond the customers' control or capability that threaten their ability to perform. In other words, customers may know what to do and when to do it, but they might not have the resources to accomplish tasks.

The elements of access reflect Albert Bandura's concept of environment in social learning theory—the environment is a specific force that shapes behavior. Because of this, access helps you shape coproduction experiences in a variety of ways so that customers are able to perform better with greater satisfaction. As shown in Figure 6.1, access is a hierarchy of seven specific physical resources.

At the foundation of the hierarchy rests *policies*, which provide the rules for the coproduction experience. *Processes and procedures* provide the script for how customers are expected to perform (and how companies respond to their performance). Since coproduction involves *people*, companies have some choice in who performs coproduction tasks. To make tasks simpler or

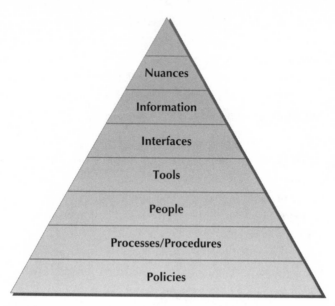

**Figure 6.1**    The seven levels of access that shape coproduction experiences.

more convenient, *tools,* such as self-service technologies, are used to supplement or enhance experiences. Additionally, *interfaces,* such as the floor plan of a store or the ergonomic design of a product, have an effect on customers' ability to complete tasks. Furthermore, *information,* such as nutritional labeling on food, helps customers make better choices. Coproduction experiences are rounded out through the inclusion of *nuances,* which subtly influence performance through sights, sounds, smells, and tastes.

In the design of customer experiences, *touchpoints* are key situations from which customers derive experiences. A touchpoint is an event that occurs when a customer is in direct contact with some aspect of a company. There are human touchpoints, such as an 800-number support line or when a customer interacts with a salesperson in a store. Additionally, there are nonhuman touchpoints, such as a customer's interaction with a product or a self-service technology (SST), like an automated teller machine (ATM). Touchpoints can be physical, whereby customers become involved through touch, sight, smell, hearing, or taste. Or they can be conceptual, whereby customers become involved through thinking, reflection, or emotion. Some touchpoints are obvious, such as pushing a button, while others are subtle, such as pulling into the parking lot of a store. Throughout these different channels, the aim is to coordinate the design of the touchpoints so they provide a consistent experience.

For example, Lands' End, the catalog retailer, designs its ordering touchpoints so the experience one has when ordering products from a live person is consistent with ordering products through its website. This is a good example of decision by design, not default. A great company tries to influence, lead, and "train" its customers at each of these key contact points. A not so great company does not give thought to these predictable influence points and therefore misses out on tremendous opportunities to condition the customer.

When you design coproduction experiences, you can enhance customer performance by providing performance-oriented touchpoints. These touchpoints enable customers to perform tasks better, faster, easier, and with greater accuracy. Through *access*, companies open the door for customers in terms of better ways of doing things. Yet if these access points are absent, poorly conceived, or poorly designed, the coproduction experience suffers. Consider the following situations.

## Customers (and Employees) Are Not Trusted

This leads to policies and procedures that are constraining. Consider online retailer Outpost.com, a division of Fry's Electronics. Buying goods is extremely easy. Choose what you want, enter your credit card, and within a day or two your goods arrive at the doorstep. But if something is wrong with what you ordered—incorrect, damaged, not working, not the right part, and so on—the PITA factor appears. You have to call a service representative, plead your case, and if the representative is convinced, you are awarded a return materials authorization (RMA) number. Other companies might require you to pay a restocking fee! However, when trust is strong, policies are more humanistic. Contrast the Outpost.com experience with buying and returning goods through Gap.com. Don't like what you bought? You can return unwashed, unworn, or defective items at any time. An RMA number is not necessary. Return the item through the mail or bring it to any Gap store. If the Gap sent you an incorrect or defective item, they'll even reimburse you for return shipping. If getting in is easy, then getting out should be easy as well. Consistency is the basic building block of trust. Without it, over time people will not trust the company.[1]

## There Are Obstacles Beyond the Customer's Control

A new location for a food market was having its grand opening. This location had been in the works for a year, and throngs of loyal customers were looking forward to the new store. Management decided upon having a "hard opening," meaning that the day the store opened would be heavily pro-moted (this is in contrast to a "soft opening," where the store is opened qui-etly for a few days to work out the bugs before the official, publicized "grand opening"). Advertisements were run, the media was alerted, and announce-ments were sent to customers. The response was overwhelming! Hundreds, if not thousands, of customers showed up on the grand opening day. They were there to buy. They bought until the store's systems to process credit and debit cards went down for two hours. No backup system, not even carbon charge card forms, was in place. Customers abandoned their carts and left the store dissatisfied. Customers did show their commitment to doing business with the store by showing up, selecting items to purchase, and trying to pay. A better plan was obviously necessary.

## There Is a Simpler Way

Users of a photocopying machine were having significant trouble replacing the toner bottle. When they went to replace the bottle they would slide the bottle across the top of a track rather than within the track. This caused the bottle to spill toner powder in the machine, which then necessitated the need for a service call to clean the spill. It was frustrating and expensive. The com-pany's first thought was to train the customers, but clearer heads prevailed. Instead, a line was painted on the bottle, and another line was painted on the inside of the photocopier. Instructions on the bottle were changed. Now when the line on the bottle lined up with the line in the photocopier, the bot-tle was in the correct position and could be slid safely, without mess, into the track. Training the customer would have been costly. By relying on similar experiences, the company found a simple and cost effective way to allow the customer to be successful.[2]

## The Right Person Is Not Performing the Task

Just as salespeople qualify customers in terms of need, creditworthiness, and likelihood of purchase, companies must ensure that the right people are per-forming coproduction tasks. For instance, a variety of companies, such as Macromedia, a developer of multimedia and web development software tools, and PeopleTrack, a human resources information system developer, have what are called *customer participation programs*. The aim of these programs is to recruit customers to participate in product development activities, such as evaluating the functionality of new products. Of course, if the wrong type of customer is selected for these programs, the value of the coproduction experience is low. Thus customers are required to complete questionnaires that determine if they are the right person to perform these specific coproduction tasks.[3]

Access is a significant force in enabling customer performance. In our research for this book, we collected hundreds of critical incident stories from customers. These stories describe how companies have helped (or hindered) customers from achieving goals. In 72 percent of the stories, customers attributed *access* as the primary force that enabled them or restrained them from being effective coproducers. Many of the enabling stories reflect the coproduction experiences of this storyteller:

> This story starts off when I was younger and my dad and I would go hit golf balls at the local golf course down the street from our house. We would go about two or three times a week and buy two large buckets of balls to hit. When we'd arrive at the golf course we'd go to the pro shop and buy our golf balls. There would be a person in the golf shop that would get a bucket and scoop balls into it. This was not a very long process but sometimes the person would be busy answering phones or there would be no balls for the person to give us. So we would have to wait around for five or ten minutes just to get golf balls. Then after getting our balls we would carry the buckets and our bags all the way down to the golf range, which sometimes would cause us to spill our balls. After a while the golf course put in two golf ball dispenser machines by the range. So now we buy some tokens at the golf shop, walk down to the range, put tokens in the machine, and the machine pours a bucket of golf balls. This is great because now we can buy as many tokens as we want and just head straight to the range without waiting. Also, we no longer have to carry the bucket down to the range. This was a big improvement and was an excellent idea for people who just like to hit balls.

Let's now look at each of the seven elements that shape coproduction experiences.

## ARTICULATING POLICIES

The foundation of access rests upon your company's adoption of appropriate policies. Policies are rules that govern the behavior of both customers and employees in the coproduction experience. Policies help set expectations and help form the primary rules of thumb that customers and employees use to make decisions. For example, airlines have policies that aim to reduce the frequency of disruptive passengers. Similarly, the story of the California World Fest (Chapter 2) describes policies that shape the coproduction experience in a musical event, such as the height of chairs and where people may dance. Policy formation is a company responsibility that defines and protects the coproduction experience the company desires to promote.

Most policies involving coproduction experiences begin with simplicity in mind and then, unfortunately, end up complicated. The starting point for a basic individualized, transactional policy is if customers don't like the good (or service), they get their money back. Indeed, the simplicity of such a policy is delightful. But the myriad of interpretations quickly threaten the economic viability of the company. Thus, a variety of quantitative conditions become added, such as the length of time a customer has to decide (30 days), the condition the product needs to be in when returned (resellable; unworn, unwashed, unused), the documentation required (store receipt), and the financial responsibility for shipping costs. These conditions are most often codified in the warranty that accompanies the good or service.

A danger of individualized policies is that as they become more complex they can become monsters. Their logic or restrictiveness threatens the customer's experience. Take a bank's overdraft policy. The basic coproduction experience here is that the customer writes checks and the bank pays the checks. The customer is responsible for writing checks within the money available in their account, and the bank is responsible for crediting customer deposits quickly and processing the checks. If the customer has insufficient funds, a penalty is assessed. However, as overdraft fees have become a profit center for banks (estimated to account for 32 percent of all non-interest income a bank receives), some banks have tightened policies such that these fees are maximized. One policy is the prioritization of payment. If several checks come in on the same day, a prioritization scheme that processes the largest check first can clear out an account with that one check. This then causes overdraft fees *for each* of the checks remaining in the queue. We are sure a customer could devise a different order of payment that would be logical and balanced. Needless to say, Paul Nadler, a professor of finance, suggests that a phone call to the customer in such situations would result in a coproduced solution that results in greater loyalty rather than the possible defection attributable to an ill-structured policy.[4]

Beyond policies that govern transactions and product usage, you can establish policies that govern the social environment in which coproduction experiences occur. Some of these policies are driven by legislation. For example, *no smoking* policies in restaurants and other public places tend to reflect local ordinances. Similarly, policies such as *no shirt, no shoes, no service* have roots in local health and safety codes and the cultural desires of customers. A majority of policies should be designed by companies to create an environment in which customers like to spend time, free from hassles or distractions.

We recently took a ride on the Coaster, a California train service that runs between Oceanside and San Diego. After taking our seat a conductor walked by to check our tickets, then handed us a card entitled Coaster Passenger Code of Conduct. The card listed 16 specific policies associated with riding the train, from the basics such as smoking, littering, and radios to such things as *consideration*—avoiding acts that are disruptive or threatening to other passengers.

Sure enough, we were fortunate to observe the policy in action. Several gentlemen seated at the opposite end of the car were a bit too disruptive in their conversation and merriment as the train proceeded southward. As the train approached the next stop, a conductor approached the group, handed them another code of conduct card, and explained to them that they had violated the code of conduct. When the train stopped in the station, he asked them to leave and escorted them off the train. Although these types of events occur infrequently on the Coaster, we applaud the conductor who took the initiative in maintaining the experience expected by customers and described in the policy.

Our experience as patrons of Southwest Airlines correlates with this situation and expands our definition of policies in coproduction experiences. If you haven't flown Southwest, you need to know that Southwest doesn't offer assigned seats. Customers receive boarding cards that assign them to a boarding group. It used to be a number—1 through 130—which determined boarding order, but now the numbers have been replaced by boarding groups—A, B, or C. Thus there is a bit of "coproduction competition" as passengers jockey to be first on the plane to get the best seats.

Several years ago, as Southwest flights became fuller, pre-boarding lines were frequently abused by some passengers. It was not uncommon to see able-bodied people holding boarding pass number 130 (a high number that ensured a middle seat in the back of the plane) cheat the system by using the pre-boarding line. Gate agents, desiring to avoid confrontation (we know, we asked), turned a blind eye to such behavior. Accordingly, those of us who followed the rules didn't find such behavior amusing, letting the cheating passenger, gate agent, and Southwest know in no uncertain terms our displeasure with their lack of enforcement. Southwest heard our complaints and changed the policy. Now, pre-boarders could only sit in rows 10 and higher. Whoops! This policy was immediately challenged by the people for whom pre-boarding was designed—the elderly and the disabled—and was quickly rescinded by Southwest. But Southwest fortunately came back with a better, brilliant system. It started issuing blue sleeves, into which boarding passes could be inserted, to passengers that met the requirements for pre-boarding. Thus, when a passenger checked in at a gate, he or she could request a pre-boarding sleeve and presumably be vetted by the ticket agent as to eligibility. Ticket agents could also provide the sleeves to passengers who obviously needed pre-boarding. With this solution, cheaters were thwarted, gate agents were able to avoid confrontation, and passengers in the regular boarding lines could visually verify enforcement of the pre-boarding policy. Passengers had greater comfort knowing that the "credentials" of pre-board passengers were being checked (even if they really weren't—Southwest successfully classically conditioned the rest of us to associate "vetted" with the blue sleeve).

The "co" in a coproduction experience means that the company is doing some of the work as well, either through an employee or technology. While the previously discussed policies govern customer behavior, other consistent policies should govern employee behavior in terms of how they support the coproduction experience. Ritz-Carlton Hotels is an innovator in policies that contribute to one of the best brand experiences in the world. Through *the credo, the motto, the three steps of service, the basics,* and *the employee promise,* Ritz-Carlton describes a set of guidelines that define the employee's role in the coproduction experience. For example, employees are empowered to take care of customer problems and needs with the standard of performance of "resolving the issue." Complaints are owned by the employee who receives the complaint, until the complaint is rectified. When guests need help finding something in the hotel, employees must escort them to the desired location. When employees hear of a guest's preference, they must record the preference. Of course, Ritz-Carlton's policies work because the company is also careful to select people who have values, capabilities, and desires consistent with the policies.

## SPECIFYING PROCESSES/PROCEDURES

All companies should have an ideal script of how they'd like customers to perform. A lot of these scripts, not surprisingly, favor the company. Consider the story of Al Yeganeh, the real-life, surly soup purveyor who became immortalized as the "Soup Nazi" on the television show Seinfeld. For over 20 years Mr. Yeganeh built an extraordinarily successful business selling high-quality soup from a small storefront in New York City. The shop's Zagat rating is higher than some top restaurants! Because of the quality, there is very strong demand. When the shop is open it is not uncommon for a line to form that stretches around the block.

High demand, a long line, and a set of values with an unrelenting focus on quality yielded a transaction process high on efficiency but low on social graces to which many of us are accustomed. To ensure everyone who wants soup can get soup, Mr. Yeganeh enforces a rigid, militaristic process in the coproduction experience:

### Ordering Procedure

1. When you walk in move immediately to the right.
2. Order your soup with no enthusiasm at all.
3. Put your money on the counter and move to your left.
4. Take your soup and do not give any comments.

Failure to follow this process results in expulsion and the admonishment, "No soup for you"—the catch phrase popularized by the Seinfeld show.[5]

Processes don't have to be as rigid and militaristic as Mr. Yeganeh's. In fact, his new franchises are not required to follow the process that made the original shop famous.

You can streamline processes to be efficient for the customer and company, as well as appealing in their simplicity. Amazon.com is one the leaders in stripping out steps and actions customers must perform to complete transactions. After placing their first order, customers may participate in the patented 1-Click ordering process. As you browse for products you click the 1-Click button for the products you want to buy. Anything you order within a 90-minute period starting with the first item is consolidated by shipping address and availability. Since Amazon already possesses shipment and payment information, the customer does not have to suffer numerous, subsequent decision steps.

The design of processes and procedures for coproduction experiences requires balancing three attributes: control, steps, and handoffs.

## Control

Control reflects the level of the company's oversight involving the coproduction experience. The tendency is to give the customer more control in how a task is accomplished. However, left to their own devices, customers can create numerous processes for accomplishing coproduction tasks. Some processes they create may be dangerous and thus must be reigned in to avoid injury. For example, when replacing bulbs in LCD computer projectors customers should first unplug the device (to avoid shock), then wait until the bulb cools (to avoid burns). Skipping these steps might cause injury. Other processes customers create may result in annoying other customers. When customers proved themselves incapable of placing seats in an orderly and fair fashion at the California World Fest, the promoter had to step in and design a process to maintain a harmonious coproduction experience.

However, in the absence of control, customers can help companies create some innovative solutions. A great example of this is a social ecology experiment undertaken at the University of California, Irvine, some time ago. When some buildings were built, no paths between the buildings were constructed. Instead, the university laid grass between the buildings. When the university opened the buildings, the people using the buildings walked across the grass to get from one building to another. Since people naturally adopt the easiest way to accomplish tasks, paths naturally emerged in the grass, identifying the optimum routes. When these routes were well established, the university replaced the worn paths in the grass with concrete sidewalks.

## Steps

As the number of steps in a coproduction experience increases, so does the PITA factor. We know that one step, such as Amazon's 1-Click service, is the benchmark for easy-to-use procedures. For many products, such an ideal benchmark is currently unattainable due to technical limitations or legal restraint (Amazon was awarded a patent on the 1-Click process and is actively defending it). Thus, what is a reasonable number of steps for a process or procedure?

Here we take the lead from some experiments performed by George Miller in the 1940s. Miller was the researcher who gave us the rule of 7 +/− 2. This rule describes the size limits of a person's short-term memory, being five to nine "chunks" of information. When people receive information, it first goes into short-term memory. Then, after some initial processing, it may move to long-term memory. Miller found that people were most able to recall lists of items, steps in a procedure, and so on if those lists or steps were structured within the 7 +/− 2 limits. Thus, if a process or procedure extends beyond nine steps, we have a pretty good idea that it will be difficult for people to remember and use.

Too many steps can negatively affect any coproduction experience. Consider the experience of several AT&T Wireless managers as they tried to use the company's mMode service. This service provides customers news, email, stock quotes, directions, and other information through their cell phone. The product was a hit with techies, but average consumers were not warming up to the service—and the company wanted to know why. Spurred by their design firm, AT&T managers participated in a scavenger hunt in San Francisco, using their cell phones and the mMode service to find a variety of goods and services, from music CDs to Walgreen's generic ibuprofen. The managers quickly discovered the tasks were too difficult using mMode. There were too many steps and too many clicks. Embarrassingly, they found themselves referring to newspapers and phone directories to complete the tasks. The experience of the managers was shared by customers in AT&T Wireless stores, who also found it difficult to access favorite web pages. These findings led AT&T Wireless to redesign the coproduction experience, simplifying the service and reducing the number of steps it took to get answers.[6]

## Handoffs

Handoffs occur in coproduction experiences when one employee hands a customer or task off to another employee during a process. Some handoffs are internal to the company. This is seen in restaurants, where one person (the waiter) takes your order and another person (the expediter) serves the food. In restaurants where the interaction was not designed (and thus is in default mode) the expediter has no clue which guest gets what and must disturb the guests to inquire, "Who gets the pasta?" Other handoffs involve the customer. We find this in various sales settings. The simple situation is when a clerk hands off a complaining customer to a manager because policies limit the clerk's authority in resolving the issue. This further frustrates the customer in many instances by making the customer explain again and relive the situation that is causing the problem. Hence, the customer's bad memory of the encounter only grows stronger.

A more complex situation occurs with car dealers. When we shopped for our Dodge truck, we were first met by a low-level "qualifier," who showed us a couple of cars and determined our level of interest. We must have passed the test, since we were quickly handed off to a more experienced salesperson who started the price negotiations. As the price negotiations got down to the last $500, we were then handed off to the closer, the guy in the suit and the no-nonsense demeanor, who seals the deal. To sign the papers we were handed off to yet another employee. While such a process may have some redeeming value to the dealer, it certainly didn't respect our notions and desires for efficiency.

Customers despise handoffs in coproduction experiences because they are so inefficient. Susan Glover, vice president and chief quality officer of Adventist Healthcare System in Rockville, Maryland, suggests that too many handoffs in hospital procedures can reduce the patient's confidence in the care the hospital provides. For example, when patients begin the intake process they often have to see different clerks who ask them the same questions over and over. Patients end up having to wait until the next person they see is free. The information they receive from one person to the next is often conflicting, raising uncertainty, confusion, and frustration. The solution is obvious. Remove handoffs wherever possible. If the handoff is necessary, enhance it such that information flows with the process and guidance is consistent.[7]

## IDENTIFYING PEOPLE

Coproduction experiences, by their very nature, involve people, both customers and employees. Employees help customers in numerous ways by providing customers information, educating customers about product usage, and helping customers complete transactions. While the selection and training of employees is an important topic (for which there are numerous texts that can guide the reader), our focus here is on how companies select customers and determine whether customers are able to perform various coproduction tasks.

Age, gender, height, weight, physical capacity, and so on form an initial set of criteria for whether customers can participate in coproduction experiences. Laws prohibit people who are under 21 from participating in various vices, from visiting bars to gambling in casinos. Curves, the fitness franchise, allows only women members. At amusement parks, if you are not as tall as the sign, you are prohibited from certain thrill rides. In the car rental industry, drivers under the age of 25 aren't permitted to rent cars. On a recent trip to Ireland the father of one of the authors (who is over the age of 65), discovered that while he could rent a car, he wasn't permitted to rent a minivan. Further investigation revealed that the skinny Irish roads and impairments of the older generation don't mix well for a safe drive through the Irish countryside.

A similar selection criteria is used by Zero-G, a company that offers customers a weightless experience. The company uses a modified Boeing 727 to fly parabolas—10,000-foot arcs—in the sky. At the top of the arc, customers experience 25 seconds of weightlessness. Such flights have trained astronauts for over 40 years. Now, for $2,950, ordinary folks can try it was well. But there are some selection conditions. Customers must be medically fit—no heart ailments or pregnancy. Additionally, an iron stomach is desired, as airsickness is a common effect experienced by even the hardiest astronauts.[8]

Companies are, in some cases, required by law to make certain accommodations for customers to participate in coproduction experiences. For example, the Americans with Disabilities Act (ADA) prohibits the exclusion of people with disabilities from everyday activities. Common places where this law has significant effect are public transportation, restaurants, theaters, and grocery stores. The ADA affects businesses of all sizes.[9]

The above criteria discuss the conditions for inclusion in various types of experiences. When companies want to shift more work to customers, then they must focus on *capability*.

Capability defines whether customers have the knowledge, skills, and attitudes to perform certain tasks. Consider the profile of customers who are allowed to sit in the exit row of a commercial aircraft in the United States.

- No physical or mental disabilities (glasses are OK)
- Must be able to hear, speak, and understand English well
- Must be over 15 years of age
- Must be able open the emergency door in an emergency
- Must be willing to act as part of the crew in an emergency

In any coproduction experience, whether it be opening the emergency exit or using a Home Depot self-checkout system, companies must discover the nature of coproduction tasks. Through task analysis methodologies, it is relatively straightforward to discover the knowledge, skill, and attitudinal components of the task. These can then be compared to the capabilities of customers to determine if there is a match (or if additional expertise is required, which we discuss later in the book).

A similar analysis can be used to determine if employee tasks can be shifted to customers. The first step is to determine if the task is simple. Simple means the task involves low-level knowledge, skills, and attitudes. For example, think about the actions involved with filling a car with gas. Unscrew cap. Lift nozzle. Turn handle. Place nozzle into hole. Squeeze. They are all simple motor skills involving limited hand-eye coordination. The procedure is short—five steps. Since the nozzle has automatic turn-off when the tank is full, there is no problem solving. Thus, if a minimum wage employee is doing the job and it takes less than ten minutes to train the basics, then perhaps the job could be done better by the customer.

The next thing to consider is customers' accrued experience and conditioning. If a customer is a blank slate, in terms of not having prior experience performing certain tasks, then convincing them to take on more work is an uphill battle. Imagine if 30 years ago gas stations jumped cold turkey from full service to self service the way it is today—with pay-at-the-pump terminals and not an attendant in sight. We suspect that customer reaction to such a coproduction experience would be entirely different than it is today.

However, what makes customers doing more work today more viable are the experiences customers are acquiring in a variety of situations. Self-service gas and ATMs have created a class of customers comfortable with doing things themselves. They have learned the basic scripts these devices offer, and when similar experiences become available in grocery stores, airports, restaurants, and so on, they already know the script of what they are supposed to do. Plus, if the experience has offered them benefits, such as faster transactions, then they will begin to demand control of certain tasks. For example, as a guest of a hotel, we would like to do the work the desk clerk does. We think that with certain technologies, we can do it better, faster, with greater accuracy, and with more satisfaction. That confidence comes from our experience with airlines, grocery stores, banks, and gas stations.

Many customers these days are required by their employers to use computers, web pages, and other tools to perform daily jobs. Here again companies have the opportunity to transfer skills people learn on the job to the work of being a customer. At many companies employees must use a web browser to maintain their human resource profiles. This basic skill then extends to customers being more able and willing to maintain information associated with their credit card, bank, telephone, and cable services.

## DEVELOPING TOOLS

Look in any kitchen drawer, any basement workshop, or the desk in any office and you'll immediately appreciate people's love of tools. These labor-saving devices take us beyond what we can do with our own bodies, whether it be mixing dough, hammering a nail, or communicating with a colleague. Tools are the lifeblood of efficiency and effectiveness. Often, they are quite a bit of fun.

It goes without saying then that ideal coproduction experiences rely on the presence of tools to make customer work easier and more fluid. Even a simple coproduction task, such as writing a check, can be thwarted by the absence of a basic tool—a pen. Tools also enable customers to willingly take on more work, evidenced by the overwhelming acceptance of ATM machines. Jonathan Velline, who heads up ATMs for Wells Fargo, says that, ". . . if I didn't have ATMs, I wouldn't have customers." ATMs are so popular that 92 percent of banking customers feel that a convenient ATM is a critical feature when they choose a bank. Others consider ATMs more essential than email.[10]

With one ATM for every 284 people in the United States, ATMs have spawned a cascade of similar self-service technologies (SSTs). In 2004, with the exception of Oregon and New Jersey, the vast majority of gas stations in the United States had pay-at-the-pump technology. Delta Airlines had 846 self-service check-in terminals in 83 airports. Kroger had 1,400 stores with self-service checkout lanes, and Home Depot had 850 similarly equipped stores. Hilton Hotels is expected to roll out SSTs in 45 hotels that allow guests to check in without seeing a clerk. Research firm IHL Consulting Group estimates that in 2003 U.S. consumers spent $128 million at kiosks. This was an 80 percent increase over spending in 2002. By 2007, they estimate spending will exceed $1.3 billion.[11]

In Lone Tree, Colorado, McDonald's has tested a self-service system that enables customers to place and pay for orders without the help of a McDonald's team member. The nine kiosks, located at the front counter, provide an icon-based interface that enables customers to order the products they want. After payment, using either cash or credit cards, the system provides the customer an order number. When their order is up, they exchange the number for their food. The extension of this system is that kiosks are also available in the children's PlayPlace. Parents can keep an eye on their kids while they place the order. When the order is ready a McDonald's crewmember delivers the food directly to the table.[12]

These tools are becoming more accessible to a wide variety of people. Bank of America, Wells Fargo, and Fleet Bank have introduced ATMs with voice-guided technology. This enables people with impaired vision to process transactions safely and securely.[13]

Technology is driving more and more innovations that shift work to customers. In Hong Kong, electronic money cards are a huge hit. In 1998, Hong Kong's subway operator, MTR Corporation, took a gamble on how people pay for transportation. It implemented an electronic money card technology that aimed to replace pocket change. The money card stores value, which customers can replenish from time to time at automated machines. The card is held over a reading device, such as at a turnstile. The reading device subtracts the cost of the ride and the customer is allowed to pass. Because the card may be read through leather and plastic, customers don't even have to take the card out of their wallet or purse. They simply wave the card over the reader and they are on their way.

But the wave of acceptance didn't stop with rides on subways and buses. Stores, such as 7-Eleven and Starbucks, began accepting the cards for customers to purchase newspapers, soft drinks, and meals. City parking meters and municipal pools also accept the card. All totaled, 12,000 locations in 2004 were accepting the card and the card was being used in 1 to 2 percent of all cash transactions.[14]

Another tool that is less intrusive than SSTs and money cards are radio frequency identification (RFID) chips. These chips may be embedded in products, much like UPC barcodes are stamped on products. Thus, when goods are brought into a store, a scanning device detects their presence and adds them to inventory. When customers select products and check out, another scanning device detects the products (without the need for every product being scanned separately) and calculates the total. At home, scanners track the consumption of inventory and the associated software sets plans for the next shopping trip.

It is easy to see, based on the last two stories, where all this is headed in terms of coproduction experiences. RFID chips combined with electronic money cards essentially mean that customers can walk into a store, load up their cart, and walk out. No checkout, no clerks, no hassle. The customer does all the work. Can the coproduction experience get any simpler or secure? Yes it can. And it will.

In 2004 Piggly Wiggly supermarkets in South Carolina started testing a fingerprint identification system to speed supermarket checkout. Shoppers enroll in the program by "registering" their finger. They scan their finger, then swipe their loyalty card and several payment methods, such as a credit cards and debit cards. Thereafter, when they check out of the store all they do is touch their finger to the pad at the checkout station, enter their phone number, and select the payment option. Thus, to follow the above RFID chip story, a money card wouldn't even be necessary. A customer's financial information is associated with their finger scans, creating a one-touch process, similar to Amazon's 1-Click process. A customer might not even have to stop at a finger scan station. The finger scanner could be standard equipment on the grocery cart.[15]

All this talk of technology enhancing coproduction experiences is exciting and fun, but does not excuse us from forgetting about tools that don't require electricity. While web-based reservation systems, package-tracking tools, and account management forms are at the forefront of coproduction experiences these days, simple, paper-based performance tools such as checklists, forms, and other conventional devices also help guide customer performance in numerous ways.

Conventional tools are found in many different contexts. Our CPA uses a paper-based tool called a Tax Planner to help guide us through the process of preparing our taxes. Our favorite sushi restaurant provides a handy card showing pictures of the various types of sushi they make, along with a checklist on which we can indicate what we want. Ski areas enhance the coproduction experience by providing self-service tool stations both in the lodge and on the mountain. These stations provide flat-head and Phillips screwdrivers, pliers, and crescent wrenches that enable skiers to make minor repairs and adjustments. For backcountry travelers, National Parks such as Yosemite rent bear-proof bins for storing your food. Grocery stores and bookstores, such as Barnes & Noble, have restrooms so you don't have to run home. Public parks have "poop bag" dispensers that provide the necessary materials for cleaning up after your pet. Hotels provide soap and shampoo. Restaurants offer toothpicks. Fireworks shops provide matches. Women's clothing stores provide chairs so men can sit (so women can shop longer). The list goes on.

Whether technology-driven or on a simple sheet of paper, tools are ubiquitous elements of a coproduction experience. They enable customers to willingly take on more work so that they can unlock more value. Consider the experiences of another of our storytellers:

> I have been snowboarding for six years and have been to quite a few resorts over the years. What I have noticed is long lift lines that are caused not by people waiting for a chair, but by the lift operator that is checking everyone's tickets. This seems to cause people to get a little upset and I know that it gets a little upsetting for me because the time you wait for the lift operator could be another few runs for the day. I had never seen a solution for this problem until I was a senior in high school. A group of friends and I took a trip to Salt Lake City for a day of snowboarding. We decided to go to Solitude. When we

went to the ticket office and bought our tickets they handed us these little cards that looked like credit cards and they had strings to hang around the neck. We did not understand, but we figured we were soon going to find out.

We went to get in line at the ski lift, but there was one problem: there was no line. There was just a place to swipe your card and a gate to walk through. The gate looked like one of the gates you walk through at a baseball game, were you walk through it and a turnstile turns for the next person. Anyways, we snowboarded the rest of the day and there were no lift lines. If there was one it was short and it was not caused by a lift operator checking tickets—it was because there were not enough chairs for everyone. This was one of the best and most efficient days of boarding I have ever had. From a consumer's point of view this was a great investment on Solitude's part because my friends and I were happy and no one was complaining that the lift operator was taking too long to check tickets. I think that this was a great thing to have and it should be at every ski resort because it is so efficient.

## DESIGNING INTERFACES

As customers engage in coproduction experiences they physically touch the product or service through an *interface*. An interface helps guide customer performance. Virtually everything customers interact with in a coproduction experiences has an interface, for example, the attitude and demeanor of the store clerk, the device that swipes a credit card, the knobs on a stove, and the buttons on the microwave oven.

Some interfaces are subtle, to the point where we don't even notice them, such as the non-slip grip on a kitchen knife. Other interfaces are obvious, such as the ringing, blinking, gated interfaces of a railroad crossing.

Interfaces are not tools, but they are parts of tools. An ATM, for example, is a tool, but a subcomponent of that ATM is its interface—the slots, the screen, buttons, and the device that spits out the cash. Similarly, the American Airlines web-based reservation system is a tool which consists of interfaces for entering destinations, selecting flights, making the reservation, selecting seats, and paying.

Products, such as computers, stereos, drills, cameras, and so on, rely on interfaces to enhance customer performance. The absence of a good interface means the coproduction experience suffers. Tasks are difficult and inefficient and customers don't get a lot of utility and enjoyment out of the experience. Consider BMW's iDrive, a single-knob device for controlling 700-odd functions, such as the radio and satellite navigation, found in 7-series models. The interface has received a lot of criticism from experts, the press, and customers. Usability expert Donald Norman calls iDrive, "Bad design." *USA Today* says iDrive, ". . . manages to complicate simple functions beyond belief." *Auto Review* describes iDrive as, ". . . not simple, no matter how clean it looks to the naked eye." Regardless of how well-intentioned an interface is, there needs to be a balance between form (iDrive looks real cool) and function (but I can't use it safely while driving) in terms of aiding customer performance.[16]

When interfaces are intuitive and fluid, customers relish the experience with the product and achieve superior performance. Take, for example, Apple Computer's new iPOD MINI, a smaller-sized version of the original iPOD. Its new click wheel interface now makes it easier to navigate the 1,000-odd songs the device stores. Additionally, it saves space by integrating more buttons. BusinessWeek's IDEA awards jury was so impressed with the new iPOD MINI and its interface that the product was awarded a gold medal for outstanding design.[17]

Interfaces can also be found in various nontechnological settings to better guide customer performance. At Stew Leonard's, the highly regarded, service-oriented food store chain in Connecticut, customers follow a path (the store's interface) that twists and turns through the store. Unlike regular grocery stores with their ordered aisles, this path is designed specifically so customers will see every product Stew Leonard's sells. You start at the "bags of the world" display (which has photos of customers holding Stew Leonard bags in exotic locations), then proceed through the bakery, produce, and then into the dairy (which is quite impressive). Then it is through general groceries until you get to the checkout area. If you are there just to get a box of cereal, then the Stew Leonard's interface might not be all that helpful. But then again, if you are just buying cereal, Stew probably doesn't want your business. Stew Leonard's aims for volume and is in the Guinness Book of World Records as being the store with the highest sales per square foot.

The troubles of a mother led to the improvement of the interface for applying sunscreen. With regular bottles of sunscreen, the interface is minimal. You squeeze the stuff into your hand and start wiping it over your body. Messy, but it works. For some people, this was inconvenient, so companies came up with a different interface—a spray bottle that would mist sunscreen over your body. But it was Kelly Moreno's son's refusal to put on sunscreen that led her to invent yet another interface—Swipes. Think of an individually packaged baby wipe that has sunscreen on it. Now you can apply sunscreen by just wiping it on with no mess or sprays.

We find the interface at Subway® sandwich shops particularly interesting. It consists of a glass partition/counter that separates customers from the sandwich makers (Figure 6.2). At the starting end of the counter (furthest away from the cash register), the customer and sandwich maker have their initial interaction. The customer places the order and the sandwich maker asks what kind of bread. The customer responds then watches as the sandwich maker selects the bread—visually confirming the right choice. Next, the sandwich maker starts making the sandwich where the customer can see it being made. The sandwich maker asks the customer's choice about several options—mustard, mayo, Italian dressing, and so on. The customer responds and again has visual proof. By the time the sandwich gets to the end of the counter the customer has seen everything that went into the sandwich. Through the interface (and as part of the process), the customer has visually verified that all instructions were carried out by the sandwich maker. Thus, when the customer sits down to eat there are no surprises.

Photo Courtesy of Subway® Restaurants.

**Figure 6.2** Subway's sandwich making counter. This interface makes the entire sandwich-making process visible to the customer.

Another way to think about interfaces is the amount of space a business provides customers and the ease of access. Here's another story:

> In my neighborhood there were three convenience stores competing with each other, Chevron, Winner's Corner, and AM/PM. All three stores are located in the same area. Chevron provides gas and they

have wide open space around the shop. Customers can easily park, fill up with gas, and purchase drinks or snacks. I find this is very convenient when I use the store. Winner's Corner has narrower space, but they have more items than Chevron. Both Chevron and Winner's Corner are located next each other, but I feel Chevron provides more space for the customer, making it easier to access. AM/PM was located one street away from these two places. It had narrow spaces and was very hard to enter the shop—which is not useful. It is no wonder that AM/PM is now closed.

## CREATING INFORMATION

Information consists of messages communicated throughout the coproduction experience that shape and modify behavior. As component parts of an interface, information includes such textual things as signs in a grocery store denoting product prices, labels on product packages, and messages displayed on computer screens. Information can also be conveyed through symbols, such as arrows painted on automatic doors indicating which way is in and which way is out, or a light on a taxi that indicates whether it is in or out of service. In other words, information is words, pictures, signals, and even textures, such as braille, that help customers perform better. In this context, information has several purposes.

**Stimulating Action.** Information causes customers to initiate action. A stoplight that changes from red to green cues drivers to go. A message on an airline check-in kiosk that reads, "Insert Frequent Flyer Card," cues the customer to insert the card. The chimes in your car cue the driver to fasten the seatbelt.

**Making Decisions.** Information helps customers make decisions. Labels on products, such as nutritional information and technical requirements, help customers decide if a product is right for them. It also helps them compare the product to other choices. Male and female signs on public restroom doors help customers decide which door is the *right* door.

**Communicating Feedback.** Information helps customers learn results. After performing actions, information communicates feedback associated with those actions. Plug in a battery-charging device, and a green light illuminates. Do something wrong on your computer, and a dialog box appears informing you of the mistake.

Appropriate usage of information is strongly influenced by how people perceive information. In their classic work on message design, Malcolm Fleming and Howard Levie suggest several principles regarding perception.[18]

1. Perception is relative. Customers are not precise scientific instruments who can offer a quantitative measure for everything they perceive. Rather, customers take in information and process it in relation to experiences, the context of a situation, and the specific need they have for the information. Thus there may be slight inaccuracies and individual differences between two or more people. In coproduction contexts, this can cause disagreement over the fullness of a cup, the size of a portion, the loudness of music, or the cleanliness of a restroom.

2. Perception is selective. Customers can devote their attention to only a few pieces of information at one time. What they select to perceive is dependent on their current actions and the packaging of the information. If the coproduction environment is noisy, then it may be difficult for a customer to concentrate on an information processing task, such as placing an order.

3. Perception is organized. Customers naturally form relationships and groupings of various types of information. As such, companies can increase the speed of customers' retention of information by designing the information in such a way so it is already grouped. A restaurant menu that groups dishes by fish, beef, pork, and chicken enables customers to be more efficient in their choices compared to a menu that has no discernable structure.

4. Perception is set. Through experience and conditioning, customers expect to perceive certain types of information. When we use a self-checkout lane at the grocery store we expect information at the end of our transaction telling us the total of our purchases. Similarly, when we turn off a device we expect all indicator lights to dim and for it to stop making noise. Some cars that we have owned have a cooling feature that is very disconcerting. After parking the car and turning off the ignition, cooling fans will still run if the engine temperature is too high. However, our expectation is that when we turn off the ignition, everything turns off.

The effects of perception can be seen in the following story. In 2004, the National Car Rental location in Tampa was moved out of the airport parking garage to a remote location elsewhere on the airport property. However,

Photo taken by authors. Used by permission of Vanguard Car Rental USA Inc.

**Figure 6.3**  Information in the form of this steering wheel sign can't be ignored. It eliminated customer complaints about getting lost when returning cars to National's Tampa Airport location.

the primary signage at the airport still directed travelers to return rental cars at the main terminal. There were signs for the National location, but they were small in size and not easily perceived due to the *perception is selective* principle. According to a return agent we interviewed, customer performance was a mess. "Customers were chewing us out big time," recalls the return agent. "Customers would follow the signs to the main terminal to return the car, and then they'd be turned back and told to find us out here in the boondocks."

To solve the problem, National provided customers enhanced information in the form of a job aid (Figure 6.3). When customers select their vehicle, a large sign hanging on the steering wheel provides step-by-step instructions for returning cars. Textual instructions are on the front, and a map is on the back. The size and placement of the sign cannot be ignored by customers. It set customers' expectations and provided them the information they needed to take action. Complaints were virtually eliminated.

## COORDINATING NUANCES

For us, nuances top off the access environment. Nuances focus on activating low-level reflex responses, akin to classical conditioning. They involve such devices as aroma, lighting, tastes, music, and other sensory cues that are subtle and in the background. Our subconscious notices nuances, but the anticipated reaction is definitely conscious. Carnivals in the United States are interesting examples of this. A carnival has a certain aroma to it. It is a sugary sweet greasy aroma that for many of us triggers a Pavlovian salivation response. When we smell that aroma we know what we must have—a doughy, deep-fried confection covered with powdered sugar.

In his book *Emotional Branding*, Marc Gobé takes the reader on a journey through the various types of nuances that build an experience. From sounds to scents, each nuance helps shape customer responses in subtle ways. Gobé describes five specific categories of nuance.[19]

1. Sounds that transport
2. Colors that mesmerize
3. Tastes that tantalize
4. Shapes that touch
5. Scents that seduce

*1. Sounds that transport.* Sounds trigger actions ("Attention Kmart Shoppers"). They also provide feedback about the result of an action, such as the laughter of Tickle-Me-Elmo when he is—tickled. Sounds can also transport customers to different places and different feelings. For example, want to create a sense of boredom or sadness? Then use sound that is slow in tempo, low in pitch, and low in loudness. For pleasantness? Use a sound that is fast in tempo, low in pitch, and high in loudness. Want people to buy more products? Then include in the experience music they like.

The U.S.S. Midway museum in San Diego uses sound as an effective means of enabling customers to tour the entire aircraft carrier on their own. Upon boarding you are given a digital audio device and headphones. At various points around the ship there is a numbered placard indicating which audio clip to play. You enter the number into the device and the sounds of the aircraft carrier come alive. Narrators describe the part of the ship you are experiencing and background sounds set the context, whether the roar of a jet for flight-ops, or the clanking of pots and pans in the mess hall.

*2. Colors that mesmerize.* Colors can confuse performance as much as they can help. The color red, for example, has specific meanings to people in the United States. Stop, danger, avoid, hot, and so on. Green, on the other hand, communicates go, a-okay, system is ready, and so on. Switch them, and what does one get? Confusion. That's why on Applied Biosystems genetic analyzers, a green indicator light always means things are okay with the instrument, while red means something is wrong.

As Gobé describes, colors affect other emotional states. Remember ROY-G-BIV—the mnemonic for the colors of the rainbow? Research shows that colors with long wavelengths, such as red, trigger arousal. Colors with short wavelengths, such as blue, trigger relaxation. Gray gives one a sense of professionalism. Want to add a bit of dependability? Then add a bit of navy blue. Black and white? Black is the color of authority and power, while white symbolizes innocence and purity.

*3. Tastes that tantalize.* Food is the bond of friendship. It makes people feel at ease. It is also pleasurable. Many bookstores, notably Barnes & Noble, include a café as part of their coproduction experience. Here patrons can browse a book while enjoying a cup of espresso and a biscotti. Other stores, such as Costco, offer food samples as part of the experience.

*4. Shapes that touch.* In many coproduction contexts, customers are directed not to touch (that customer trust issue again). But in some stores, such as the Sharper Image, the experience is all about touching. Everything in the store is available for you to try, from the remote-control race cars to the massaging chair. Touch is what gets you in, and touch is what gets you to take something home.

Gobé suggests that touch is critical to experiences. So many products these days are wrapped so tightly that we cannot feel them before we buy them. We would rarely consider buying a book that is shrink-wrapped, would we? We want to hold the book in our hands, feel the cover, and flip through the pages.

Customers also want products that ensure performance through touch. Cutting meat with a knife that slips in your hands is a recipe for disaster. So is a tile floor that becomes extremely slippery when wet.

Related to touch is the overall sensations our bodies feel in coproduction experiences. A car that vibrates too much may diminish the driver's comfort experience, whereas a stiff suspension improves the performance experience. When one of our clients opened a new store the freezers made the store very cold, alienating an older generation until the problem was solved.

*5. Scents that seduce.* Neuropsychologist G. Neil Martin believes that scents have strong powers in changing behavior. Historically smells have enabled humans to avoid harmful behavior and make the process of eating food more enjoyable. Natural gas, for example, contains a scent additive (mercaptans) that enables people to detect gas leaks.

Martin suggests that there is both anecdotal and empirical evidence that supports the influence scents have on other kinds of behavior. Studies have shown that if the same odor is present during a task involving the encoding and retrieval of information, recall is enhanced. A chocolate aroma also appears to increase recall. In another experiment, a pleasant-smelling air freshener had a significant effect on plans people formed for a future negotiation task, in terms of setting higher goals, perceiving greater mastery, and desiring a higher share of funds. In practice, however, this scent resulted in greater monetary concessions than in a negotiation setting without scent.

Marketers have experimented with aromas in terms of customers buying more, staying in stores longer, and viewing the environment as positive. In one study, researchers found that shoppers found a store environment more pleasing when it had the aroma of lavender, ginger, spearmint, or orange than an unscented store environment. Another study found that customers perceived a lemon- or coconut-scented disinfectant as more powerful in terms of disinfecting than other aromas (and the lemon/coconut aromas were also found to be pleasing).[20]

## SUMMARY

In this chapter we discussed *access*, a force that provides customers the tools and resources they need to perform. Through the principles associated with access, companies can simplify customer tasks and help customers overcome obstacles that enable them to do more work, reduce costs, and unlock greater value.

Access comprises a hierarchy of specific tactics that are related to certain performance problems. For example, if customers are acting as anarchists, *policies* offer a means to guide the behaviors of both customers and employees. If customers experience confusion, then companies might simplify *processes* to improve customer performance. Some coproduction experiences are appropriate for certain kinds of *people*, hence selection enables companies to choose experiences that are right for them.

Because our bodies can only do so much, *tools* are important performance aids that enable us to perform beyond our natural capabilities. *Interfaces* make using tools easier. When companies need to stimulate action, aid decisions, and communicate feedback, *information* is the conduit of choice. Finally, *nuances* help shape reflexive behaviors through sight, sound, taste, touch, and hearing.

Access has a lot of power to influence performance, yet it can't encourage customers to perform when they don't see or feel the need to perform. Motivating customer performance is the role of incentives, which we discuss in the next chapter.

# CHAPTER 7

## STRUCTURING INCENTIVES

*Reward to encourage goodness; punish to deter evil.*

—Chinese proverb

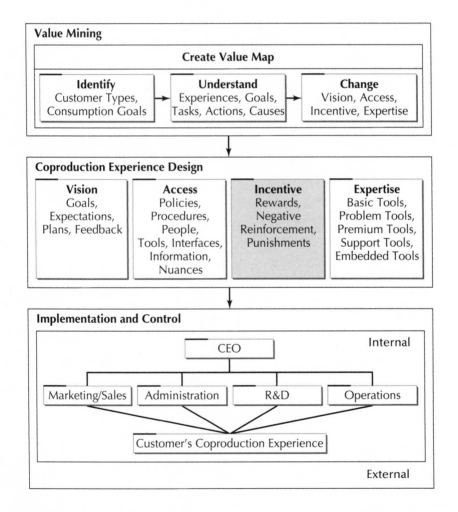

I n this chapter, we examine the third element of the Coproduction Experience Model, *incentive*. Throughout the history of modern commerce, *incentives* (and its opposite, *disincentives*) have had a significant impact on customer behavior. Free gifts, premiums, rebates, and discounts encourage customers to buy more goods, shop more frequently, and tell others of their experiences. On the other hand, extra fees, denial of service, and even arrest encourage customers to plan ahead, avoid trouble, and do the right thing. We start this chapter by clarifying three key concepts: positive reinforcement, negative reinforcement, and punishment. Next, we provide a set of principles for linking the ideal incentive or disincentive to specific situations. The chapter concludes with three sections that show you how you design incentives and disincentives into coproduction experiences by:

- Creating rewards that encourage desirable customer performance
- Structuring intentional negative reinforcement to shape customer performance
- Crafting punishments that discourage undesirable customer performance

## THREE KEY CONCEPTS

Knowing how to use incentives and disincentives in coproduction experiences requires a general understanding of three key concepts, *positive reinforcement, negative reinforcement*, and *punishment*.

- Positive reinforcement, also known as *rewards*, is when a customer receives something of value after responding or performing in a certain way. Receiving a 500-mile bonus when booking an airline ticket online is an example of a reward. The result is that the behavior of booking online is strengthened.
- Negative reinforcement describes the presence of an annoying or painful experience that is removed only after the customer responds or performs in a certain way. An example is when a customer quickly vacates a hotel room to escape the painful scream of a fire alarm. The result is that the behavior of vacating is strengthened.
- Punishment is when a customer receives something of negative value, such as a fine, after responding or performing in a certain way. Getting your season ticket at a ski area revoked after getting caught skiing out-of-bounds is an example of a punishment. The result is that the behavior of skiing out-of-bounds is weakened.

Reinforcement (positive or negative) encourages select behaviors. Punishment discourages select behaviors. To better understand the dynamics of these concepts, imagine that you are a consultant helping the owner of a trendy club design a better coproduction experience for customers. The customer goal you are trying to understand is *gaining access to the club*. Because of the popularity of the club, customers must line up to gain entry. The club owner has evidence that the current experience is a mess, which causes customers to complain more frequently. As part of the analysis, you do some fieldwork, observing the line outside the club on several different nights. Your analysis reveals six different outcomes, as illustrated in Figure 7.1.

In your report, you show the club owner that on some nights the wrong customer behavior gets rewarded and the right customer behavior gets punished. For example, customers who cut the line might be rewarded with quicker access into the club—the cause being a lenient doorman. This success conditions customers to use this strategy more frequently. Alternatively, on some nights customers who wait patiently and quietly never gain access to the club. In essence, these customers are being punished. They are doing exactly what you want them to do, but they never get the reward for doing it—access to the club. Because of this, these customers might choose alternative entertainment—defecting to another club. Thus, when considering incentives as part of a coproduction experience, companies should aim to reward goodness, punish evil, and avoid experiences that reward bad behavior and punish good behavior.

**Incentive/Disincentive Strategy**

| | | Rewarded | Negatively Reinforced | Punished |
|---|---|---|---|---|
| Customer Performance | Doing the Right Thing | Performance: Customers wait in line patiently. Reward: Customers gain access to the club. | Performance: Customers wait in line patiently. Negative Reinforcer: The club's doorman doesn't nag or hassle the customers. | Performance: Customers wait in line patiently. Punishment: Customers never gain admittance to the club. |
| | Doing the Wrong Thing | Performance: Customers cut the line. Reward: Customers gain access to the club without the wait. | Performance: Customers cut the line. Negative Reinforcer: The club's doorman hassles the customers and orders them back in line. | Performance: Customers cut the line. Punishment: The club's doorman sends the customers to the end of the line or unconditionally refuses them entry. |

**Figure 7.1**   Incentive/disincentive strategies and their effects.

What the story above demonstrates is that you must handle incentives and disincentives carefully. The potential for misuse and unintended consequences is quite high. A humorous example is illustrated in a Dilbert® cartoon that is a favorite of software engineers. The pointy-haired boss institutes a program whereby engineers are rewarded for each bug they find in their software code. Of course, the reward only drives the software engineers to add more bugs to their programs, thus perpetuating a vicious cycle.

Customers are virtual Houdinis in their ability to get rewarded for doing unintended things. Consider the story of David Phillips, a civil engineer in Davis, California. Mr. Phillips is known to many as the "Pudding Guy." In 1999 Healthy Choice foods ran a promotion for its line of packaged food products. It offered a reward of 500 frequent flyer miles for every 10 UPC barcodes redeemed by customers. The intention of Healthy Choice was to sell more of its product. Unfortunately, the company might not have thought through how customers might view this offer. Mr. Phillips thinking was quite the opposite. He wanted to take his family on vacation to Europe. He concluded that the Healthy Choice offer could get him there inexpensively.

After visiting several stores, Mr. Phillips determined that Healthy Choice chocolate pudding, at $0.25 per package, offered the best deal to achieve his goal. He proceeded to visit every single Grocery Outlet store in his area and bought the entire supply of Healthy Choice chocolate pudding—12,150 containers. This made him eligible for 1,215,000 frequent flyer miles for a cost of only $3,037.50. Additionally, Mr. Phillips allocated over one million miles to American Airlines and instantly became a lifelong member of its million-miler club, earning him even more perks. The ill-fated promotion, which was estimated to cost Healthy Choice $25,000, perhaps earned them some "free" promotion. We think the only winners in this contest were the Pudding Guy, who took his family to Europe, and food banks throughout central California, who feasted on pudding for some weeks thereafter.[1]

Incentives trigger *behaviors*, which result in *outcomes* that have *consequences*. We call this the B-to-O-to-C model. The incentive Healthy Choice offered did motivate customers (behavior) and resulted in the sale of more pudding (outcome), which is positive. Unfortunately, the consequence turned out to be negative, especially for Healthy Choice, since the cost of the incentive was substantially more than the revenue Mr. Phillips generated. Companies must design incentive programs such that behaviors are activated, outcomes are achieved, and consequences are positive.

## SITUATIONS CALLING FOR INCENTIVES AND DISINCENTIVES

To successfully integrate incentives into coproduction experiences, you must first consider what incentives make sense in certain situations. In contrast to the other forces in the Coproduction Experience Model, incentives are strong medicine that can be habit forming for both the customer and the company in disastrous ways. Companies should select incentives carefully and not rely on them as the sole driver of desired customer performance. Incentives and disincentives are the right strategy to shape specific customer behaviors only when certain preconditions are satisfied:

1. The customer has a clear *vision.*
2. The customer has the necessary *access.*
3. The customer has the required *expertise* (which we discuss in the next chapter).

In the absence of any of these preconditions, an incentive triggers the desire to perform. However, customers won't be able to achieve a positive outcome if the goal is not clear, they don't have the right tools, and they don't have the necessary skills.

The bottom line on incentives (and disincentives) is that they are useful when the customer is able to perform, but for some reason chooses not to. So why does a customer choose not to perform? As shown in Table 7.1, several possible situations are attributable to the design of the coproduction experience.

The first two situations aim to enhance the coproduction experience by adding a reward or punishment to the experience. Rewards can drive desired customer behaviors, such as trying a new online ordering service. Punishments, on the other hand, can reduce undesired customer behaviors, such as smoking on an airline.

The second two situations are associated with unintentional outcomes. The coproduction experience itself might be punishing customers inadvertently, or the coproduction experience rewards undesirable behavior. In these cases it is best to remove the unintended punishments or rewards.

The following sections elaborate these key principles.

### 1. The Coproduction Experience Should Reward Customers When They Do Things Right

This situation reflects the most well-known kind of incentive—the delivery of a reward when customers exhibit the right kind of behavior. Many sales promotions leverage this type of conditioning, whereby a purchase by a

**Table 7.1    Incentive/Disincentive Scenarios for Coproduction Experiences**

| If the Coproduction Experience... | Then | Solution(s) | Example |
|---|---|---|---|
| Does not reward customers when they do things right... | Customers won't do what you want them to do. | • Provide rewards | When launching its e-commerce site, Southwest Airlines offered double rapid rewards points for people who booked tickets online. |
| Does not punish customers when they do things wrong... | Customers keep acting badly and become a PITA factor to the company and other customers. | • Clarify and enhance policies<br>• Levy penalties<br>• "Fire" customers | Carnival Cruise Lines asks customers to sign a policy statement regarding "no smoking" on a ship. If a customer violates the policy, Carnival asks the customer to leave the ship at the next port and fines them $250. |
| Unintentionally punishes customers... | Customers will avoid the experience and perhaps defect to a competing experience. | • Remove punishment or<br>• Offer a moderating reward | Equipment damage causes long lines and wait times at a ski lift on opening day (punishing skiers). Resort offers skiers a free ticket voucher to moderate the punishing experience. |
| Unintentionally rewards customers for doing something wrong... | Customers will keep doing the wrong thing, becoming a PITA factor to the company and other customers. | • Eliminate rewards<br>• Ignore the behavior you don't want | Unpleasant/ aggressive customers receive a higher level of service (reward). Resolve by providing equal levels of service to both pleasant and unpleasant customers. |

customer is followed by a rebate, premium, or contest entry provided by the sponsoring company.

Aside from rewards that stimulate purchase behavior, many companies use rewards to solve novel problems or help drive customer adoption of new programs and services. A novel problem that a Tahoe ski resort faced was a limited number of parking spots. On sunny spring days parking lots would fill up before the resort reached skier capacity. Obviously, this cost the resort in terms of potential revenue. To solve this novel problem, the resort tried several ideas to maximize the number of skiers who could access the resort. The first idea was to provide people who carpooled—defined as three or more skiers in the car—a special parking area close to the resort. The reward was a shorter walk to the lodge. There were numerous logistical issues with this solution, primarily the fact that so many skiers took advantage of the program that the special parking area would run out of room. Thus, the following year the reward was changed. Instead of a special parking area, people who carpooled each received a raffle ticket. At 11 A.M., the guest services director would hold a raffle at a designated location. The rewards were quite good—typically a $50 gift certificate at a local restaurant. The resort also experimented with other nonfinancial rewards to solve the parking problems. A successful strategy involved opening a chairlift 30 minutes early, rewarding people who parked in a secondary lot next to that lift with an extra 30 minutes of skiing (or first access to fresh powder).

When launching new services, rewards help condition customers to the new way of completing tasks. When Southwest Airlines introduced its e-commerce website, customers still believed using the phone to make airline reservations was easier than using the website. Why would anyone change to something that was perceived as being more difficult? The learning curve associated with using the website was a barrier to adoption. Southwest Airlines successfully overcame this barrier by providing an enticing reward to stimulate usage and help customers unlearn the old way of doing things. Customers who booked Southwest flights online received an extra rapid rewards point. This enabled customers to earn free tickets twice as fast.

Banks are using a similar tactic to get customers to pay bills online, which is part of a cost cutting and customer retention strategy. For the most part, these online services are free to customers. The problem is getting customers to shift their work from paper to cyberspace. Citibank, Wells Fargo, and Bank of America, just to name a few, offer cash to customers to use online banking. Citibank offers the richest purse—up to $200—depending upon how many bills you pay. U.S. Bancorp used a different tactic. Customers who used online banking were entered into a contest that offered a $10,000 cash prize. These incentives pay off in several ways. Customers who use online banking are better customers. They have more accounts and higher balances, and make fewer calls to support lines and branches.[2]

To get customers to perform when they otherwise would not, rewards are the best approach to help condition behavior. Rewards provide the push customers sometimes need to adopt new ways of doing things.

## 2. The Coproduction Experience Should Punish Customers When They Do Things Wrong

Well-designed coproduction experiences establish a clear set of rules that govern customer behavior. The rules are established to ensure that all customers have the opportunity to unlock as much value as possible from goods and services. When customers break the rules, the coproduction experience suffers and customers impacted by the rule breaker may defect to a more desirable alternative.

Ideally, a coproduction experience should integrate punishments for undesirable behavior. A humorous example of this is a series of advertisements that ran from 1965 to 1989 featuring Mr. Whipple, the cranky grocery clerk. The advertisements were for Procter & Gamble's Charmin toilet paper. The setup in the ads was that customers found Charmin so irresistibly soft that they would squeeze it right there in the store. For Mr. Whipple, this behavior was a no-no, probably because he couldn't easily sell the crumpled merchandise. Thus the advertisements regularly had Mr. Whipple popping out from behind store displays, chastising his customers with the words, "Ladies, please don't squeeze the Charmin!"

While Mr. Whipple's escapades are fantasy, there are companies who zealously guard their coproduction experiences with a diligence that would make Mr. Whipple proud. Carnival Cruise Lines had a simple "no smoking" policy aboard its ship, Paradise, for nearly six years. Carnival really meant it. When customers checked in for their cruise, they were required to read a policy statement and sign a coupon attesting to their understanding of the policy. The policy advised customers that smoking is not allowed anywhere on the ship, and that possession of smoking material violated the policy. Sanctions for violating the non-smoking policy included debarkation and a $250 fine. Additionally, customers were not entitled to a refund and had to pay their own expenses to get home from the debarkation point.

Through this policy, numerous customers who violated the rules were disembarked at the very next port. In one interesting case, cabin stewards found a pack of cigarettes in a cabin occupied by some teenagers. The mere possession of cigarettes violated the ship's policy and a Carnival officer ordered the teens (and their parents) off the ship in Ocho Rios, Jamaica. These customers were then on their own to find their way back to Miami.[3]

The buzz in cruising circles suggested customers approved of the policy and commended Carnival on their enforcement of the policy when Carnival removed customers from the ship. However, in Fall 2004, the company rescinded the no-smoking policy due to a redeployment of ships. According to Carnival President and CEO Bob Dikinson, "When we analyzed our redeployment strategy, the *Paradise*, based on its size and attributes, was the obvious choice to offer a fresh new short cruise alternative from California. And with only one ship operating that program, we could not limit it to non-smokers."[4]

As illustrated in the stories above, punishments can take many forms. The range is bordered by verbal reprimand on one end to arrest and prosecution on the other. Most punishments, however, tend to take the form of financial penalties. These penalties are typically invoked when the customer violates an explicit or implied contract with a company. Some restaurants charge a no-show fee if a party fails to show up on time for a reserved table. Cable companies charge a late fee if you don't pay the monthly bill on time. Banks charge additional fees if you write a check that bounces. Canceling a cell phone contract before the contract period has ended might subject customers to early cancellation penalties.

A survey conducted by professors Eugene H. Fram and Michael S. McCarthy investigated customer perceptions of penalties. For the most part, customers don't universally consider penalties unfair. Many customers believe that penalties have a purpose, especially if the penalty is associated with "fair compensation for losses" for a business. This fairness rule extends to customer negligence, such as when a customer breaks a glass in a fine crystal shop. The proprietor expects the customer to pay for the broken item as a penalty for the negligent behavior. But companies who cross the fairness line, whereby penalties become a "method of business revenue enhancement," earn the loathing of customers who will defect at the earliest opportunity.[5]

## 3. The Coproduction Experience Should Not Unintentionally Punish Customers

When we go out to dinner with our parents, we know we're in for an awful time if the restaurant we choose is loud. An elevated noise level, due to music, conversation, or horrible acoustics, is punishing for our parents. They can't stand it. They want nothing more than to leave the restaurant as soon as they can.

Given the principles of negative reinforcement, customers do not have the patience for experiences that are punishing. A customer's conditioned response to such situations is to leave.

When designing coproduction experiences, you must determine whether the planned or existing experience has a punishing effect on customers. This is easy to do. Just ask the customers who quickly abandon coproduction experiences. With regards to one of our retail clients, customers who abandoned grocery carts identified several punishing factors associated with their experience:

• Store was too cold
• Store was too crowded
• Could not find products
• Checkout lines were too long
• Credit card payment system wasn't working
• Employees were unhelpful and at times surly

Punishing coproduction experiences aren't limited just to services. Products can be full of annoying punishments. They might not work, have faulty assembly instructions, or by design be just plain annoying. The "welded plastic" packaging that many products come in these days is one example. While companies such as Costco, Wal-Mart, Best Buy, and Circuit City demand these types of packages to prevent theft, consumers hate them. Getting the package open is punishing in more ways than one. It is not easy, it takes time, and the ripped plastic frequently cuts your fingers. The risk increases when customers use knives and scissors to assist in the job. One slip, and you are off to the hospital for stitches. In 2002, over 1,400 people ended up in the emergency room due to mishaps with today's new theft-proof packaging. It is getting to the point where customers will choose a product based upon its packaging. Companies like Thomson Consumer Electronics and Sony are adding perforations and "cut here" lines that guide customers in the proper way to open the packages. Hopefully this kind of design change will reduce the punishment customers experience when buying these products.[6]

We have even found ourselves being punished when we thought we were being rewarded. One of the perks of possessing an airline-branded, platinum-level credit card is a free companion ticket for travel in the continental United States. Receiving the reward is no big deal—just pay the

$150 annual fee and the reward arrives in the mail a month later. But using the reward is extraordinarily punishing. Instead of making your reservation using the regular frequent flyer reservations number (Punishment #1—Convenience), you need to call the "promotions desk," which puts you into an annoying holding pattern for some time (Punishment #2—Time). If you pass this initial screen of your vigilance, you are ultimately connected to an agent who proceeds to inform you of the various redemption fees associated with the "free ticket" (Punishment #3—Unexpected Costs). You are then booked on a flight that has as many stops as technically possible (Punishment #4—Convenience). But all that is easy compared to what's to come. You are then instructed that you have 24 hours to get to an airport to redeem your companion ticket at the ticket counter (Punishment #5—Convenience). So the next day you rush to the ticket counter only to be punished even more by a sign that reads "Customers for today's flights only" (Punishment #6—Convenience). Then, if you finally get to a counter you find ticket agents who haven't been trained to process companion coupons. They have to call the "promotions desk" to get the instructions and special codes so the computer system can complete the transaction (Punishment #7—Time). By design? Perhaps. It sure is a great system to limit the number of customers who actually want to use the companion tickets.

The solution to punishing coproduction experiences is simple. Remove the punishing factors. If such an obvious action is not possible, then consider providing a reward to offset the punishment. This latter situation occurred at a Lake Tahoe ski resort. On opening day in 2004, the resort's primary lift, a high-speed six-pack, broke down. A lightning storm the previous night damaged the lift's electronics. People waited for the lift to open. For two hours the line didn't move—it just grew bigger. The wait was punishing, and everyone who had come to the ski area pumped-up and excited now looked upon the resort as a bunch of incompetents. However, the resort acted quickly, explaining the problem and giving people who purchased tickets a voucher for a free ticket. Season pass holders were rewarded with free drinks at the bar.

## 4. The Coproduction Experience Should Not Unintentionally Reward Customers When They Do Something Wrong

We've experienced many situations where customers are rewarded for exhibiting undesirable behaviors. At one end of the scale we have customers who are complacent—doing as little work as possible. We call this the *co-dependent customer effect.* By appearing helpless, inept, difficult, self-important, charming, or disinterested, these customers can shift the tasks they are supposed to be doing back to the company. The customers' aim is to extract more value from the company than they are entitled to, hence the reward. If the company ends up doing the tasks for the customers, the customers are essentially rewarded in terms of time, convenience, and self-appreciation. Furthermore, they now have the leverage to demand and expect such services again and again. The customer becomes conditioned and the company gets trapped.

One of the situations that disgusts us the most is the amount of trash customers leave in their wake. In movie theaters, sporting venues, and other public events, customer laziness in cleaning up after themselves is perpetually rewarded. Their complacency is their reward—they don't have to spend the time, make the effort, or deal with the mess if they just walk away from it. After all, "someone else" will take care of it. It is unfortunate that this behavior is so strongly conditioned in our society.

Another frequent target of complacency is filling out forms. Many businesses require forms to initiate services or conduct transactions, such as bank account applications, loan applications, and so on. The expectation and design of many of these forms is that the customer fills them out. However, by making frequent mistakes, claiming ignorance regarding certain questions, or writing illegibly, customers can easily shift the task back to the company, and bask in the reward of having less paperwork to do.

At the other end of the scale, the most dangerous situation is when customers are rewarded for being unpleasant, whether it be demanding special privileges, abusing service workers, or extracting more than they are entitled to from a company. We believe this is dangerous because it perpetuates a cycle of customer behavior that can have a negative effect on the job satisfaction of frontline employees and the experience of other customers. Consider an experimental study conducted by William R. Swinyard of Brigham Young University. To investigate how the mood of salespeople and the behavior of customers influence service levels, subjects were asked to play the role of a salesperson in either a department store or a discount store. In that role they experienced one of two scenarios: a pleasant/non-aggressive customer who attempts to return merchandise and an unpleasant/aggressive customer who attempts to return merchandise. After reading the scenarios subjects completed several scaled measures, including a customer service effort scale. Swinyard surprisingly found that unpleasant/aggressive customers received a higher level of service than did the pleasant/non-aggressive customers. If such an effect is left unchecked, it can result in either:

- Customers learning to become more unpleasant/aggressive to extract more from the company
- Customers who don't like being unpleasant/aggressive switching to a competitor

Neither option is desirable, which leads Swinyard to recommend that salespeople, "... be trained to provide equivalent levels of good service to both non-aggressive and aggressive shoppers." Such a strategy aims to eliminate rewards tied to undesirable behavior. However, such advice is contradictory in light of service principles such as the customer is always right, and it's human nature to do whatever it takes to avoid and minimize conflict.[7]

## CONCEIVING REWARDS

Companies must design rewards associated with coproduction experiences thoughtfully and carefully. Rewards can do a lot of good for a coproduction experience, such as aiding the shift of work from company to customer that was so important to Southwest Airlines' e-commerce strategy. However, given the nature of rewards and human behavior, poorly designed reward schemes can trigger undesired and unanticipated behavior (like the Pudding Guy). In this section we discuss the key principles for designing coproduction rewards, which include:

- Setting clear objectives
- Defining the nature of the reward
- Selecting the form of the reward
- Timing the reward
- Establishing reward conditions

### Setting Clear Objectives

The first step in designing rewards is to set a clear objective regarding the desired outcome of the reward. Based upon the analysis discussed earlier in this book, you should know the general nature of the problem or opportunity you want to address. To address these problems and opportunities, you want customers to behave differently. Rewards can shape that behavior.

Generally speaking, rewards address two primary objectives, *performance* or *loyalty*. Performance describes the work customers do in conjunction with consuming goods and services. The reward motivates customers to perform differently. For instance, in exchange for extra bonus points, customers start booking airline tickets online rather than over the phone. For completing a customer training program, customers get free or low-cost access to a special technical support service. Or, for a monetary reward, customers will lose weight, reduce smoking, or be compliant with some other kind of treatment regimen.

Loyalty describes the customer who a company rewards when the customer purchases a good or service, repeatedly patronizes a specific company, or does not defect to an alternative. The reward essentially "buys" the customer's loyalty. Consider these strategies:

- Sales promotion, where coupons, discounts, and rebates influence product preference
- Loyalty schemes, where supermarket club cards, airline frequent flyer programs, and free birthday desserts at restaurants influence company preference
- Retention and recovery programs, where apologies, free drinks, vouchers, gifts, and other gestures compensate a customer for a punishing experience with the aim of retaining the customer

When designing coproduction experiences, the primary focus of rewards must be on performance-oriented objectives. The reason is that in coproduction experiences you are often asking customers to do more than simply make a good or service choice. You are asking customers to adopt new skills, take a risk in trying something new, or change the way they do things *after* they have made the choice to purchase a good or service. You should use these rewards to condition the long-term performance behaviors that are beneficial to the company. There will always be cross-over effects, where performance rewards stimulate loyalty, and vice versa. If our aim is to help customers do more work, reduce costs, and unlock more value, then rewards should be structured to achieve those aims.

Marten Transportation Ltd., a trucking company in Mondovi, Wisconsin, had a very specific performance objective in mind when designing a coproduction experience for its customers. It wanted to reduce the time its trucks had to wait at customer sites to be loaded and unloaded. According to Randy Marten, president of the company, most of the inefficiencies take place at the receiving end of the process, when trucks are full and are waiting to be emptied. Marten's strategy for achieving its objective included *vision*— it set goals for acceptable turnaround times, *access*—it shared loading-time information with its customers, and *expertise*—it worked with companies to help them eliminate wasteful practices. The customer reward for desired performance—greater utilization of Marten's fleet—was lower prices. The strategy has cost Marten some customers, but also reduced the rates for many others, increasing loyalty. According to Marten Vice President Timothy Nash, "It's not about punishment. If you can change behavior, everyone wins in the end."[8]

## Defining the Nature of the Reward

There are literally thousands of ways to reward customers, and new ones are being invented every day. The most important principle about rewards is that the customer, not the company, is the one who perceives the value of the reward. The value customers expect will be different based upon the nature of a company's products, the complexity of product tasks, and the segmentation of customers.

The question, then, is what do customers value the most in rewards? In their research on customer loyalty and reward programs, professors Grahame Dowling and Mark Uncles guide us in identifying eight factors that contribute to the design of a successful customer rewards program:[9]

1. **Cash Value.** The reward has to have sufficient cash value to trigger the desired performance. Market research can help you pinpoint the amount that is right for your context.

2. **Range of Choices.** The more choices associated with the reward, the more power the reward has in influencing behavior. For example, giving customers the freedom to select from a list of prizes or travel to one of multiple destinations is more powerful than locking them into a single reward.

3. **Aspirational Value.** A reward that is linked to a customer's aspirations (such as arranging for the customer to meet with a favorite professional athlete or celebrity) will have more power than a lifetime supply of laundry detergent.

4. **Likelihood of Achieving the Reward.** The customer must believe the reward is attainable. Otherwise, motivation wanes and performance is extinguished.

5. **Reward Scheme Ease-of-Use.** Once the customer performs the desired behavior, getting the reward should be easy. For example, when using online ticketing services, performance rewards are automatically added to your account. You don't have to fill out special forms, redeem coupons, or perform other nuisance tasks.

6. **Belonging to a Program.** Membership in a group is a very strong performance motivator. Airlines offer silver, gold, and platinum classifications. Microsoft awards customers with competency certifications, such as MSCE, MCT, and MCDST.

7. **Accumulation.** For some customers, the badge value of accumulating rewards, such as airline miles, points, privilege cards, and so on, enables them to brag to friends and family about their expertise.

8. **Mapping.** The reward offered has some natural linkage or relationship to the good or service. For example, airlines offer miles. Restaurants offer desserts, drinks, or some other food item. A recent offer we received from Bank of America offered money. Finally! We never quite understood why banks gave away toasters.

## Selecting the Form of the Reward

The most appreciated reward for customers is when a product or service works as promised—which is referred to as the *primary* reward. Beyond that, a reward can take on many different secondary forms, varying from intangible to tangible, as illustrated in Table 7.2.

*Recognition* rewards can be very powerful motivators. They are typically inexpensive, intangible, and easy to deliver. The simplest form of recognition is verbally acknowledging when the customer does something correct. This form of recognition is typically offered privately, but can also be provided publicly. Other rewards in this category increase the level of public exposure, such as featuring a customer in an advertisement. Related to recognition are rewards that provide customers access to *special services*. These might include club membership, dedicated customer support telephone numbers, or special lines.

Companies can also reward customers with *collectibles*, which are rewards that need to be accumulated over time before they can be converted into something tangible. An example is hotel rewards, where award levels (such as 25,000 points for a free hotel room) motivate continued performance. *Vouchers*, which include coupons for free or discounted products, are similar to collectibles but provide a more immediate offer. An advantage of vouchers is that redemption rates are typically low, which results in lower program costs.

Tangible rewards include immediate *prizes*, such as trips or vacations, or *financial* instruments, such as cash. For example, in 2004, Bank of America initiated a campaign to encourage existing customers to begin using online banking services. Bank of America offered a one-time award of $25, credited to the customer's account, if the customer paid a bill online by a specific date.

Table 7.2 **Examples of Rewards**

| Reward Form | Examples |
|---|---|
| Recognition | • Verbal acknowledgement, such as "Good job!"<br>• Designating the customer "Customer of the Day, Week, Month, Year," and so on<br>• Giving the customer an award for achieving a goal<br>• Displaying customer's work in a store, such as a photograph a customer took or a craft a customer produced<br>• Featuring the work of your customer in promotional materials<br>• Featuring the customer in promotional material |
| Special Services | • Club membership<br>• Special lines<br>• Dedicated telephone numbers<br>• Single point-of-contact<br>• Reserved parking spots |
| Collectibles | • Miles<br>• Points<br>• Stamps |
| Vouchers/Coupons | • Free or discounted product<br>• Two-for-one deals<br>• Partner discounts |
| Prizes | • Steak knives<br>• Toasters<br>• Vacations |
| Financial | • Cash<br>• Rebates<br>• Direct discounts |

Of all the rewards a company can offer, customers prefer cash. A survey of 407 customers by Maritz Loyalty Marketing showed that 61 percent preferred cash, followed by free merchandise (57%), gift certificates (46%), members-only discounts and offers (38%), special benefits or upgrades (13%), free travel (11%), and free event tickets (10%).[10]

## Timing the Reward

Like feedback, rewards are most effective when customers receive them immediately after exhibiting the desired performance. The reason for this is that if rewards are delayed, the customer might exhibit other undesirable or irrelevant performances and associate those performances with the reward. In other words, customers might associate the reward with the wrong performance.

However, you should be cautious in the execution of an experience involving immediate secondary rewards. The goal of any coproduction experience must be to shape behavior in such a way whereby the experience itself becomes the reward. In most situations it is counterproductive to have continuous secondary rewards—customers become conditioned to perform only when a reward is being offered. For example, if you offer discount coupons too frequently, customers withhold their purchases until you launch the next program. In these situations, performance is bought by you for a short time period. When the program is over, performance evaporates. Continuous rewards often diminish performance, rather than maintain or increase performance.

Primary rewards, such as consistent product performance or fluid service transactions, must become incentive enough for the customer to effectively perform. To achieve this, reward strategies should adopt a variable reinforcement schedule leading to the withdrawal of secondary rewards.

Variable reinforcement means that the delivery of the reward does not occur every time the customer performs. Sometimes you get the reward, and sometimes you don't. This is the logic that drives gamblers to play slot machines. Every once in a while the slot machine pays back a few coins, which motivates continued performance. The scheduling of such variable reinforcement can take the following forms, as outlined by B.F. Skinner:

- **Intermittent.** The company rewards the customer whenever it feels like it, for example, when you check in for a flight and you find yourself upgraded to first class.
- **Fixed Ratio.** The company rewards the customer every nth performance. Hotels offer these kinds of rewards as stay ten nights and the eleventh is free.
- **Variable Ratio.** On average, the company rewards the customer every nth performance, but the time gap between rewards varies. An example is the slot machine.
- **Fixed Interval.** The customer is rewarded on a regular basis. Members of Southwest Airlines Rapid Rewards receive a birthday card every year from the company, which includes some kind of discount coupon.
- **Variable Interval.** The customer is rewarded on a regular basis, but sometimes sooner and sometimes later. American Airlines does this for customers who meet minimums for its Gold and Platinum frequently flyer designations early. The customer does not have to wait until the end of the year to realize membership.

The ultimate aim of a rewards scheme is withdrawal. This is where the secondary reward is removed, and the primary reward maintains customer performance. Earlier in this chapter we discussed Southwest Airline's program for motivating customers to use its e-commerce site to book tickets. Southwest kept the rewards program running about six years, until the degree of customer conditioning was so high that customers would book tickets online whether a reward was offered or not. Southwest Airlines withdrew the double points, and customers continued to book tickets online.

## Establishing Reward Conditions

None of us wants to be the executive who approves a program that creates another Pudding Guy. Reward programs must have limitations that govern the upside so the program can't spin out of control. The following are some key conditions associated with rewards programs.

- **Time-limited.** Programs should encourage customer performance by a certain date. For example, Bank of America's online banking offer asked that customers pay one bill by 11/19/04. Additionally, programs should always have an expiration date—which can be extended if the company desires.
- **Dollar-limited.** Programs can specify a dollar limit of the reward. For instance, the Bank of America online banking reward was limited to $25.
- **Volume-limited.** This limits the number of times the customer can claim the reward, such as, "one per household."
- **Availability-limited.** Airlines allocate only a certain number of seats on each plane available in exchange for frequent flyer miles. Additionally, they use blackout dates when rewards are not valid for redemption (such as during holidays).
- **Person-limited.** To ensure the person who performed is the person who gets rewarded, rewards should designate who the reward is for.
- **Transferability.** Some rewards may be transferred to other people, such as family members. Other rewards may not be. Additionally, companies typically prohibit the barter or sale of rewards.
- **Tax liability.** Rewards should indicate whether there are tax consequences, and if so, who bears the tax burden.
- **Subject to change.** The general catch-all condition if the company discovers its program has some undesirable upside that was never imagined.

## STRUCTURING NEGATIVE REINFORCEMENT

To refresh your memory (as this is a complex and often misunderstood concept), negative reinforcement aims to strengthen behavior by removing something unpleasant when the customer performs correctly. In essence, it is the customer's choice whether an experience is pleasing or not. For coproduction experiences, companies often design *intentional* negative reinforcement to achieve certain goals. However, it is more often the case that negative reinforcement is *unintentional*, which causes customers to defect.

### Intentional Negative Reinforcement

Intentional negative reinforcement happens for a purpose. It is *by design*. There are certain coproduction experiences where you want customers to feel uncomfortable, to the point of fleeing. For instance, companies may not want customers to enter certain areas of a store or building. Through architectural design, some spaces can make customers feel happy and secure. In a hotel lobby, comfortable chairs, artwork, decorated walls, carpeted floors, and pleasant music encourage customers to "hang around." However, if customers wander "backstage" in a hotel, they experience a spartan, utilitarian environment of linoleum floors, cinderblock walls, and white paint. The design of this space subtly tells customers that they don't belong there, hence the desire to get back to more desirable environments. Obviously, it is less expensive to have this kind of utilitarian environment in non-customer areas, but there is a sociological purpose as well.

Another example of intentional negative reinforcement relates to safety. If there is an emergency in a store, such as a fire, the store wants to make the customers' experience so unpleasant that the customers will choose to flee. Ear-splitting alarms, flashing lights, and other annoyances act as negative reinforcement, encouraging the customers to leave, and leave quickly.

For intentional negative reinforcement, the presence of or participation in an annoying or painful situation is always the customer's choice. The expectation, however, is that the customer will choose to leave the painful experience in favor of a more pleasant experience. Thus, for the design of coproduction experiences the objective is to make the spaces where companies want customers to be pleasant. Correspondingly, spaces where companies don't want customers to be should seem unpleasant. If you don't want customers in non-public spaces, design them so they are uncomfortable for customers. If you don't want customers in a room when there is a fire, make it unbearable. However, if you don't want customers to visit competitors, make the experience your company offers more pleasant, which has the effect of making the competitor's experience unbearable. Use the techniques of *vision, access, incentive,* and *expertise* to achieve these aims.

## Unintentional Negative Reinforcement

More often than not, it is unintentional negative reinforcement that threatens a coproduction experience. It occurs *by default* and can come to life any number of different ways. Perhaps it is the lack of cleanliness in a store, the attitude of a clerk, or the checkout line that makes customers uncomfortable. Perhaps the product itself, such as car purchase, auto repairs, or insurance, triggers an avoidance reaction. For the most part, unintentional negative reinforcement reflects the PITA factor.

Most companies have programs in place to discover unintentional negative reinforcement. Through customer surveys, mystery shopping, interviews, or simple observation, companies can discover what features of a coproduction experience customers don't like. These ideas were discussed in Chapter 4, being part of the process for discovering where value hides. Thus the strategy for overcoming unintentional negative reinforcement is to practice the techniques of *vision, access, incentive,* and *expertise* associated with a coproduction experience.

## CRAFTING PUNISHMENTS

The aim of punishment is to discourage or weaken specific customer performances. For example, if a customer steals, then a punishment—arrest—is applied. Unlike negative reinforcement, the customer does not have the choice of whether the punishment is applied or not. When a customer violates a law, norm, or policy, the intention of the coproduction experience is to levy a punishment to encourage the customer not to perform that way again. Thus, an effective punishment strategy for coproduction experiences has:

- A clear policy
- Objective sanctions
- Systematic monitoring
- The guts to follow through

This also sets an example for the customers that are performing appropriately.

## A Clear Policy

It is unfair to punish customers if there is no policy that governs behavior. As we discussed in Chapter 6, companies establish policies to govern the social environment in which coproduction experiences occur. Some of these policies are driven by legislation. For example, *no smoking* policies in restaurants and other public places tend to reflect local ordinances. Similarly, policies such as *no shirt, no shoes, no service* have roots in local health and safety codes and the cultural desires of customers. The majority of policies, however, are designed by companies to create an environment in which customers like to spend time, free from hassles or distractions.

A clear policy defines the rules of the coproduction experience. Communicating it clearly ensures that customers are aware that it exists. Most ski areas, for example, have a clear policy on skiing out-of-bounds: You can't. The policy is clearly communicated in signage, ropes, and the small print of the ticket. The policy is in place because the danger to the skier and anyone who might be asked to rescue that skier is significant. If a skier violates the policy, the result is a significant sanction, such as confiscation of the skier's ticket or pass.

## Objective Sanctions

Sanctions are the consequences of violating law or policy. A sanction is objective if it describes exactly what will happen if a customer violates policy. For example, if a customer writes a check with insufficient funds, the bank levies a fee of $30. Such sanctions are clearly described in the bank's terms and conditions documents.

Sanctions fall into two primary categories, *nonfinancial* and *financial*. Nonfinancial sanctions draw their power from social stigma or personal inconvenience. For example, the "bad chair" pile at the California World Fest described in Chapter 2 has a bit of both. The social stigma is having other customers observing the offending customers finding their chairs in the pile. The personal inconvenience is threefold: having your chair removed, having to find it in the pile, and having to find another spot for your chair. Nonfinancial sanctions can range from a simple verbal reprimand ("please stop handling the fine china") to arrest and prosecution by law enforcement authorities. They may also include firing customers, denying services to customers, publication of the customer's name in a public record (for example, mechanic's liens), and the redoing of certain tasks, such as having to recomplete a loan application if the first one completed was illegible.

Financial sanctions draw their power from simple economics. Customers don't want to lose money or pay more than they have to for a good or service. Thus companies who have customers that habitually write bad checks, pay bills late, frequently change their minds, or return rented items late encourage customers to change their behavior by levying a fine.

The most successful sanctions are those that have been adopted by competitors in a specific industry. When this occurs, competitive pressures associated with the presence of sanctions and their magnitude are diminished. Building on research by professors Eugene Fram and Michael McCarthy, Table 7.3 examines some of the sanctions that are common (or that are gaining a foothold) in several consumer-oriented industries.[11]

**Table 7.3   Example Sanctions**

| Industry | Example Sanctions |
| --- | --- |
| Airlines | • "No Fly" list for disruptive behavior<br>• $75 for changing reservations<br>• Full fare for lost tickets (may be refunded pending an investigation)<br>• $10–$20 penalty charged by travel agents for cancelled tickets<br>• Missed flight for being late |
| Automobiles | • Fees for early cancellation of leases<br>• Fees for early cancellation of insurance policies (UK)<br>• Denial of insurance based upon driving record and claims |
| Banks | • Penalty for early withdrawal of a CD<br>• Penalty for too many withdrawals on a money market account, either a fee or switching the account to an interest-bearing checking account<br>• Fees if balance falls below a threshold level<br>• Late fees for late payments on loans<br>• Fees for writing or depositing a check with insufficient funds<br>• Repossession for failure to repay loans |
| Car Rentals | • $25 to $100 no-show fees for reservations<br>• "Filling fee" for returning a car without a full tank of fuel<br>• Penalties for driving in restricted areas (such as off-road)<br>• Denial of service based upon driving record |
| Child Daycare | • $5 per minute penalty if parent is late in picking up his or her child |
| Cellular Phones | • $25 cancellation penalty for early cancellation of service |

Table 7.3    Example Sanctions (*Continued*)

| Industry | Example Sanctions |
|---|---|
| Credit and Debit Cards | • Late fees in addition to interest charges<br>• $25 penalty for paying your credit card in full<br>• $25 penalty for account inactivity in a six-month period |
| Cruises | • 25%, 50%, even 100% penalties if passenger cancels trip<br>• Disembarking passengers for policy violations |
| Hotels | • One night's room charge if room not cancelled by a certain time<br>• $25 to $50 early departure fees |
| Medical Services | • Full charge of office visit for late or no-shows |
| Restaurants | • $50 no-show fees for reservations<br>• Refusal of service for inappropriate dress |
| Retail Stores | • 15% restocking charges for returned merchandise<br>• Paying the full price of goods that the customer breaks or damages |
| Ski Areas | • Confiscated ticket or pass for skiing out-of-bounds<br>• Confiscated ticket or pass for skiing too fast |
| Trains | • $20 penalty for returned tickets<br>• $20 fee for changing tickets<br>• Disembarking passengers for policy violations |
| Video/DVD Rental | • Paying for replacement of damaged videos/DVDs<br>• Late fees for videos/DVDs returned after the due date |

## Systematic Monitoring

It can be expensive, inconvenient, and psychologically draining for a company to extensively monitor customer performance and levy sanctions when appropriate. Hiring employees to watch and monitor customers is costly. Furthermore, since people tend to avoid confrontation, it may be difficult for employees to play the role of police officer. Companies do not go into business to be the police, but that's the role they often need to assume to ensure that coproduction experiences offer the greatest value to the largest number of customers.

The most effective monitoring strategy is one that is automatic and system-driven. Data acquisition is typically low cost and human involvement is minimal. For instance, if a customer's bank balance falls below a minimum level for the month, the account management system automatically applies a fee. No human intervention is needed to monitor the infraction and apply the sanction. Similarly, car rental companies have begun experimenting with "black box" monitoring. Like aircraft black box recorders, a vehicle's black box monitors the customer's driving habits in a rental car. Data regarding excessive speed, off-road driving, sharp cornering, and hard braking is collected during the rental and downloaded upon return. Behaviors that negatively affect safety, wear-and-tear, and maintenance result in penalties, increased rates, or service denial.

The more employees get involved in monitoring tasks, the more variable the outcomes can become. The reason is based upon the subjective nature of people's perceptions. One person might classify a customer's behavior as intolerable, while another might classify the same behavior as permissive. A clear policy, appropriate training, and management support is critical for such a program to work.

In some companies it is possible, even preferable, to have customers monitor the performance of other customers. Customers have long served in varying capacities as informants, alerting companies to shoplifters and vandals. For example, eBay has made self-monitoring a critical element of its coproduction experience. All eBay buyers and sellers can determine acceptable and nonacceptable buying and selling behavior. Using eBay's feedback and rating system, buyers can report positive or negative experiences associated with a particular seller. Too many negative experiences tarnishes the seller's reputation, reducing the number of buyers who will patronize the seller. In this structure eBay doesn't take the leadership role in policing the actions—customers do.

## The Guts to Follow Through

Punishing customers should be the last resort considered by companies who want to weaken specific customer behaviors. Punishment is unpleasant business—companies don't like to do it and customers don't like to receive it. But in the late 20th century, due to customer-oriented competitive strategy, customers have become conditioned to the belief that they are always right, that they can do no wrong. Stew Leonard proclaimed this on a piece of granite: Rule #1: The customer is always right. Rule #2: Re-read rule #1. Such fundamentalism makes for great headlines, but in our experience it sets up managers, employees, and other customers for failure.

The fact is that there are right customers and there are wrong customers. On the wrong side of the fence are customers who are rude, uncooperative, demanding, and unable to be satisfied. They are high-maintenance and expensive, both financially and psychologically, to keep in check. Service expert Chris Lovelock calls these customers "jaycustomers." They might be desirable in terms of target segmentation, but their stupidity, irrationality, and illegal actions exceed a tolerance threshold. Common sense demands action, if not for the survival of the company, then for the psychological wellness of the employees and other customers.[12]

Automatic systems make it easier for companies to follow through on the conditions associated with their policies. Change a non-refundable airline ticket and the penalty is assessed automatically if the customer consummates the transaction. However, there is more willingness of companies to take subjective action. We find this willingness in both urban legends and actual practice. Like Southwest's Herb Kelleher, Gordon Bartholemew, president of Continental Airlines, is also featured in one of these legends as the crusading chief executive who personally banished a customer from his airline after a customer verbally assaulted one of the company's flight attendants. First Chicago Bank, on the other hand, is more systematic in its handling of customers who are unprofitable or cost a lot to serve. The first option is to require customers to change the behavior. If this doesn't work, the second option is to require customers to pay more for services. If results still aren't forthcoming, the third option is to require customers to find another bank.[13]

As discussed earlier in this chapter, customers are more willing to accept punishment if the punishment is associated with the customer's personal negligence or free choice. If the penalties are due to unavoidable circumstances or if customers suspect penalties as having revenue-generating motives (rather than recouping of costs), customers will be more vocal in their displeasure and more apt to defect to alternatives.

## SUMMARY

This chapter examined how *incentives* help shape coproduction experiences. The purpose of incentives is to encourage customers to perform in a way they might otherwise not. Companies can use incentives to strengthen desired customer behaviors, or use them to weaken undesired behaviors. The need for incentives occurs when vision, access, and expertise alone do not result in the desired customer performance.

Incentives come in three primary flavors: positive reinforcement (rewards), negative reinforcement, and punishment. Companies use rewards and negative reinforcement to strengthen desirable behavior, whereas punishment aims to weaken undesirable behavior. For example, if a company wants to encourage customers to use a new system or service, a reward, such as cash, points, or prizes, works best to encourage adoption. Punishing customers in a case such as this, perhaps by charging them extra to use the old system, results in dissatisfaction.

While it is best for companies to design incentives into coproduction experiences, sometimes incentives (or disincentives, as the case might be) appear unexpectedly. Experiences, through such nuances as loud music, cold temperatures, and other annoyances, can be punishing to customers, causing them to avoid the experience. On the other hand, some experiences can reward undesirable behavior. Customers who get better service when they complain more are essentially being rewarded for their complaining behavior. This initiates a vicious cycle whereby customers attain satisfaction through increasing unpleasantness.

In coproduction experiences, rewards are clearly more desirable than punishments. Rewards must focus on performance and not just loyalty. The nature of the reward must reflect the desires of customers, not necessarily the company. Rewards can be nonfinancial or financial, however, in most cases customers prefer cash. Companies should structure rewards so they don't become an annuity for customers. The aim is that the reward should condition customers such that the withdrawal of the reward does not have a significant effect on the conditioned performance.

Punishments do have their role in coproduction experiences. There are times when customers violate a law, norm, or policy that is detrimental to the coproduction experience. Such behavior might incur unexpected costs, or impact the experience of employees and other customers. In these cases punishment is appropriate, provided it is not perceived by customers as unavoidable or as a scheme for generating revenues. Punishments in coproduction experiences, therefore, must be based upon clear policy, objective sanctions, and systematic monitoring. Furthermore, companies must have confidence to follow through on their promised sanctions.

## CHAPTER 8

# ENHANCING EXPERTISE

*Education costs money, but then so does ignorance.*

—Sir Moser Claus

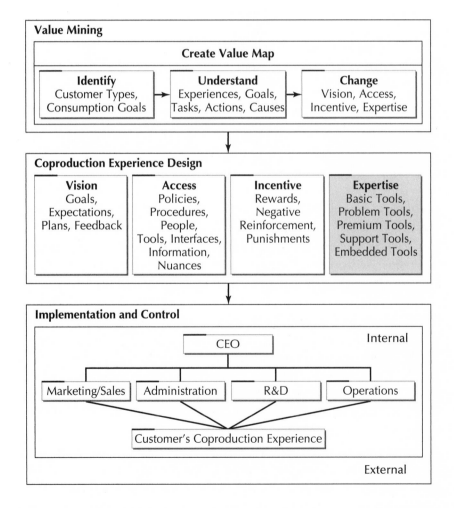

In this chapter, we examine the fourth element of the Coproduction Experience Model, *expertise*. Expertise reflects the knowledge, skills, and attitudes customers develop that enable them to be effective coproducers. We start this chapter by discussing the nature of expertise and what it means in the context of coproduction experiences. We follow this with a discussion of the situations in which the development of customer expertise—through customer education—would be worthwhile. The chapter concludes with a roadmap for customer education design that guides you in:

- Creating basic tools that orient customers to goods and services
- Planning problem tools to hand-hold customers during usage
- Developing premium tools to teach customers high-level skills
- Publishing support tools to guide choice and usage
- Integrating embedded tools into goods and services themselves

## THE NATURE OF EXPERTISE

On the surface, expertise is a simple concept. It means that a customer can perform product-related tasks successfully. This can be as basic as distinguishing a nut from a bolt, or as complex as shimming a wall so that cabinets and countertops can be installed level. But as one digs deeper into what a customer must really know to accomplish product-related tasks, one recognizes that expertise is a rich, multifaceted concept.

The road to expertise begins with increasing levels of *familiarity*. Familiarity involves specific experiences a customer has with a product. These experiences might be abstract, such as information gleaned from advertising and friend's word-of-mouth stories, to more concrete experiences that include salesperson demonstrations and personal tryouts. When a customer adopts a product or service, the frequency and intensity of usage further build familiarity until expertise begins to emerge.

From a quantitative standpoint, a customer who has expertise expends *less effort* performing tasks—that is, the expert customer can perform tasks faster with fewer errors. Think about the first time a customer uses a bank ATM. Since the customer isn't familiar with the technology, the concepts, and the process of the ATM, the transaction takes a long time. The customer must read each of the screens and respond by pressing the correct button. Of course, incorrect buttons are pressed and the customer must spend additional effort recovering from mistakes. However, as usage increases, the customer acquires competence and the transaction requires less and less effort. Speed goes up, errors go down. Performance therefore increases and we can say that the customer has expertise.

As effort decreases, another element of expertise increases—*automaticity*. Automaticity means that customers are essentially operating on autopilot, performing tasks fast without much conscious control. We call this *unconscious competence*. This means a customer can multitask and still successfully accomplish product-related tasks. For example, a frequent ATM user can not only withdraw money from the machine but at the same time carry on a conversation on a cell phone. Similarly, a customer who visits the Starbuck's drive-through every day can be operating a vehicle and rattling off exactly what is wanted without thinking about it too much—iced Venti, triple-shot, half mocha, half white mocha, ice to the second line, non-fat milk, and only filled 3/4 of the way.

So what is expertise? It is a customer's ability to perform tasks fast, without error and without having to think much about the specific behaviors the task requires. Expertise is important to customers since it enables them to unlock more value from the goods and services they use. It is also important to companies since it reduces the cost of providing customers services, as well as increases switching costs—making it more expensive for customers to defect to competing solutions.[1]

## Cornerstones of Expertise

Customers develop expertise through practice and repetition. During these activities, customers build two kinds of knowledge, *content-oriented knowledge* and *process-oriented knowledge*. These two kinds of knowledge form the cornerstones of expertise.

Content-oriented knowledge reflects the knowledge of "what is." Identifying certain parts of a product, noticing the differences between two competing products, and recalling certain facts about a product, such as its nutritional values or performance specifications, are examples of content-oriented knowledge. Content-oriented knowledge is what enables customers to "talk-the-talk."

Process-oriented knowledge reflects the knowledge of "how to." Assembling a product, using a product, making a deposit using an ATM, booking a hotel room online, and using a self-checkout system at a grocery store are examples of process-oriented knowledge. Process-oriented knowledge is what enables customers to "walk-the-walk."

For a customer to have expertise it is clear that the customer must possess both kinds of knowledge. This is illustrated in a study conducted by Vikas Mittal and Mohanbir Sawhney. Their study investigated the effects of

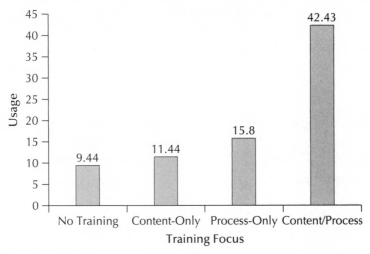

**Figure 8.1**    Usage Effects of Content and Process Knowledge. Adapted from Mittal and Sawhney (2001).

content-oriented training and process-oriented training on the usage of a Gartner Group web-based information service. In the experiment, subjects were divided into four treatment groups. The first group received training in the content and process associated with the service. The second group received training only on the content, while the third group received training only in the process. The fourth group received no training. As shown in Figure 8.1, the results show that the performance of the content/process group was, on average, three times higher than the other groups. Over time, the subjects in the content/process group increased their usage, while usage in the other groups remained flat or in some cases decreased.[2]

## Developing Customer Expertise

The results of Mittal and Sawhney's study suggest that if customers are not supported in some way, at least initially, performance is not as strong as it could be. This has a lot to do with the *initial success factor*. When trying a new good or service, if the customer does not experience initial success—that is, accomplishing a task to a reasonable performance standard—future performance diminishes. Why? Because initial success is a primary reward. This reward stimulates motivation to repeat the behavior. If satisfaction with the good or service remains high after each performance, the loop continues, building the customer's expertise. This relationship is illustrated in Figure 8.2. Initially, customer education provides the customer the first bit of knowledge

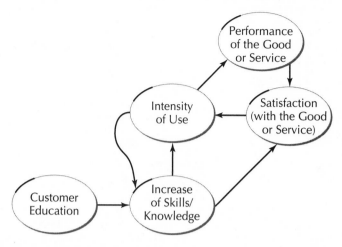

**Figure 8.2**    Initial success with a good or service triggers a loop of increasing usage intensity, expertise, and satisfaction. Adapted from Hennig-Thurau, Honebein, and Aubert (2005).[3]

and skill about a good or service. Based on the level of knowledge and skill acquired, the customer will use the good or service to some level of intensity. The good or service responds by delivering some level of performance related to achieving a goal or task. How well it achieves the goal or task contributes to the level of satisfaction the customer experiences—the primary reward. If the experience is rewarding, the customer intensifies usage, building additional knowledge and skill and unlocking more value from the good or service.

A second factor affecting the development of customer expertise is the *power law curve*. This curve illustrates the phenomena of customers learning basic knowledge associated with a good or service rather quickly with minimal effort. However, once this basic performance level is reached, noticeable improvement beyond this basic level is often slow and difficult to attain.[4]

For example, at a new interactive, participative restaurant called Stir Crazy, customers quickly learn the ropes on their first visit. The customer's task is to select various stir-fry ingredients, add them to a bowl, then hand the bowl to a wok chef who adds meat and noodles and fries up the whole concoction as the customer observes. As shown in Figure 8.3, between the time customers step into the restaurant for the first time (0 in the graph) and when they leave (1 in the graph), the increase in knowledge and skills is exponential. The service staff, instruction-oriented menus, small booklets,

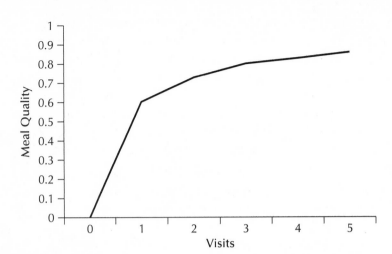

**Figure 8.3**  Hypothetical Power Law Curve for the Stir Crazy Experience. Customers become proficient during their first visit, but improvements to their meal are less dramatic over time.

and the observation of other patrons provide a rich learning environment. Customers develop concept knowledge, such as being able to distinguish between the various ingredients, especially the eight different sauces. They also develop process knowledge—knowing how to fill up their bowl, selecting the right volume and proportion of ingredients, and delivering it to the wok chef. For the newly initiated the first experience delivers lots of new knowledge and skill and a reasonably good meal—so much so that the customer is inclined to repeat the experience. However, in subsequent experiences (visits two through five in the graph) the incremental increase in taste and quality will not be as significant as the prior experiences. In the case of Stir Crazy, it is naturally more difficult to learn the nuances of volume, proportion, and flavor combination that differentiate the good meal from a great meal. Unlocking more value from the experience becomes increasingly more time consuming as the detail of knowledge and skill becomes more complex. At some point in time customers maximize their competence. To grow beyond this "paper ceiling," customers might need to enlist the services of a coach or mentor.

To ensure that the power law curve continues to increase at a rate that increases the cost of defection, we introduce a third factor affecting the development of expertise. It is called the *zone of proximal development* (ZPD). Conceived by the Russian psychologist Lev Vyostsky in the early 1900s, the

ZPD describes the range of expertise a person cannot exceed without the assistance of a more experienced mentor. Just as school children need a teacher to help them increase their reading level and perform increasingly complex mathematical calculations, customers need a similar support structure that helps them continually increase their expertise with a good or service.

The principles associated with the initial success factor, the power law curve, and the ZPD suggest that a strategy for developing customer expertise must start with a significant educational experience at the beginning of the customer relationship. This increases the probability that the customer will experience an initial success, paving the way for repeat performances. As the customer continues the relationship, additional support structures insure that incremental gains in expertise are realized.

Such a strategy is employed by WebEx, a provider of web-based conferencing services. For new users of the service, WebEx provides a variety of customer education solutions to teach the basics to first-time users. These tutorials are either self-instructional, in the form of an interactive tutorial that is accessed online, or a live demonstration by a WebEx specialist. These solutions enable customers to run their first conference successfully— essentially reaching a basic level of performance. After that first experience, WebEx aims to build customers' expertise in other areas of the service through regular email-based information and tip sheets. These enable customers to incrementally adopt new skills associated with the product, which might include computer sharing, screen recording, and the creation of canned, narrated presentations.

A similar experience awaits those who visit Build-A-Bear® Workshops, a new retail concept store. Your experience starts when you walk in the door. You are immediately greeted by a Master Bear Builder$^{SM}$ associate. This person is your guide and coach (and, of course, salesperson) who leads you through the Build-A-Bear® Workshops process.

The first step is to choose a bear skin, of which there are more than 30. Next, customers can then record a personalized sound that can be integrated into the bear. When the bear is hugged, the sound plays. The Master Bear Builder then helps the customer fill the bear with stuffing, add the bear's heart, and stitch up the bear. Then it's off to a station where the customer can fluff and brush the bear. After that, a kiosk system helps the customer name the bear, generate a birth certificate, and register the bear in a tracking service (in case it ever gets lost). Finally, customers can accessorize the bear with various clothes, appliqués, and jewelry. The process ends when the customer pays for the experience and carts the bear home in its own house. This entire process is supported with web-based experiences that explain the process through interactive examples and video commercials. The company even offers materials to schools for teaching friendship, identity, diversity, and mutual respect.[5]

As shown in these examples, it is impossible for companies to teach customers everything there is to know about a good or service in one session. The development of expertise takes time. Companies must be specific in identifying the knowledge customers must learn to have initial success. Furthermore, there must be a roadmap for the knowledge customers must acquire to ensure ongoing, incremental improvement of performance and the building of their expertise.

## The Role of Customer Education

There are many ways for customers to build their expertise. Customers informally learn how to use goods and services through direct experience and the informal observation of other customers. Web-based communities and monthly user groups provide a more structured forum for learning everything from general product principles to in-depth techniques. Third-party organizations, such as the Red Cross, Federal Reserve Board, and Consumer's Union, offer *consumer education*—content that teaches people how to be better consumers. When a company invests in improving customer expertise in relation to the goods and services the company markets, the methods employed by a company fall under the label of *customer education*.

Customer education reflects the process companies use to build the skills of customers over time. While the customer education process may start long before the customer ever purchases a company's products, a majority of customer education occurs when the customer intends to use a service or has purchased a product. According to research conducted by the Corporate University Xchange, the topics most frequently addressed in customer education programs include:

1. Product Knowledge
2. Technical (non-IT)
3. Management
4. Leadership
5. Technical (IT)
6. Sales
7. Customer Service
8. Orientation to Organization or Industry[6]

Companies invest in customer education for a number of reasons. Some invest because they must, as defined by law. Numerous government organizations such as the U.S. Food and Drug Administration (FDA) or the U.S. Consumer Product Safety Commission (CPSC) mandate certain levels of customer education for goods or services that fall within their authority. When not mandated by legislation, legal liability associated with certain goods and services drives companies to invest in customer education as a secondary form of insurance. But for the most part, companies invest in customer education to establish a competitive advantage. Specifically, customer education programs have been shown to:

- Stimulate trial and adoption of goods and services
- Establish barriers to diminish switching
- Reduce the cost of support and service
- Increase customer satisfaction and repeat purchase[7]

For many technology-oriented, business-to-business companies, customer education is a multi-million dollar business. Microsoft, Hewlett-Packard, IBM, Cisco Systems, and Unisys, just to name a few, have profit-oriented customer education divisions to teach businesses and their employees a variety of skills associated with products and business processes. These customer education programs feature complete curricula and learning paths for various topics, as well as certification exams. For example, Hewlett-Packard offers customers certifications in five specific areas:[8]

- Sales
    - o Accredited Sales Professional
    - o Accredited Sales Consultant
- Presales
    - o Accredited Presales Professional
    - o Accredited Presales Consultant
- Integration
    - o Accredited Platform Specialist
    - o Accredited Integration Specialist
    - o Accredited Systems Engineer
    - o Master Accredited Systems Engineer
- Operating System
    - o Certified Systems Administrator
    - o Certified Systems Engineer
- Developer
    - o Certified Systems Developer

What can these "certified customers" do? Accredited sales professionals (these would be resellers of HP products, not HP employees themselves), for instance, would have the skills and competency to translate a set of customer business requirements into a proposal that recommends a set of HP goods and services. Additionally, these sales professionals would be able to communicate the advantages of HP products and technologies to a generalist audience. This level of expertise is important to ensure that HP's distribution channel can effectively position and sell HP's products in a competitive marketplace.

## Expertise as a Competitive Strategy

Since its inception, Home Depot has made the enhancement of customer expertise a focal element of its competitive strategy. Its founders, Bernie Markus and Arthur Blank, realized early in their careers that customers don't visit hardware stores just to browse. Customers come to those stores with a specific problem in mind, such as fixing a leak, repairing an electrical switch, painting a room, or replacing the floor in the kitchen. Furthermore, customers are there because they want to do it themselves. The pair speculated that if they could help customers be successful with a simple task, such as fixing a valve in a toilet bowl, they could migrate the customer to become a more serious do-it-yourselfer. The more serious the customer became, the more the customer's lifetime value would increase.

Thus the Home Depot strategy of teaching customers was born. It started with the now-familiar weekend clinics that offer instruction in various home improvement tasks. Home Depot began advertising these clinics as a way to enhance the expertise of its employees. The effect was that if customers perceived Home Depot as being knowledgeable, customers expected that knowledge to be transferred to them. Customers who had never fixed a leaky bathtub found that the orange-aproned employees could not only guide them to the products and tools that could fix the leak, but could provide them impromptu advice and tutorials on how to actually repair the leak.

The success of the expertise strategy expanded in a number of different ways. More and more topics were added to the clinic curriculum. This also led to another natural extension—Kid's Clinics—which started building the expertise of future customers by teaching them to build birdhouses, signs, and animal figures. Suppliers were encouraged to provide point-of-sale, self-instructional educational materials that could be displayed near products. Pergo, a manufacturer of laminated flooring products, provided single-page job aids with step-by-step explanations of how to install the flooring pieces. The company hired certified kitchen designers to help customers design projects which customers could then build themselves. Home Depot also established relationships with the Discovery Channel to produce home improvement television programs, and Better Homes & Gardens to produce home improvement books bearing the Home Depot brand. As the Internet gained prominence, Home Depot developed e-learning programs available for free on its website.[9]

As the Home Depot example shows, the development of customer expertise further enhances the customer's overall performance. Even if customers have *vision* (knowing the problem to be fixed), *access* (the necessary parts and tools), and *incentive* (eliminate nagging from a spouse), the final component that makes the whole coproduction experience come together is the *expertise* an individual must have to accomplish a task successfully. Developing expertise, however, is not easy or inexpensive. Companies must make a significant investment to discover the learning needs of their customers, organize the content customers need, and deliver it in an appropriate format. Customers must invest time to learn new knowledge and acquire new skills, whether it be in formal courses or through on-the-job experiences. Because of this expense companies often focus their efforts on vision, access, and incentives in an attempt to create successful coproduction experiences that leverage the customer's existing expertise. The millions of people who now book travel reservations online never needed to attend an Online Booking 101 course. Rather, an intuitive user interface, some bonus miles, and relaxed reservation change policies were sufficient to stimulate the customer-driven, on-the-job training program that built expertise in record time.

## SITUATIONS CALLING FOR ENHANCED EXPERTISE

As we discussed at the beginning of this chapter, customer education can be expensive. It also carries a greater degree of risk in its ability to resolve customer performance problems than other factors in the Coproduction Experience Model. Companies must selectively know when to use customer education and how extensive their customer education programs should be in light of certain conditions.

The level of a company's investment in customer education varies depending on context. Competition, opportunity, customer segments, industry norms, liability risk, regulations, and the nature of products are the typical dimensions upon which a company bases its decision. Within these dimensions customer expertise and product complexity are the most worthwhile

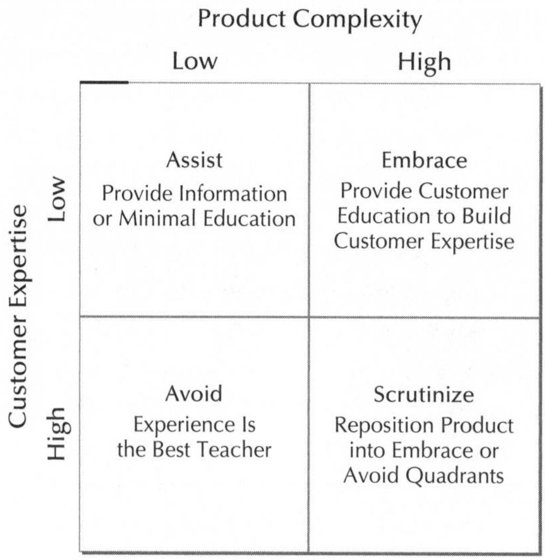

Product Complexity

| | Low | High |
|---|---|---|
| **Low** | Assist<br>Provide Information<br>or Minimal Education | Embrace<br>Provide Customer<br>Education to Build<br>Customer Expertise |
| **High** | Avoid<br>Experience Is<br>the Best Teacher | Scrutinize<br>Reposition Product<br>into Embrace or<br>Avoid Quadrants |

Customer Expertise

**Figure 8.4** Investments in customer education focus on situations where customer expertise is low and product complexity is high.

in making customer education investment decisions since they are core factors influencing customer performance (Figure 8.4).

Before we look at the situations of assist, embrace, avoid, and scrutinize, let's first discuss the two dimensions in this model, customer expertise and product complexity.

## Customer Expertise

As discussed in the first part of this chapter, customer expertise reflects the level of effort a customer must expend to complete a product task, as well as the automaticity that is apparent when performing that task. *Low customer expertise* describes a customer who performs slow and has numerous errors. *High customer expertise* describes a customer who performs fast with few errors.

A high level of customer expertise is evident in the following story. We were traveling to a conference and a colleague of ours happened to be on the same flight. We had rented a car and invited the colleague to ride with us to the conference. Once off the plane, we said, "follow us," and took off through the airport. We navigated our way through the terminal and boarded the rental car bus at the curb. Once at the rental car location, we hopped off the bus, went to the nearest car on the Emerald Aisle, threw our bags in the trunk and headed toward the checkout gate. We flashed our Emerald Aisle card and driver's license, and then we were on our way. Our colleague, who was in the back seat, finally spoke. "How did you do that?" she asked. "Do what?" we responded. She reflected for a moment, and then spoke. "How did you get through the airport so fast, get your rental car, and get on the highway without ever once being slowed down? I'd still be in the terminal." We chuckled, "Expertise, my dear, expertise."

## Product Complexity

Product complexity reflects the degree of difficulty inherent in a good or service. The lower the complexity, the easier a task is for a customer. What makes a product complex? The level of *component, coordinate,* and *dynamic* complexity associated with a product (Figure 8.5).[10]

- Component complexity is the nature of the product itself. Products that have numerous parts, require numerous steps to complete tasks, and have numerous information cues are more complex.
- Coordinate complexity is the nature of actions surrounding the product and its tasks. Products whose tasks are performed infrequently, with no fixed sequence, and in different locations are more complex.
- Dynamic complexity is the nature of the environment in which the product is used. Products that customers may use in varied environments, such as outside (in the field) rather than in an office, are more complex.

Figure 8.6 shows the results of a survey we conducted in which the complexity of several electronic products was evaluated using a ten-item

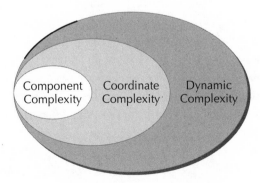

**Figure 8.5**    Relationship between Component, Coordinate, and Dynamic Complexity.

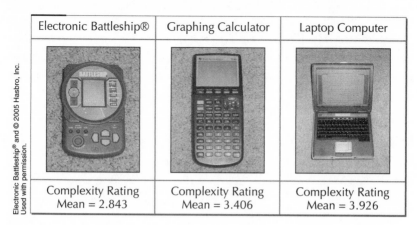

| Electronic Battleship® | Graphing Calculator | Laptop Computer |
|---|---|---|
| Complexity Rating Mean = 2.843 | Complexity Rating Mean = 3.406 | Complexity Rating Mean = 3.926 |

Electronic Battleship® and © 2005 Hasbro, Inc. Used with permission.

**Figure 8.6**  Complexity comparison of three electronic computing products.

complexity scale. A rating of five means that the product is very complex, while a rating of one means that a product is very simple. Electronic Battleship (a computer version of a classic board game) has low product complexity. It has few parts, is very sequential in usage, and isn't designed to be used in various conditions. The expected level of customer education for this product would be low. The laptop computer, on the other hand, has high product complexity. Its numerous parts, various software applications, dynamic nature, and connectivity to other goods and services contribute to its apparent complexity. We expect customers would require significant support to develop expertise with this product.[11]

Like goods, we can also classify services as simple or complex. For example, getting a haircut has relatively low complexity for the customer. There are few parts, actions, and information cues. There is a specific sequence of actions in a controlled location. Furthermore, there is little or no state change (one's hair isn't rapidly growing during the haircut nor does a haircut take place in a windy and wet storm). Thus the expected level of education a customer might need to get a haircut is relatively low. Before the haircut, the customer must be able to choose a style or indicate what the stylist should do. During the haircut, the customer must learn to follow the stylist's directions, for example, "Tilt your head forward." After the haircut, the customer must learn how to check the stylist's work.[12]

Financial management, on the other hand, is very complex. This complexity is compounded when the customer takes more responsibility for investment decisions. There are numerous parts (cash, CDs, bonds, equities, futures, commodities), numerous actions (buy, sell, short sell, reinvest dividends), and numerous information cues (newspaper, online quotes, newsletters, broker advice). While the act of buying and selling has a specific sequence, the timing of those events is variable, as is the frequency and intensity. The dynamic complexity is significant, as the markets are always in a state of dynamic change. Therefore, the expected level of education a customer needs to be successful with this service is quite high.

## Customer Education Investment Strategies

By matching the level of customer expertise with the level of product complexity, you can determine the relative level of investment in customer education for a specific product. The four different investment strategies are:

- Assist
- Embrace
- Avoid
- Scrutinize

### Assist

Low expertise and low product complexity suggest a strategy of *assist*. Due to the low-involvement nature of products in this quadrant, customers may need only information or minimal education, such as simple product instructions or a short user manual, to orient them to a product and its uses. Since the risk of error is low, direct, purposeful experience with the product is the best teacher and customers will develop most of their expertise through usage. Customers will rapidly move from a low level of expertise to a high level of expertise, minimizing the value of any substantial customer education due to the absence of reuse and ongoing reference. In short, information and education in this quadrant is a throwaway, consumed once and then never used again.

The following story illustrates the strategy of assist. In this story a customer who has low expertise with a very simple product (bread) wants to learn more about the product. Through a simple, low-cost, one-on-one tutorial, the storyteller illustrates how he developed the customer's expertise (and sold more bread in the process):

> I work at the greatest grocery store on earth (in my opinion), Trader Joe's. Trader Joe's is "your unique grocery store," as our logo suggests. We carry all kinds of specialty items other grocery stores most likely do not carry, and we provide exceptional customer service every day.

I was busy stocking some coffee when a customer stopped me and asked if we had any rice bread. I knew that we did. I took her to our bread section and showed her the two different rice breads we carry (Rice Almond and Brown Rice). She looked over the packaging of both products, viewed the breads through the see-through parts of the packaging, and then asked me what they tasted like. I told her I hadn't tasted them and didn't know. However, I also told her, "Let's find out!" I quickly took out my box cutter, opened both packages of bread, and gave her some to taste. I also tasted both breads as well. She politely and humorously said, "I'll break bread with you my friend." We did a sort of cheers with our pieces of bread, and it was fun. She loved the Brown Rice bread and asked me several more questions about the bread, which I answered with integrity and honesty. She decided to buy the whole shelf of bread—I believe this was about six loaves—because she was going to freeze it. She told me this was her first time in Trader Joe's and she couldn't believe that I opened the product for her to taste right there. She also said she would definitely be back to shop soon.

## Embrace

Low experience and high complexity suggest a strategy of *embrace*. This is the sweet spot for customer education because in this quadrant customers are highly involved and expect to spend significant effort developing complex behaviors. Thus companies should plan significant investment reflecting the time it takes to develop complex behaviors and the support required to minimize the threat of rejection due to error and dissatisfaction. Additionally, since the likelihood of future reference and referral is high, instructional materials must be designed to ensure longevity—an additional expense. However, companies have conditioned customers that education in this quadrant typically involves a cost, which enables an organization to recoup some or all of its investment.

If you look at companies that offer significant customer education programs, it is evident that high product complexity and low customer expertise are driving their investments. In the financial service category, Charles Schwab offers a variety of educational solutions to build the skills of its customers. These solutions include live seminars at its branches, webcasts through its website, and a range of printed materials that help customers understand the basics of investing to developing a retirement plan. In the home improvement category, Home Depot follows a similar strategy, with its in-store clinics, point-of-purchase instructional displays, and web-based How-To Clinics.

In business-to-business contexts, companies with very complex and specialized products make substantial investments in customer education. Applied Biosystems, a provider of instruments, reagents, and software systems for genetic analysis, has a multifaceted strategy. When customers buy products they receive the usual educational materials—user manuals, product bulletins, 800-number service support, and in some cases, interactive CD-ROM tutorials. During product installation, field support engineers provide basic instruction on how to run experiments. Furthermore, for a fee, customers can attend hands-on training classes at Applied Biosystem's training labs. Here they can learn everything from DNA chemistry techniques to how to use and maintain their instrument systems.

## Avoid

High expertise and low product complexity suggest a strategy of *avoid*. Customer education investments in this quadrant are not prudent because the incremental knowledge associated with the product has little or no value to a consumer with high expertise. Additionally, customer education may annoy the customer, distract the consumer from the task, and detrimentally increase the time it takes to reactivate a purchase. The customer in this quadrant is seeking efficiency, where a "just the facts" orientation is sufficient.

Consider the following experience of one of our storytellers as he tried to offer a little customer education to a customer in a Blockbuster Video store. In this situation high customer expertise (the customer knows how to pick a video and probably find it as well) combined with low product complexity (both in terms of the product itself and the strategies the store uses to merchandise the products) contributes to making additional help or education unwanted.

> When I was 17 years old I got a job at a nearby Blockbuster Video store. Blockbuster never got too busy during the day so I was always scheduled to work the night shifts between five and midnight. At Blockbuster, employees are trained to greet every customer that walks through the door. They are also trained to talk to every customer that was on the floor looking for movies to see if they needed help finding anything. These are not at all hard things to do except for the weekends when we had large volumes of customers walk through our doors. And it's especially hard to talk to every customer

looking for movies on the busy nights. Friday and Saturday nights
were our busiest nights. No matter how nice we were to customers
it always seemed they hated us talking to them. I remember one time
I was assigned to work the floor. I hated working the floor because it
was a Friday night and most of our customers on weekends were as
rude as can be. I was walking around the store's back walls were all
the new releases were located and I went up to a customer and said,
"Hi! Is there anything I can help you find?" She quickly snapped
back at me, "NO! CAN'T I JUST [expletive] LOOK WITHOUT
ANYONE BOTHERING ME!" I was completely surprised with her
response, replied, "Sure," and walked away.

These situations require careful service design and training of employees.
One does not necessarily know the customer's expertise or the complexity
of their task. We are not advocating that companies avoid opportunities to
establish customer relationships. The bond of sharing expertise with a customer can result in stronger relationships with the customer. Instead, perhaps
training a clerk to read nonverbal cues would guide the decision to approach
or avoid the customer. For example, a customer obviously in deep thought
doesn't need the interruption. If this type of customer needs help, he or she
will likely ask for assistance—and having an employee nearby solves his or
her immediate problem.

## Scrutinize

High experience and high complexity suggest a strategy of *scrutinize*. This is
perhaps the most challenging quadrant since studies show customers with
high levels of expertise can become complacent. Expert customers are more
likely to experience more product use errors due to overconfidence or mis-
applied rules than nonexperts. Because of this, experts may attribute defection or discontinuance decisions to the product rather than themselves.

This does not suggest that customer education investment in this quadrant be avoided entirely. Pharmaceutical companies successfully provide
continuing medical education (CME) to physicians as a means of building
relationships and fostering product adoption. This form of customer education is mandated by law. In other contexts expert customers may perceive
customer education in this quadrant as a waste of time. Why? Because of the
power law curve. Customers are smart enough to recognize that the additional effort required to learn new skills or refine existing skills associated
with a product or service is not worthwhile. In this situation, it is more likely

that new learning or performance improvement comes from direct experience with the good or service, perhaps coached, but not from a traditional educational event.

Investment in this quadrant might best be allocated to reposition a product in such a way to minimize the effect of product complexity or consumer expertise, essentially moving the consumer back into the *avoid* or *embrace* quadrants. For example, a complex product might be simplified over time, reducing customer errors and making the need for customer education moot. Alternatively, a product (or the tasks associated with a product) might be manipulated to address different uses. This is similar to installing new software on one's personal computer. Product complexity remains high, but the new software shifts the customer into a low expertise state, enabling the company to offer additional educational services to build the customer's expertise once again.

## A PROCESS FOR DEVELOPING EXPERTISE

Building customer expertise is a process, not an event. Throughout a customer's relationship with a company, its goods, and its services, the opportunity for the customer to learn something new exists at each touchpoint. Learning may occur independently, or it may be facilitated in some way by the company, a third-party, or even another customer. Regardless of the context or source, companies that plan for this process of continuous customer learning will be better positioned to enable customers to do more work and unlock greater value.

### Customer Education Roadmap

An approach for determining what methods a company should use to develop customer expertise is the Customer Education Roadmap (Figure 8.7). This roadmap defines the various components that are part of a customer education system, and illustrates the paths of escalation and reference.

As depicted in the diagram, customers start their journey toward expertise with *basic tools*, such as an instruction manual. This familiarizes customers with the product and starts them on their journey toward the initial success. *Embedded tools* in the product, such as user assistance or voice-driven prompts, provide just-in-time knowledge for the task. If the customer runs into problems during execution of the task, *problem tools*, such as a telephone customer service representative, help the customer navigate troublespots. When put together, these three tools focus primarily on the helping the

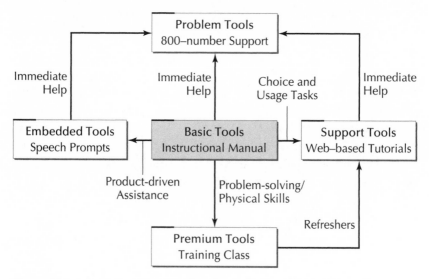

**Figure 8.7**   A Customer Education Roadmap. (*Adapted from Hennig-Thurau (2000)*).[13]

customer develop the minimum expertise necessary to achieve initial success with a good or service.

For longer-term development and expertise enhancement, two other tools come into play. *Premium tools*, which typically involve formal training, are included in the system if tasks associated with the product are very complex or require physical skill. *Support tools*, such as web-based information and tutorials, focus on aiding the customer in the ongoing development of expertise.

## Basic Tools

The starting point at the center of the roadmap is *basic tools*. For products, these are typically self-instructional materials that support initial success, such as user manuals, job aids, videos, or CD-ROMs. Content associated with these basic tools tends to be limited to the core functionality of the product. For example, when you open the box of a new TiVo® digital video recorder, the basic tools include visual aids on the packaging that identify the key components, a poster that explains how to connect the system, and a user manual (Figure 8.8). These materials help the customer perform the initial preparation tasks associated with the product, but do not address high-level skills such as planning a week's worth of program recording.

Sony's Personal Computing division in Europe has taken what we think of basic tools one step further. During a nine-month period in 2004, customers

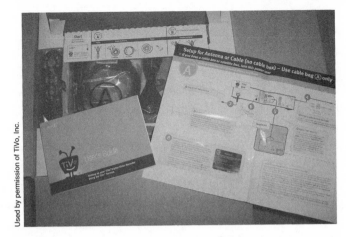

Used by permission of TiVo, Inc.

**Figure 8.8**   Basic Tools that come with the TiVo® Digital Video Recorder System: Instruction-based packaging, wiring poster, and user's guide.

who purchased a specific Sony computer system received a free, telephone-based training course. Sony provided customers a special toll-free number. When customers called the number, a Sony representative provided customers a short course on basic computer setup, functions, and operations.

In service contexts, basic tools are often supplemented or replaced by an employee who can explain the operation of a service. An example of this is the concept restaurant Buca di Beppo. Unlike other restaurants where each customer orders an individual entree, at Buca di Beppo all meals are served "family style" and must be ordered for multiple people. Since new customers aren't familiar with this process, the table's server supplements the textual instructions listed on the menu: "Hi, my name is Stephanie and I'll be your server. Have you ever been to Buca di Beppo before? No? Okay then, let me explain how things work around here." The server continues by explaining how the ordering scheme works and offers guidance on what amount of food a table might need.

## Embedded Tools

For some products it is possible to include embedded tools that provide customers immediate instruction, expertise, and assistance in completing product-oriented tasks. These are very similar—if not the same—as the tools we discussed in the Access chapter. A voice-prompt GPS navigational system in a car is an example of an embedded tool. It provides just-in-time knowledge to the driver so the driver can learn how to get to a specific address or location.

But such embedded tools must be implemented carefully, otherwise they become annoyances. In the 1980s car manufacturers experimented with electronic voice alerts (EVAs) in cars. For example, if a door was open a voice would announce, "The door is ajar." If fuel was getting low, the car would say, "Please check your fuel level." While good in theory, such devices were ultimately discontinued as customers found them to be extraordinarily annoying.

Software products have for a long time embedded help systems into their products. Microsoft Office products feature the Office Assistant, the sometimes-annoying paperclip character to whom one can go for advice and guidance. Depending on how the user configures this tool, the Office Assistant might be active or passive. As an active tool, the Office Assistant interrupts the user from time to time when it notices a specific sequence of actions, wanting to show the user how to do a specific task, such as creating a business letter. As a passive tool, the Office Assistant remains on screen, seemingly watching the user work. If the user needs help, the user can click the Office Assistant, which responds by displaying a field into which the user can ask the question.

## Problem Tools

In most cases companies expect basic tools to jump-start customers' development of expertise so customers can have an initial success with the good or service. However, if the basic tools are not well designed, unforeseen problems occur. If customers have insufficient expertise, customers will need a helping hand to overcome these rough spots. That's where *problem tools* come into play. Problem tools are typically in the form of another person, in-person, on the phone, or accessible through synchronous text messaging. Alternatively, these tools might also be in the form of an interactive voice response (IVR) system accessible from a telephone, an expert system built into a website, or both.

One recent innovation in this category are software tools collectively labeled as *live help*. These systems enable companies to monitor user experiences on websites and interactively assist customers as they complete tasks on websites. Using these systems, companies can:

- Monitor web traffic and view the navigation paths of customers
- Co-browse, whereby company representatives can help customers complete online forms and demonstrate how to navigate through a website using a shared pointer
- Engage in live chat with a customer to answer questions and provide advice and support

In a survey of 40 financial services firms, Forrester Research discovered that over 50 percent of those companies had either deployed or were considering deployment of live assistance for sales, support, collaboration, and co-browsing. Proficient Systems, Inc., a leading provider of solutions for live assistance, finds that these kinds of tools significantly boost the satisfaction customers experience online. Their research of over 7,000 customers shows that over 94 percent of customers who participate in live assistance rate their customer experience as being good to excellent. Furthermore, 91 percent of customers said that they would be very likely or more likely to engage the service again because of live help. So when customers engage this service, where do they see the value of the experience? Proficient's research suggests the following:

- 41% Asking specific questions directly of a product expert
- 19% Saving time by having help to access the relevant information quickly
- 18% Helping with online research and buying needs
- 16% Learning about other product or service offerings
- 14% Getting more explanation about price
- 12% Getting assistance with placing an order[14]

## Premium Tools

While basic tools drive initial success with a product, premium tools tend to develop expertise associated with skill-oriented tasks that are related to the product or service. Nikon digital cameras, for instance, come with basic tools (user manual) that teach customers how to use the product. However, through its Nikon School, Nikon offers customers the opportunity to develop expertise not only with its cameras, but also with the art of photography. The Nikon School curriculum offers fee-based, instructor-led courses throughout the world in basic digital photography, advanced digital photography, and other associated photography topics.

We classify premium tools as specific customer training experiences, whether they be instructor-led or self-instructional. These experiences are typically formal in nature, with the customer registering to take the training, and are organized in a curriculum of one or more modules.

The category of premium tools is inclusive of other forms of training content, distribution, and management. For instance, computer hardware and software manufacturers are testing the feasibility of offering free, skill-based, problem-oriented courses in retail stores. The driving force for offering these courses is the maturing of the marketplace. While most households have a personal computer, many do not understand how to unlock more value from that resource—limiting the sale of upgrades, consumables, and companion products. Microsoft and Hewlett-Packard are partnering with such retailers as Circuit City, CompUSA, and MicroCenter to offer courses in digital photography, digital music, home office, and wireless networking. Contract instructors from MarketSource LLC, who are specially trained not only in the technology, but in acting, public speaking, and establishing emotional connections, teach the classes. In the home office class, customers learn techniques for creating professional-quality documents, faxing, scanning, and emailing. In the digital music class, customers learn how to copy music to a computer or digital music player, organize the music, and listen to it.[15]

Not to be outdone, cell phone service providers are also offering customers classes on how to unlock more value from their cell phones. French cell service provider Orange has equipped recreational vehicles to be mobile training classrooms. These classrooms are parked in high-traffic shopping areas and offer customers courses in how to use various cell phone services and features. In the United States, Sprint offers customers courses in retail stores, as described by one of our storytellers:

> I am a sales representative for Sprint. We have just started offering customers a course on how to work the cell phones that we sell. In the course we cover everything from adding a friend or family member to the phone book to assigning a number to voice command. Since we have started offering this course we have gotten 23 percent more prime customers and our churn percentage has decreased. We now have educated our customers, which in turn brings more business our way. As long as we can keep all ages in tune with how cell phones are developing and how the various features can be useful to them we will continue to run this course.

To stimulate discovery learning among customers, companies often sponsor skill contests. These contests push customers to use products in such a way that rewards the development of expertise on the part of the customer. Agfa, a marketer of photography products, sponsors a monthly photography contest. Customers electronically submit their entries, and other customers help Agfa select a winner through an online voting process. Nabisco sponsored a contest in which customers competed to achieve Bachelors, Masters, and Doctorate degrees in Snackometry. In the contest customers completed tests that assessed the customer's knowledge of Nabisco's sensible snacks. One of the more popular skills contests is the World Series of Poker, sponsored by Binion's Horseshoe Casino in Las Vegas. This event stimulates thousands of people to build their expertise in playing poker, including those who only choose to watch the event on television.

## Support Tools

For the most part, support tools are 24/7/365 web-based resources that offer customers just-in-time knowledge to solve novel tasks associated with products. These tasks are usually purchase-oriented or usage-oriented in nature. For purchase-oriented tasks, the tools help customers understand the nature of products and the criteria used to select products. For usage-oriented tasks, customers want information that helps them develop a plan or complete a task.

For example, a customer interested in buying a replacement depth finder for a boat probably doesn't have sufficient knowledge to make an informed choice. The products are durable—boat owners perhaps purchase one every five or so years—so customer knowledge about the product class is likely low. Customers forget the terminology, the technology, and the product elements. Thus, before buying a new depth finder, customers want to develop a basic level of expertise so they can ask the right questions, consider the right features, and make the best choice. West Marine Products, a boating products retailer, has long specialized in this form of support. Through web-based technologies, West Marine offers customers West Advisor, a set of web-based resources that help customers learn about various boating products.

> **Product Assistant.** The purpose of this tool is to help customers narrow down a specific product. For instance, customers might know they need an anchor, but they don't know the type or size. By asking the customer a series of questions, the Product Assistant ultimately presents a list of products that meet the customer's criteria. The process also helps the customer learn the criteria that is most important in selecting a specific product.

> **Interactive West Advisor.** The purpose of this tool is to demonstrate specific psychomotor skills associated with boating. Using digital videos, the Interactive West Advisor demonstrates for customers how to wakeboard (setting up, getting up, and first moves) and how to tie various boating knots (bowline, figure eight, clove hitch, and so on).

**The West Advisor.** The purpose of this tool is to provide customer core-level knowledge regarding various products and their technologies. These text-based articles each cover a specific boat-oriented topic, from wind generators to eating well at sea. The articles themselves don't recommend specific products, but links associated with the article direct customers to products that relate to the concepts in the article.

**BoatTest Videos.** These videos, developed by a third party, provide overviews of various marine electronic products and techniques. Demonstrations illustrate everything from using electronic charts on GPS navigation systems to techniques for reducing noise on VHF radio systems.

Both Home Depot and its competitor Lowes offer a similar set of web-based support tools for tasks relating to home improvement. These include:

**Calculators.** Need to determine how much paint you'll need to paint a room in your house? Determine how much lumber you'll need for a project? These and other useful calculators help customers collect the right data and perform specific calculations.

**Design Tools.** Need to build a deck, select plants, design a garage, or choose a paint color for your living room? These software tools help customers do the actual design and provide content to build their expertise.

**How-To Videos.** These videos use third-party content licensed from the television show *This Old House.* Experts such as Norm Abrams demonstrate the finer points of installing drywall, freeing a paint-stuck window, and removing poison ivy.

**Interactive Tools.** These multimedia presentations provide step-by-step instruction in understanding key household systems, such as heating/cooling, irrigation, kitchen/bath, and plumbing.

In many cases support tools rely on content generated not only by the company, but by third parties as well. In some cases customers even become contributors to an ever-growing knowledge base of content. Macromedia, provider of various software tools for multimedia and web-based publishing, provides discussion-board forums for each of its products. In these forums customers can post questions related to product-related tasks, and get answers from other customers as well as Macromedia employees.

Support tools don't necessarily need to be electronic. User groups that meet on a regular basis virtually or in person provide a means for customers to learn from other customers and company representatives. Companies may sponsor customer events such as user meetings, or microevents within the context of a larger third-party conference.

## SUMMARY

In this chapter we discussed *expertise*, the knowledge and skill customers possess to accomplish product-related tasks. Expertise is expensive to develop, for both the company and the customer. Both must invest time, effort, and financial resources. Even with that investment, success isn't always ensured. The development of expertise is at times fickle, due to the complexity of the product, the design of the customer education, and the capabilities of the customers.

We know customers have expertise when they can perform tasks quickly, without error, and with some degree of automaticity—which means that customers don't exert much cognitive effort when completing a task. Content knowledge and process knowledge are the cornerstones of expertise, and research shows that both must be addressed in customer education programs to deliver the greatest return on investment.

The process of developing expertise relies on the customer having an initial success with a good or service. Such a success provides a primary reward and ensures that a loop of product usage and skills development is maintained. Customers can easily abandon a good or service if they don't have this initial success, hence the importance of ensuring that customers have appropriate aids and training materials. In most situations the initial success correlates to a rapid learning curve. In a single experience customers can acquire a level of expertise that makes them minimally proficient with a good or service. However, as suggested by the power law curve, additional expertise can take a long time to develop as the number of learnable skills become fewer and their relative complexity increases exponentially.

The techniques companies use to help customers develop expertise are collectively referred to as customer education. Customer education describes a process of instruction that systematically builds customer expertise. Customer education programs link together a variety of instructional methods that efficiently, effectively, and appealingly develop customer expertise. Through customer education, companies can speed the adoption of products, erect switching barriers, reduce service and support costs, and stimulate greater customer satisfaction.

Customer education is most appropriate when companies face situations in which customer expertise is low and product complexity is high—hence our recommendation that companies *embrace* customer education in that quadrant. If product complexity is low, then companies are better off using strategies that assist the customer. This assistance tapers off as customer expertise increases to a point whereby companies cease offering assistance unless the customer specifically asks for it.

The process of developing expertise relies on a variety of different instructional methods, each used to address certain aspects of the customer's experience. *Basic tools* are used to get the customer started, and should be supported by some kind of *problem tool*, such as a telephone hotline. For very complex products companies can offer *premium tools*—specific instructor-led and self-instructional programs that formally build customer skills. Informally, *support tools* primarily rely on 24/7/365-accessible content to provide just-in-time knowledge for purchase and usage tasks. Finally, *embedded tools* add instructional methods to the product itself, in the form of text-based aids and voice-oriented cues.

Since customer education relies upon various communication channels to pass knowledge from a source to a customer, companies must take care in managing the various channels. Desirable expertise that has taken weeks, months, or years to develop can be discredited in a single event over which a company has little or no control. In the next chapter, Navigating the Pathways of Learning, we'll suggest some strategies for ensuring consistent communication to customers.

# CHAPTER 9

# NAVIGATING THE PATHWAYS OF LEARNING

*To learn virtue takes three years; to learn evil, one day.*

—Chinese proverb

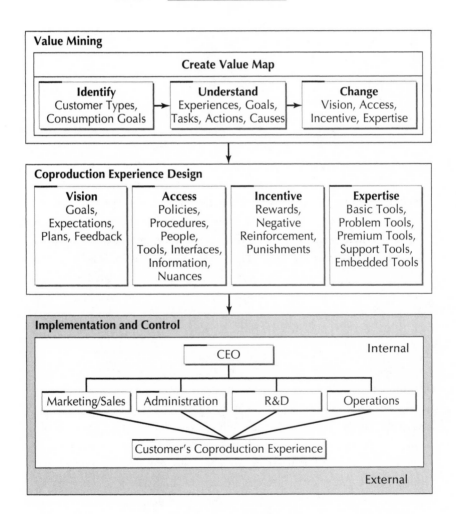

I n this chapter, we examine the external level communication forces that can impact the effectiveness of coproduction experiences. You will contribute significant resources to the design of coproduction experiences. However, your work can become undone by communication channels you do not control. Macro forces external to a company's well-designed plans have a powerful effect on conditioning customer performance in ways that might be inconsistent with the coproduction experiences you design. We start this chapter by discussing which communication channels are controllable, and which are not. The chapter concludes with six principles for controlling the uncontrollable, which are:

1. Enforce the rule of law
2. Model ethical behavior
3. Establish expertise
4. Recruit desirable models
5. Own the context
6. Encourage articulation

## KNOW WHAT SOURCES ARE CONTROLLABLE

Since much of human behavior is learned, you must pay particular attention to the sources from which customers learn. Whether the source is another customer, an employee, an article in the newspaper, or a blog, customers are continually influenced to think, act, and perform in specific ways by a wide variety of messages. Ideally, the influence is positive, whereby the customer learns to do good, generating greater value for both the customer and the company. Yet there is always the threat that through missing or incomplete messages, or the observation of others' inappropriate behavior, customers learn evil.

Through the observation of inappropriate actions, customers can learn inappropriate behavior almost instantly. However, the learning of appropriate behaviors is entirely feasible, requiring consistent conditioning of acceptable performance through multiple communication channels. It is through these communication channels that vision, access, incentive, and expertise become known to customers. Thus, before you implement a coproduction experience, it is important to analyze the communication channels through which customers become conditioned. In this analysis, you must determine which communication channels are controllable (and which are not) and the relative influence each channel has on coproduction experiences. Once this analysis is complete, you can shape the communications infrastructure to support coproduction experiences.

When companies implement coproduction experiences, they need to communicate the elements of vision, access, incentive, and expertise to their customers consistently across various communication channels. A communication channel describes any provider of information that is ultimately received by customers. Communication channels include salespeople, advertisements, other customers, even goods and services themselves.

Communication channels are essentially the social learning equivalent of observable models. It is through these models that customers learn norms, the rules for desirable behavior, as well as information that helps them make better choices. Thus the objective for an effective coproduction experience is to manage the greatest number of communication channels through which to disseminate vision, access, incentive, and expertise.

Yet you can't control all the pathways from which customers learn. While theoretically possible, total control is an economic impracticality. Control assumes that there is a formal agreement or understanding between parties, and that the controlling party has some capability of rewarding desired behavior (or punishing undesired behavior). Essentially, the bottom line on control is that if one doesn't pay, one doesn't control. So, by following the money trail, one can begin to understand the sources one controls, the sources one doesn't control, and the sources that reside in a region between control and no control (Figure 9.1).[1]

The top of Figure 9.1 lists the various communication channels over which you can exert considerable control. These include such channels as products, policies, and company media. As you start moving down the list, the level of control you have becomes weaker and weaker, until it is virtually nonexistent.

Another force depicted in Figure 9.1 is society's conditioning to the meaning of messages from the various channels, in the form of *perceived technical expertise* and *trusted evaluative judgments*. Communication that is more strongly controlled by a company is typically seen by customers as being technically accurate. For example, technical specifications for a product are more believable if they come from the company rather from your Uncle Fred. On the other hand, communication that is weakly controlled by companies is typically seen as more trustworthy in subjective, evaluative judgments. Thus, if Uncle Fred attests to the quality of Guinness stout found in the pubs of Ireland, his opinions are more acceptable to us than the Guinness advertising that blankets the country.

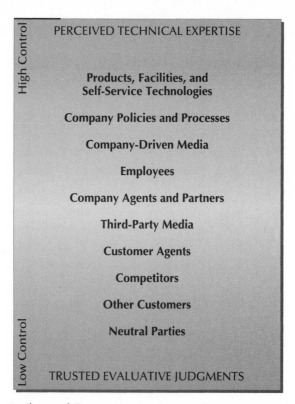

**Figure 9.1**    Attributes of Communication Sources. Customers perceive technical expertise with high control sources, whereas they trust evaluative judgments from low control sources.

In the following discussion, we introduce the various communication channels that are known to influence the good and bad within customers. We also provide examples showing how several companies put those channels to work to influence desirable customer performance.

## Products, Facilities, and Self-Service Technologies

Three channels over which you exercise the strongest control are products, facilities, and self-service technologies (SSTs). Since you can "program in" the communication these channels provide and can replicate them such that consistency is maintained, they have become reliable means of shaping behavior.

Products are constantly communicating with customers, either actively or passively, to shape desirable, consistent behavior. In terms of active communication, automobiles provide many performance-enhancement messages. Cars talk to you when your seatbelt is unfastened and "idiot lights" illuminate when a taillight has burned out. Similarly, computers emit tones, beeps, and tunes when you do things right as well as when you do things wrong. Passive communication, on the other hand, describes features designed into products that limit or enable performance. For example, Cuisinart® food processors have a safety lockout design that renders the device inoperative until the cover is closed and the hopper is in place. Through this simple design, correct setup is quickly communicated by the function of the device. Other products, such as battery chargers for portable electric drills, feature physical jigs in their design to ensure batteries may only be inserted the correct way—eliminating the age-old performance problem of putting a square peg into a round hole, which damages the device.

When you walk into a store or a place of business, the design of the facilities contributes to activating certain customer responses. At our dentist's office, muted colors, plants, and soft music communicate relaxation, which contributes to making patients more compliant. Even the venerable Victoria's Secret underwent a significant change in their store design in 2002. They abandoned the cushy pink, Victorian-era, fantasy boudoir design. Now they have a design that signals a flashy, supermodel runway feeling. The purpose of the makeover? To condition customers to associate Victoria's Secret with *racy* and *upscale*. Vice President for Store Design Kathleen Baldwin led a team that changed virtually everything, from the lighting to the type of music that is played. In the redesign, five key principles emerged, which are being applied to all stores:

1. Offer shoppers an enticing entryway
2. Bring the bustle to the center
3. Class up the color scheme
4. Make the catalog come to life
5. Put the merchandise on the menu[2]

Self-service technologies (SSTs) offer a similar level of control by the company. The company owns the script of what customers can and can't do with SSTs. ATMs, for instance, quickly condition customers that nothing may be transacted with the machine unless a card and personal identification number (PIN) are provided. Once access is granted, the range of choices and the actions to perform tasks is constrained to ensure success, satisfaction, and safety.

## Company Policies and Processes

The ways companies do business with customers has a powerful conditioning effect. Nowhere is this more evident than in the policies and processes companies develop regarding the purchase of their goods and services.

Consider for a moment a business in which a customer:

- Pays in advance for a service
- Pays a price that is different than what the person next to him paid
- Is not entitled to a refund if the customer decides not to use the service
- Must pay extra if the customer changes his or her mind about specific service options
- Has no guarantee that the service will be performed as promised

Taken at face value, our collective reaction to such a policy is that it is a recipe for a failed business, since no customer in his or her right mind would agree to such terms. But sadly, it is a recipe that we have all become conditioned to when we purchase airline tickets (which in some respects is a failed business). Slowly, over many, many years, airlines have shaped and conditioned us to accept this policy as the status quo. When one of the enlightened few recognizes the emperor has no clothes, the industry responds by discussing "yield management" processes, which somehow explain why we are paying $500 more than the guy sitting next to us for exactly the same seat, and suggests that such a process makes it okay. It is no wonder that in 2004, several major airlines introduced "simple pricing."

While airlines have trapped us into a system that both infuriates and amazes us, other companies have focused on policies and processes that condition us to expect surprisingly effortless transactions. During a recent visit to Bed Bath & Beyond, a big-box household accessories retailer, we shopped and then proceeded to the cash registers (another form of process conditioning). Because Bed Bath & Beyond and its competitor Linens 'n Things are relatively indistinguishable on the inside, we lost track of which store we were in. Because of this, we attempted to pay for our purchases using coupons from Linens 'n Things. "These are Linens 'n Things coupons," the cashier announced, quickly bringing us back to reality and causing us to kick ourselves for going to the wrong store. "But it's no problem," she continued, "we accept them just the same." She scanned the barcodes on the Linens 'n Things coupons, the cash register accepted the coupons, and the correct discount was displayed on the terminal. Our conditioning was complete. Bed Bath & Beyond occupied a space in our minds reserved for companies with whom it is easy to do business.

## Company-Driven Media

As with policies and processes, companies also exercise significant control over company-driven media. Website content, user manuals, product bulletins, brochures, and advertisements, to name a few, are conduits through which desired behaviors and performance may be modeled for customers.

Control for this media is high because of the group-oriented review of content. While one employee or consultant may be responsible for the initial creation of the messages, companies typically subject such communication to review by various stakeholders. Engineers, scientists, or similar experts review content for technical accuracy, lawyers review the content for legal compliance, and marketers review the content for appropriate persuasive messages and consistency.

Another characteristic of company-driven media is the presence of style guides and other tools that drive communication consistency. At the most basic level corporations typically have an image or brand "style guide," which documents how employees must implement the visual presentation. This includes such basic rules as logo placement, colors, and typographical styles. Style guides often extend to a database of approved images that may be used in company communications. These images may include abstract representations of product concepts and processes, as well as high-fidelity photographs of products and people. Organized in an online database, such as Interwoven's MediaBin Asset Server, these images are accessed by employees to use in various communication pieces. A further extension is the creation of a dictionary of terms and phrases that must be used when describing processes and procedures associated with company products. As these elements become part of the company's DNA, sales proposal templates, canned PowerPoint presentations, and boilerplate email messages emerge to further solidify control of company messages. One can recognize when tight controls are in place for company-driven media when "copy and paste" and "save as" become common tasks in the creation of communication.

## Employees

Consistency begins to wane some when communication control shifts from the group to the individual. Employee conduct is typically governed by a contractual relationship. Rewards and punishments are usually in place to encourage desired behavior. But there is a greater chance that inconsistent messages may be communicated to customers due to the inherent diversity and expertise of individuals. Business school professor Jim Donnelly, Jr. illustrates this in the following story:

> ... I was in my hometown shopping for some seafood. I drove to a food market I had never been to before. I spent a few minutes

window-shopping and then spotted the orange roughy, which happens to be one of my favorite kinds of fish. I ordered a pound of it. As the man behind the counter was weighing and wrapping it, I was praising his fish counter. "I now know where to come to get fresh fish. I'm really excited about this because I love seafood." As he handed my fish to me, he said, "If you worked here as long as I have, there's a lot of this stuff you'd never eat again for the rest of your life." As I walked to my car I thought, "I hope he wasn't referring to my orange roughy." That night I didn't finish eating all of the fish, and I haven't been back to that fresh seafood counter again.[3]

As communication devices, employees function in two main roles when interacting with customers. As *coaches*, employees take an active role in prompting, guiding, and reinforcing specific customer behaviors. For example, the predictable phrase in a retail transaction, "How may I help you?" initiates a scripted action of customer service. Similarly, "Would you like fries with that?" offers a reminder of complementary products. In most airports, identifiable Traveler Assistants guide customers to appropriate lines or in some cases happily tell customers they can bypass the line completely and proceed to the boarding gate if they possess the correct documents. Ushers in theaters escort customers to seats and facilitate the distribution of printed information. Pharmacists disseminate patient information and education to customers who purchase prescription pharmaceuticals.

As *models*, employees assume a more passive role in shaping customer behavior. Ritz Carlton hotels has long relied on the motto "Ladies and gentlemen serving ladies and gentlemen" to illustrate the kind of behaviors employees should model when interacting with guests and other employees. Simple things, such as dress, grooming, posture, nonverbal expression, and tone of voice can communicate significant information to customers about the nature of the business and its norms.

Figure 9.2 contrasts the formality of the staff at a Morton's, The Steakhouse, a luxury eating establishment, with those at Dick's Last Resort, where sassiness and rude behavior combined with buckets of food let diners experience an informal, fun environment.

At Morton's, The Steakhouse, formal dress and impeccable grooming of service staff model the formality of the dining experience, which reinforces the message that, "Jeans, T-shirts, shorts and sandals are not appropriate for dining at Morton's, The Steakhouse."[4] At Dick's Last Resort, where one of

Photos courtesy of Mortons, The Steakhouse. Outrageous fun and service photos courtesy of Dick's Last Resort.

**Figure 9.2** Employees Modeling Desired Behaviors. The formality of Morton's, The Steakhouse service staff (left) models desired customer behavior of refined elegance, while the informality of the service staff at Dick's Last Resort (right) reinforces outrageous fun and service.

the many mottos is "If the music is too loud, you're too damn old," jeans, T-shirts, shorts, and sandals are considered proper dress. Dick's features service staff in all manners of dress, from shorts to jeans, piercings to tattoos, hats to do-rags, and various other garish accoutrements. This models the partying, almost-anything-goes atmosphere where your plate is a piece of butcher paper and you can eat with your hands.

The strength of employees as coaches and models was recognized by researchers interested in understanding the nature of service quality. They developed ten general attributes that establish a baseline for how employees can effectively perform their tasks as coaches and models and assist in the conditioning of customers.[5]

1. Employees of excellent companies will be visually appealing.
2. Employees at excellent companies will understand the specific needs of customers.
3. Employees of excellent companies will tell customers exactly when services will be performed.
4. Employees of excellent companies will have the knowledge to answer customer questions.

5. Employees of excellent companies will give prompt service to customers.
6. Employees of excellent companies will always be willing to help customers.
7. Employees of excellent companies will never be too busy to respond to customer requests.
8. The behavior of employees at excellent companies will instill confidence in customers.
9. Employees of excellent companies will be consistently courteous with customers.
10. Excellent companies will have employees who give customers personal attention.

Employees always need to be "on stage" when it comes to their communications. Yet transgressions are frequent. Before getting on a plane one day we were sitting near the check-in counter. The two gate agents were talking between themselves, complaining about the pilot for the morning's flight. One gate agent says to the other, "The pilot for this flight is named 'Schmuck.' And he is one." Overhearing this, we wondered to ourselves whether the safety of the flight would be compromised in anyway by the schmuck in the cockpit.

## Company Agents and Partners

A significant drop in control occurs when customers receive communication from third parties who are affiliated with the company. These third parties include independent retailers, manufacturer's representatives, franchisees, and partners. In some of these situations there is a formal contract that governs the communication behavior of the third party. This is evident in a franchise company that sells personal safety. The company's business model is to provide free safety seminars to companies, then sell safety devices, such as pepper spray, whistles, and property-marking kits, to participants. Franchisees, who teach the seminars and distribute the products, are required to follow a very specific script when delivering safety presentations due to liability issues. Of course, whether franchisees are 100 percent compliant in this requirement is not known, but anecdotal feedback suggests that there is some freewheeling by franchisees from time to time.

Independent salespeople and retailers of a company's products tend to have more freedom in what they say about products and how they merchandise them. But, again, the nature of the contractual relationship governs the level of control. Companies with clout establish agreements that enable them to terminate distribution relationships if products are not sold or merchandised to company standards. However, the nature of many retailers is to act on behalf of the customers, helping them decide between competing products and often editorializing their preference of one product over another. Even if desired communication is supported through training and rewards, such as sales commissions, retailers retain the freedom of choice to participate or not participate in the company's programs.

Another form of agent is law enforcement. We know of nothing that communicates orderly behavior among customers more than a peace officer in uniform. One of our clients hires a deputy sheriff on weekends to enforce appropriate customer behavior, since due to regular crowding of the store, customers must line up in the hot South Florida sun and wait to be admitted. The owners of the business love to tell the true story of a middle-aged woman who grew frustrated with standing in line and became a nuisance to the other customers. The deputy arrived to resolve the issue, only to be pushed by the frustrated woman. The woman was duly handcuffed, taken to the station, booked, and released on her own recognizance. Upon her release, she returned to the store, patiently waited in line, and completed her weekend shopping.

## Third-Party Media

Independent magazines, newspapers, newsletters, websites, television shows, blogs, and radio programs are attractive sources for conditioning customers. They provide an independent viewpoint that is aligned with their readers' interests. They feature content that is more trustworthy than company-sponsored media. The editorial integrity of these sources diminishes the control companies have over the dissemination of messages, whether it is getting your message in the news, or keeping negative publicity out.

Getting a company's message in the news has become increasingly challenging since the number of pages or the amount of time available for such messages are nowhere near the demand. Yet editors desire interesting content. Through the creativity of public relations specialists, companies provide editors story ideas that advance the company's interests. In our work with public relations specialists, the strategy of *about you*, *include you*, and *by you* leverages a company's control of the editorial process. Stories *about you* describe the company, its products, its involvement in the community, and so on. Stories that *include you* incorporate a company spokesperson to comment on a related newsworthy story, typically in the role of an expert or analyst. Stories *by you* leverage specific expertise in the company to provide by-lined articles to publications on a variety of topics.

The trick is linking your message with something that is newsworthy and noteworthy that goes beyond the general new product introduction story. This increases the chance of getting a message published. Consider an article in the *Wall Street Journal* that was part of a series on success and failure in business. As a classic *about you* article, it featured entrepreneur Tomima Edmark, who in the early 1990s had a smashing success with a product called the Topsy Tail, a hair styling device that has delivered $120 million in sales. The article discusses Tomima's experience with what she termed lottery-like success with the Topsy Tail, followed by a string of products that experienced significantly less success, even failure. But the underlying message about this entrepreneur and her business was the dedication, determination, and willingness to continually innovate to recreate the original success that launched her company. Not a bad message for the customers she does business with or potential buyers should she decide to sell her business.[6]

Positive publicity is always a blessing since it offers readers the social proof they need to trust your products and the people behind them. However, when alleged product defects, illegal behavior, or financial misconduct become associated with a company, negative publicity can undo years of image building and conditioning. This is no more evident than in the case of Martha Stewart. For over 20 years she worked to build her brand, conditioning customers through books, magazines, television programs, and websites to associate homemaking elegance, sophistication, perfection, and beauty with her name. Based upon her modeling, customers learned to perform homemaking tasks more elegantly, from making the perfect pie crust to creating beautiful flower arrangements. Yet this image of perfection was significantly tarnished when in 2002 news reports began to appear alleging that she improperly traded shares of Imclone stock. Based on this news the value of Martha Stewart Omnimedia stock decreased 50 percent and in 2003 she faced government charges associated with the alleged improprieties. Throughout this process and faced with an almost overwhelming amount of negative publicity, Ms. Stewart fought to take control of communication, establishing the website www.marthatalks.com. The website promoted Ms. Stewart's innocence, published letters from supporters, and provided press releases from her attorneys. In a year, the site registered 34 million hits and had received 170,000 supportive emails. Ultimately, she was forced to resign her leadership position with the company she created and was ultimately convicted in 2004 on several counts associated with conspiracy to obstruct justice, making false statements, and perjury.

However, her communications strategy seemed to pay off. After serving prison time, her company's stock price has increased substantially and several new projects appear poised for success.[7]

## Customer Agents

Customer agents are people or organizations that provide advice or other services to customers related to the consumption of goods and services, typically for a fee paid by customers. At a high level, lawyers and accountants fall into this category as they provide advice regarding business transactions. Other advisors and consultants may be retained to provide the expertise customers don't possess.

We have hired home inspectors to inspect a home we intended to purchase, well inspectors to inspect the well that provided water to the home, and furnace inspectors to assess the operation of the home's heating systems. Since the buyer pays a fee for the advice, we perceive that the seller has little control over the communication the buyer receives. But as we reflect on our experiences after owning the home for several years and the various problems that arose, we realize that the inspectors were recommended by the realtor, who is ultimately paid by the seller. Thus, if an inspector finds faults that break up a deal, the inspector might suffer the consequences of not being recommended in the future. Perhaps the seller has more control than we perceived.

A similar agent to the inspector is the image consultant. These specialists are hired by people who are unsophisticated when it comes to selecting clothes, accessories, and other trappings, doing something with one's hair, or exhibiting correct manners in important social situations. For a fee, image consultants will take you on a shopping spree, work through your closet to eliminate anything that isn't stylish, well-fitted, or complimentary to your color palette, and offer their personal opinion and coaching on your verbal and nonverbal communication.[8]

As communication channels, customers rely on these advisors for unbiased advice and ethical behavior. Yet from a control perspective, these proxies must learn about the goods and services they advise, hence an opportunity for companies to influence the messages that originate from these sources.

## Competitors

Competitor communication takes a variety of forms, from comparative advertising to bad-mouthing and disparagement. Its purpose is to condition customers that a competing company's goods, services, and business practices are inferior. In a 2003 advertising campaign from Dell Computer,

Dell humorously warned consumers away from retailers (which obviously benefits Dell's direct-to-consumer business model). The targets of the campaign are not only the retailers, but the competing computer manufacturers who sell through retail channels, such as Hewlett-Packard. One of the ads challenges the pricing found in retail channels and features a 30-ish man who must do odd jobs, such as selling lemonade, baby sitting, and mowing lawns, so he can afford an MP3 player. Another ad spoofs a Computer Purchase Training Center boot camp, where customers in training are shown practicing critical retail purchasing skills, such as learning to say, "I don't have to settle for what's on the shelf!" illustrating Dell's strength in customizing systems that meet customer needs.[9]

The allure of comparative communication stems from the fact that it is an effective means of presenting a point-of-difference between competitors. The classic "Pepsi Challenge" campaign, which featured consumers blind taste-testing Coke and Pepsi products, represented a point-of-difference that Pepsi thought was important—taste. However, in a study of 5,000 commercials by Research Systems Corp, the difference between comparative and noncomparative ads in terms of superior persuasion was slight, showing a difference of only 3 percent (21 versus 18 percent, respectively).[10]

Although it still occurs, bad-mouthing is generally discouraged as an ineffective (and unethical) competitive strategy. In most cases companies have little control over what their competitors say and do unless the communication crosses a fine line called the Lanham Act. Created over 50 years ago by Congress, the purpose of the act is to protect businesses from various forms of unfair competition. Section 43(a) of the act addresses competitive communication, specifically misrepresentation. In the words of the Lanham Act, misrepresentation occurs when a company:

- Makes false or misleading factual representations of the nature, characteristics, and qualities of another company's practices, products, or services
- Uses the false or misleading representations "in commerce" or in connection with any services
- Makes the false or misleading statements in the context of commercial advertising or promotion
- Makes another company believe that it was likely damaged by such false or misleading factual representations

For example, in Nolu Plastics v. Valu Engineering, Inc., Nolu alleged that Valu's sales force was making false or misleading factual representations of its guide rail products. Evidence presented in the case showed that during sales calls, Valu's reps would inform perspective customers that Nolu's guide rails were made from inferior plastic (Nolu claimed its products were made from a high molecular weight polyethylene). Reps would then show customers examples of Nolu's products that had been misshapen (which could only occur if the products were exposed to temperatures beyond normal usage and operating specifications). A California federal district court agreed with Nolu that Valu's practices violated the Lanham Act and granted a preliminary injunction to enjoin Valu from continuing these misleading practices.[11]

## Other Customers

The observation of customers significantly influences the behavior and performance of other customers. Yet word of mouth, the active communication between two or more customers, is touted as one of the strongest sources of influence impacting customer conditioning. In a 2004 MediaLab study, 76 percent of consumers were "more comfortable" with a product if a friend provided a recommendation.[12] A similar InsightExpress study found that 70 percent of Americans recommend new products to friends and family, and 55 percent learn about new products from those same friends and family, more than any other source.[13]

To capitalize on the importance of word of mouth, websites have been established to provide a structured means of disseminating word-of-mouth messages (for example, see www.planetfeedback.com/consumer/). Customers are motivated to use these channels because such activities provide social interaction, economic incentives, the opportunity to help others, and enhancement of one's self-worth.[14]

The logic of the word-of-mouth communication channel is simple. When we have a good experience with a good or service, we often share our pleasure. However, if we have had a poor experience, pity the object of our wrath. Recently, a friend called us up and asked for recommendations of an optometrist in town. While we were at a loss for recommending an optometrist she should go see, we had no problem telling her which optometrist to avoid, based upon a previous, negative experience.

In one of our studies, one respondent wrote the following amusing experience:

> My roommate and I decided to get wireless Internet for our condominium. I have an Apple Macintosh computer and she has a Dell

Wintel PC. Big Box Retailer A is one of the few places that sells Apple computers in our town so we decided to take our business there. After we looked around for a while, we found the wireless stuff. We needed someone to tell us what exactly we needed for our condominium. The first lady who helped us didn't know anything about wireless systems. The next guy that helped us said that we couldn't have wireless for some dumb reason. I finally asked if I could talk to a supervisor or someone who knew what they were talking about. Since I made a big scene we were finally sold the right things and signed up for the free in-home installation. A couple days later the technician comes out to install the wireless Internet. After looking at our systems he says, "I don't know anything about Apples. I can't do this." That put me over the edge. I ended up just taking everything back and going to Big Box Retailer B.

What impressions about Big Box Retailer A do you have after reading this story? Knowledgeable? Prompt? Consistent? Focused? Consider another story from a different respondent:

I recently had an incident with the cable company's customer service department and actually ended up being a satisfied customer.

I had moved into a new apartment and called them to set up a transfer date. They said sure—no problem, and gave me a three-hour time frame that I had to be home in order to let them in my apartment, thus enabling them to set the system up (which is not that convenient and was actually a problem, but you do what you have to do). So I waited, and sure enough, once that last hour rolled around, they showed up. The guy was very friendly and hooked it all up.

The next day I tried the service out in my bedroom, where the installer had only hooked the cable up but not actually checked to see if it worked. And wouldn't you know it—it didn't work. I was mad and called the company around 11:30 at night. I didn't expect to talk to anyone, but I figured maybe it was something I did wrong and they could tell me how to fix it. To my surprise, someone actually answered the phone. I told her the problem and she set up another appointment for me. A few days later, another cable guy came and fixed everything—checking to make sure it all worked. He said the installer before didn't exactly do his job and that's why it wouldn't work in my room. He apologized.

I ended up being satisfied with how the situation was handled because they did eventually take care of everything for me, they were very nice, and they even waived my transfer fee!

Are your impressions of the cable company illustrated in the second story more favorable than the impressions of Big Box Retailer A in the first story? Obviously, the cable installation didn't go exactly as planned. However, the company did a number of things right to rectify the situation. They also created the conditions for positive feedback, including an apology and a fee refund to compensate the customer for the lost time.

Although companies can't control what customers say to one another, they can establish conditions that increase the frequency of positive word of mouth. While the basics of good service and quality influence positive customer feedback, David Fletcher of MediaLab suggests the following techniques can enhance the frequency of messages:

1. Target people who are *transmitters*. These are the 86 percent of adults who actively spread information about the goods and services they use.

2. Provide *specialist communication* that enables your company to have a deeper conversation with transmitters. As found in their research, the first stop for transmitters when they want more information is the Internet.

3. Actively engage transmitters with *multiple communication channels*. Make sure they become involved with the company's relationship and loyalty programs on a regular basis.

## Neutral Third Parties

The communication channel that has the lowest level of company control is neutral third parties. This category includes the government, nonprofit organizations, and consumer advocate groups, such as the Consumer's Union, which publishes *Consumer Reports*. The aim of this category is to maintain as much independence as possible so the channel's communication serves the public's best interest in terms of consumer protection and trustworthy evaluative judgments.

The government's primary role is to act as a regulatory body. Through various agencies, such as the Food and Drug Administration (FDA), Federal Trade Commission (FTC), Consumer Product Safety Commission (CPSC), and Department of Agriculture (USDA), communication associated with a company's goods, services, and business practices is mandated and/or regulated. For example, the FDA mandates the labeling of food products with nutritional information. This labeling ties in with other FDA programs, such as the "minimum daily requirement" and the "food pyramid" consumer education campaigns. The FDA additionally regulates the approval of pharmaceuticals as well as the communication that accompanies the drugs in terms of their claims and treatment efficacy. Of course, the legislation that drives these organizations is shaped by lobbying, offering some level of control to the company.

Nonprofit groups aim to benefit customer performance through consumer information and consumer education campaigns. Some nonprofit groups are actually industry-driven consortiums, such as the Milk Advisory Board. This organization has become famous (and quite successful) with its Got Milk? advertisements, which of course benefits the milk industry. However, many other organizations are truly independent entities and thus pride themselves on their independence and objectivity. Underwriter's Laboratories, for example, independently tests electrical devices to ensure safety and compliance with key standards. Indeed, having UL certification for a product communicates an increased level of product safety to customers. Yet independence is difficult to maintain, especially if the nonprofit organization lacks expertise. It is quite common for a nonprofit to partner with a company to produce consumer education. The nonprofit's perceived vetting of the content increases the trustworthiness of the content, yet the company has some say in shaping the message. Fleet Financial, for instance, has partnered with the National Consumers League in the past to develop consumer education programs associated with banking, credit cards, mortgages, auto loans, and other financial services and transactions.

The Consumer's Union holds the top spot in terms of independence and objectivity that is absent of influence from a company or organization. Established in 1936, the mission of Consumer's Union is to provide unbiased advice to consumers concerning goods and services, personal finance, health and nutrition, and other consumer issues. In pursuit of this mission it performs rigorous tests of all kinds of products, from washing machines to automobiles. The products it tests are not acquired directly from the manufacturer. Instead, the organization purchases products as ordinary customers do, through established consumer distribution channels. Thus the selection of products is essentially random. Through *Consumer Reports* magazine, the organization publishes the results of its tests and assigns recommendations to products that have the highest ratings. The organization's independence is topped off by the fact that these results and recommendations may not be used by a company for the promotion of the company's products.

## SIX PRINCIPLES FOR CONTROLLING THE UNCONTROLLABLE

Consistent communication is at the heart of any effective strategy that enhances customer performance. Customers must receive a consistent message regarding the behaviors that are desired through all the channels of communication that we've discussed in this chapter. However, how can a company control channels that we've described as being, to varying degrees, uncontrollable?

The key is focusing not on the uncontrollable communication channel itself, but the periphery that influences the communication channel (in other words, model the modeler). Six principles help establish the foundation for consistency and make messages emanating from uncontrollable sources more aligned with a company's interests. Figure 9.3 illustrates the hierarchical structure of the principles, which builds from the bottom to the top.

### 1. Enforce the Rule of Law

The foundation of our list is a company's obligation to its customers (and employees) to enforce the rule of law and order. A company must take

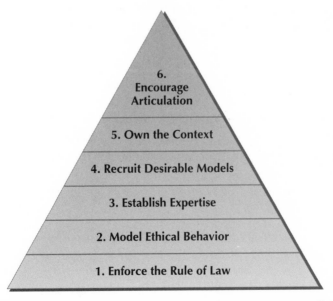

**Figure 9.3**  Hierarchy of principles for driving consistency in uncontrollable communication channels.

appropriate and visible steps to manage deviant customer and employee behavior, such as theft, fraud, disorderly conduct, or violence. For example, if customers observe employees stealing or facilitating a dishonest transaction, we would expect customers to adopt similar behaviors, especially if no punishment is forthcoming or observed. The same holds true for customers observing other customers. If a dishonest act is not stopped or punished, then over time that act will be assumed to be okay. In adopting these practices a company communicates much about its integrity and reinforces the message that transactions with the company will be fair, honest, and trustworthy.

To adopt this mindset one of the first things a company must recognize is that it ultimately controls whether it does business with a customer. In most cases a company has the right to refuse service to anyone (hospital emergency rooms, for example, don't necessarily have this option due to state laws). A company may also "fire" customers and in some cases have customers arrested if they violate criminal laws.

Airlines are pioneers in the field of enforcing the rule of law with customers. The U.S. Federal Aviation Administration (FAA) categorizes disruptive customers three ways:

**Category One.** A flight attendant requests compliance with crewmember instructions and the passenger complies with the request. No further action is required by the flight attendant, nor does it warrant a report to the cockpit, the carrier, or the FAA.

**Category Two.** A flight attendant requests a passenger to comply, but the passenger continues the disturbance, which interferes with cabin safety. This includes continuation of verbal abuse or continuing refusal to comply with federal regulations.

**Category Three.** A crew member's duties are disrupted by continuing passenger interference, or a passenger or crew member is injured or subjected to a credible threat of injury, or an unscheduled landing is made and/or restraints such as flexcuffs are used.

A category three passenger might be like a 37-year-old firefighter from Chicago. On an Aer Lingus flight from Chicago to Dublin, the man shouted abuse and sexual remarks, and punched a flight attendant. To prevent disruptions such as this, experts suggest four specific actions:

1. Make potential perpetrators aware of how the airline will respond to disruptive passengers.
2. Adopt a "zero-tolerance" policy, whereby all incidents are reported.

3. Make potential perpetrators aware of the consequences they face.

4. Implement a consistent set of measures globally.

Some airlines have adopted other solutions in addition to the ones described above. Air New Zealand, Aer Lingus, and Cathay Pacific, to name just a few, maintain lists of banned-for-life passengers. Airlines, through press releases, publish the stories of passengers who are prosecuted or banned. As for the passenger on the Aer Lingus flight, he was ultimately restrained by crew members and fellow passengers, arrested when the plane landed, fined about $1,000, and banned for life by Aer Lingus. He fared worse than Courtney Love, rock star and widow of Nirvana band leader Kurt Cobain. Ms. Love was detained by police for allegedly swearing at a Virgin Atlantic flight attendant and refusing to sit down during a flight to London. She was not arrested and subsequently had her traveling privileges restored by CEO Richard Branson, after personally apologizing to him. Needless to say, employees and unions were outraged. The message the rest of us received is that if you are famous you can do whatever you want on a Virgin Atlantic flight.[15]

## 2. Model Ethical Behavior

In those situations where the law is weak or nonexistent, ethics forms the basis for acceptable behavior. We have come to know ethics as what individuals do when no one is looking. We were taught this principle while backpacking on public land in Nevada where Native American artifacts are frequently found. One in our group found a beautiful, white arrowhead in perfect condition, last used approximately 2,000 years ago. Keeping the artifact violated federal law, yet it was so small and exquisite, just one slip into the pocket and no one would ever know. This gentleman, however, was of ethical fabric, as he secretly discarded the artifact back to the land in which he found it in such a way that he and the rest of the group to this day does not know its exact location.

If a company desires its customers to act in an ethical manner, then it should act ethically as well (and promote that fact whenever possible). Such modeling enhances trustworthiness as well as leverages the commitment and consistency of others. Imagine the message sent by Worldcom to customers when it was discovered to have defrauded investors. We're sure many customers' initial reaction was to develop their own schemes for cheating Worldcom, based on the principle of, "If they can do it, then we can do it."

We have experienced many ethical dilemmas in the companies in which we have worked and the customers we have served, and hope that our past decisions have embraced what many call "the right thing to do." One experience that comes to mind is a situation involving at the time one of Premiere Conferencing's largest customers, IBM. Premiere's teleconferencing services in some cases had over-conditioned people within IBM, to where they would use our services for the simplest of calls. It became common that when an IBM employee wanted to call another IBM employee, they would call our reservation staff and have them make the connection, mainly because it was easy for them and they didn't know we were a vendor—our staff answered the phone "IBM Conferencing." This service wasn't necessary, since the IBM employee could have called directly, for free, using IBM's internal phone system. Such calls, of course, increased our revenues and probably would have continued undetected by IBM. Yet in our minds it wasn't right. We ended up raising the issue with our contact at IBM and developed a solution to recondition IBM employees to use our services in those situations where it financially made sense. Our reputation was enhanced and could be leveraged in some cases to encourage ethical behavior on IBM's part, such as the timeliness of paying their bills.

A trend we are seeing is companies publishing (for all to see) ethical policies regarding their transactions as customer and vendor. Sybase, for example, publishes on its website a statement about its ethics and business practices. In this statement Sybase clearly lets its vendors and customers know the standards to which Sybase employees are expected to adhere. For example, the policy prohibits employees from giving or receiving gifts if such a gift in any way influences a business decision, violates any law, or might embarrass Sybase.[16]

## 3. Establish Expertise

Only after a company has addressed the issues associated with rule of law and ethics should it engage in establishing its expertise. Expertise, which reflects the knowledge and skill a company or individual possesses, has a profound effect on shaping desirable customer behavior in that experts are perceived as more trustworthy than nonexperts.

Magnetic engineering expert Thomas Potter has built a very successful business based on this principle. Tom is the founder of Reno A&E, a company that designs and manufactures magnetic automobile detection devices. These devices are used to, among many other things, detect whether automobiles are at stoplights (thus cueing the traffic signal to change appropriately). In building his business Tom has made it a point to be recognized as the engineering authority for magnetic detection. As such, he is frequently invited to give seminars and talks about the technology, its uses, and its configuration and implementation to solve novel control problems. While these talks are a key sales strategy for the company, the often generic and technical nature of the content provides customers knowledge beyond Reno A&E's products themselves, which further establishes the company's expertise. The result is a strong, positive reputation in the industry, which contributes to Reno A&E's competitive advantage.

Tom's practical experience is correlated with a study conducted with Lindora Comprehensive Weight Control, which has several weight-control clinics in the Southern California area. Through questionnaires and interviews, researchers found that expertise is a key factor for influencing client behavior. If the client perceives a health care provider is an expert, then the client is much more likely to accept the provider's instructions. Subsequent interviews with patients also suggest that provider experience plays a role as well, as illustrated in a client's comment:

> The nurses know the program inside-out; they can point to specifics in the book when offering help. They can also provide alternative suggestions when a patient doesn't like a certain food.[17]

## 4. Recruit (and Train) Desirable Models

Another interesting result found by the researchers at Lindora Comprehensive Weight Control is that if providers have more in common with the clients, specifically attitudes, then motivation and compliance increases. This finding is consistent with Bandura's thoughts on effective models, whereby attractiveness, competency, and trustworthiness are desirable attributes.

By recruiting and training desirable models, companies can have greater control over what other customers observe. Models companies should consider in this context are both employees and customers. During a recent visit to Home Depot where we used the FastLane self-checkout system, the clerk overseeing the self-checkout registers was excited, enthusiastic, and genuinely positive about the technology. She ensured we were successful, talked to us about how the system worked, and noted that she enjoyed overseeing the system because it kept her busy and she was always helping customers. She had obviously been well-trained not only on the technology, but on how to make people feel comfortable with the technology. This enthusiasm, along with our successful transaction, made us that much more enthusiastic about the system as well. Imagine if the clerk had been apathetic, slow to respond, and bad-mouthed the negative aspects of the system.

Even if the system worked for us, our trust in the system would likely be much lower.

The power of models comes from their ability to provide the social proof of acceptable behavior, thus reinforcing the consistency of other messages customers receive. One of our favorite stories about customers doing the modeling is a story about customer behavior in fast-food restaurants in the United Kingdom. When American fast food first arrived in the UK it introduced a new twist to the customer's coproduction role: clearing the table once one was finished eating. Never before were customers in the UK implicitly asked to clear their own tables, and as such most would leave their trays and wrappers on the table, requiring employees to clean up after them. Other customers would observe this incorrect behavior, and thus wouldn't clear their trays, continually reinforcing undesirable behavior. To overcome this problem McDonald's in the UK, as the story goes, hired actors to model the correct behavior for other customers. These actors, after eating a meal, would in an exaggerated fashion model the process of cleaning up after themselves for the other customers. They would noisily crumple their wrappers, collect everything on their trays, and then deposit the debris in the trash bins and place their tray on the top of the bin.[18]

## 5. Own the Context

If a company can't directly control what customers say, then the next best thing is to control where they say it. By establishing and moderating places where customers can talk, companies are in a better position to hear what customers are saying to each other and correct misconceptions or issues that may arise.

Clubs, user groups, and affinity groups have been primary strategies companies use to provide a modeling context. One of the more popular and successful has been the Harley Owner's Group (HOG), established by Harley-Davidson Motorcycles in 1983. Created to provide Harley owners a means to express their passion and pride, HOG has experienced tremendous growth, building a membership of 800,000 and a local chapter organization of over 1,100 in 20 years. These chapters, which are sponsored by local dealerships, provide localized opportunities for Harley owners to congregate and socialize. Through HOG, members enjoy a wide range of benefits, activities, and services. Members may attend monthly chapter meetings, participate in local "dinner rides," receive Harley publications, access special website features, party at special HOG Hospitality areas at motorcycle events, receive insurance and financing services, acquire travel services, even participate in affinity events, such as the ABC's of Touring contest, which encourages members to visit locations beginning with as many different letters of the alphabet as possible.[19]

## 6. Encourage Articulation

Once the context for communication is established, companies can further drive consistent communication by encouraging articulation. What this means is asking customers to express themselves in small ways, whether verbally, in writing, or through photographs, regarding positive experiences tied to a company's products, services, and business practices. For example, after a meal in a restaurant, a server might ask the dining party about their meal. When the customers respond, they are taking a stand, positive or negative. If positive, the server has just established commitment (a principle of persuasion), which increases the likelihood that the customers' word of mouth will continue to be positive. If negative, it provides the server another chance to end the meal with a positive experience, such as offering a free dessert or discounting the meal. Such a strategy can have powerful effects since customers tend to remember and recall the beginning of an experience and the end of an experience when making subjective judgments about the quality of the experience.

In the previous section we mentioned a HOG contest called the ABC's of Touring. To enter the contest members must submit a photograph of themselves standing in front of an official Harley-Davidson sign for the location, holding a copy of the latest issue of *HOG Tales*® or *Enthusiast*® magazines. In another contest, called LOH® Memories, Ladies of Harley are asked to write a one-page story that describes their favorite riding experience, along with a color photograph of them with their Harley. In both these activities, Harley encourages positive articulation by its customers, further establishing customer commitment to the brand and the products. Additionally, as judges of the contest, Harley controls the selection of winners (desirable models) to further promote a consistent message to customers in their market segment.

## SUMMARY

In this chapter we discussed how various communication channels influence customer performance. Communication channels are the conduit through which vision, access, incentive, and expertise are communicated. Yet if channels are not managed appropriately, customers can quickly learn undesirable behaviors. To ensure appropriate behaviors are modeled, companies must strive to establish consistency across the various communication channels through which customers receive messages.

The nature of communication channels naturally puts some forms of communication directly in a company's control. This is important since customers perceive communication that is highly controlled by a company to be valuable in terms of technical expertise. Products, facilities, and self-service technologies are the most tightly controlled channels due to the absence of humans in the communication process. However, as individuals become involved in communication, companies begin to lose control and inconsistent messages become more frequent.

As communication becomes less controlled by a company, customers perceive that the communication is more trustworthy in terms of subjective judgments, such as product quality and product performance. As customers become more sophisticated, they have better access to various third-party communications through such media as publications, online discussion groups, and consumer advocates. As more of the tricks associated with disreputable or manipulative marketing become known and shared, expert customers are better able to avoid being lied to. Recently some friends from Australia contacted us to announce that their daughter had won an international poetry contest and was to be honored at a special ceremony in Washington, D.C. They were excited about the honor and were planning a family trip to attend the ceremony. Even though their excitement level was high, they still did their due diligence, combing the Internet for information about the organization sponsoring the event. Their expertise and diligence paid off, as they soon discovered that these events were an alleged scam. The following week we received an email from them that linked us to a site exposing the organization's alleged fraud. On the site past participants expressed outrage when, at the event, they quickly learned that everyone attending was a winner and that promised publishers and literary agents were not in attendance.

In this age of instant communication, diligent consumers, and skeptical claims, honest companies must adopt strategies that drive greater consistency between controllable communication and uncontrollable communication. To impact uncontrollable communication, we identified six key principles that aim to "model the modelers." By enforcing the rule of law and modeling ethical behaviors, companies establish the foundation for consistency based upon principles of fairness, equity, and trustworthiness. Once these initial foundations are set, companies can then further their impact on uncontrollable channels by establishing expertise and recruiting desirable models, which are cornerstones of trust. Furthermore, by owning the context for communication and encouraging customers to articulate their feelings and beliefs toward products, services, and business practices, companies can ensure communication is more aligned with the purpose of good rather than evil.

When given a choice customers will follow the path of least resistance, even if that path has negative consequences that lessen the value for all. Through various communication channels, all customers can learn the path of least resistance. Yet expert customers recognize that acquiring greater value is as much a group effort as an individual one. To ensure that all customers have a fair and equal chance of maximizing the value embedded in goods and services, companies must consistently manage vision, access, incentive, and expertise across all communication channels. Unlike evil, good is not instantaneous. Good takes time, good takes effort, and good takes hard work.

# Chapter 10

## Embracing the Coproduction Revolution

*An ounce of action is worth a ton of theory.*

—Friedrich Engels

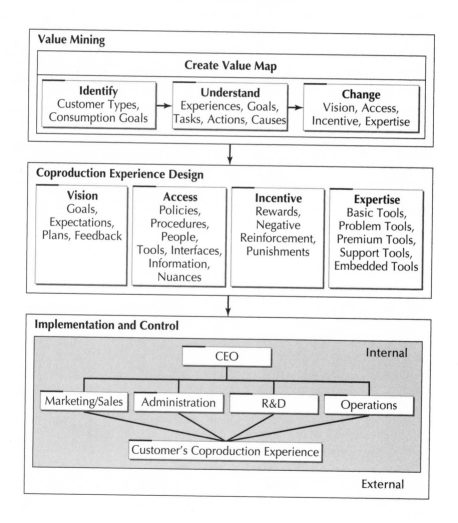

We have arranged the tools, models, stories, and insights of this book in an order that we hope has been logical, interesting, useful, entertaining, and enlightening. The adoption of the content from this book, translated into your company, is our fondest hope. In this last chapter, we reflect on what it means for companies to embrace the coproduction revolution and do-it-yourself customers. Additionally, we suggest some high-level principles for what companies can do to prepare themselves to be coproduction revolutionaries.

The belief that all companies will benefit from our ideas is a dream that we would like to one day wake up and find true. The examples, cases, and stories sprinkled throughout the book indicate that coproduction experiences are possible in virtually all kinds of businesses. Whether you sell tangible goods or provide intangible services, customers have some level of involvement in your business. How will it enhance your competitive advantage to have your customers participate in more tasks and do more work? How important is it for customers (and the company) to have better vision, access, incentive, and expertise so they can unlock more value? How must your company adapt to deliver this competitive advantage? These are just a few of the questions that you should be considering in regards to how coproduction experiences fit in your company.

So where do you go from here? Since we don't know the current state of your company and its relationship with customers, we cannot provide specific advice on what you should do first, second, third, and so on. However, what we can do is point you in the right direction by outlining eight general pieces of advice that, at one time or another during engagements, we share with our executive teams, direct reports, and clients.

- Strategic initiative, not a tactical task
- Reduce the effect of silos
- Overcome resistance from within
- By design, not by default
- Build from a baseline
- Opportunities are everywhere
- Transfer control
- Support customer sophistication

## STRATEGIC INITIATIVE, NOT A TACTICAL TASK

Coproduction experiences drive a fundamental change within a company. It is a big step to focus your company on creating experiences that involve your customers in the codesign, cocreation, and coproduction of your goods and services. As such, we firmly believe the coproduction revolution is a strategic initiative, not a tactical task.

We know through our experiences working with companies that, in fact, many companies already have adopted portions of the coproduction experience. For the most part we have discovered that the decision process in adopting various strategies was driven more by default rather than from a well thought out, long-term, strategic plan. More often than not, the tactical decisions proved to be correct. But conscious, strategic design decisions must be initiated to ensure long-term success.

Customers doing the work that traditionally was done by your employees will create a fundamental shift in the business model that you have been using. Keep in mind that in some instances there will be internal opposition to this approach. While it will be logical to agree with the strategic intent to create coproduction experiences, it will be emotionally difficult for some to comply.

Internally, your company is comfortable with the way you do business. It understands it, feels relatively safe, and has a vested interest and often a significant amount of pride in how it is satisfying customer needs. Resistance, however, comes in many forms and shapes, some covert and some overt. Often, it is centered around money.

From the perspective of a senior executive, there is risk in allocating resources to make coproduction experiences a strategic initiative. But consider this: Companies already invest a tremendous amount of time and money in training their employees. The best companies in the world tend to be the ones that invest considerably more. The investment in employee training, coupled with advertising, marketing, and public relations budgets, are interesting as points of departure to consider the investment that companies have been making in training their customers. The investment to recruit, orient, train, educate, and retain your employees has been budgeted (or should be), and is understood as important. The recruitment, orientation, training, education, and retention of your customers are most likely contained in a variety of operational budgets. The money is there. It is up to you to convince the owners of those dollars to work together to create your very own do-it-yourself customers.

The ability of any company to accomplish any goal, either strategic or tactical, is directly proportional to appropriate resource allocation. You must have the right people, the right plan, the necessary tools, an approved budget, and a time line. Most companies understand the importance of resource allocation. In an endeavor such as this it is critical that you establish a process that is not hampered by the functional organization (beware the silo). The customer experience as we have discussed crosses all the departments within your organization, so you must look at the implementation of the coproduction initiative as a cross-functional team process.

A cross-functional team with budget authority that represents all the departments that have a vested interest in creating this customer experience is the only way to ensure strategic success. The internal ownership of this type of initiative should be at the highest level possible. We encourage the CEO to be actively involved in this process.

## REDUCE THE EFFECT OF SILOS

When a company discovers disconnects within its customer experiences, it often realizes that the major problems customers have mirror the internal workings of the company. An easy way to illustrate this is the silo management structure (Figure 10.1).

In a silo structure, the customer's experience is a path through each of the departments. Disconnects occur in the white space between the silos, when the customer is physically or virtually transferred to different parts of the company (yet from the customer's perspective, he or she sees only one company, and not the individual parts). Because there is a lack of bridges, the company can unwittingly make an experience difficult when it does not have to be.

The company potholes or gaps that are frustrating to customers are almost always caused by a disconnect between the departments. For example, a sales

**Figure 10.1**  Common silos in a company and the customer's path.

promotion is sent to target customers, who then decide to come to purchase the product. At the point of purchase they discover that the product is not yet in the stores. Hence there is a disconnect between marketing and operations. In another situation, customers who receive new cell phones find that the specific steps and directions they receive to set up their phone don't work. Hence there is a disconnect between R&D's packaging design and the operations employees distributing the phones. In both cases the customer is frustrated and the company incurs the expense of responding to the customer's inability to perform, thus driving its own cost up.

The interior and intricate workings of companies will result in a series of silos being created. This creation of departments establishes certain dynamics of human performance that need to be monitored and shaped so that the coproduction experience can be as pleasurable as possible.

## OVERCOME RESISTANCE FROM WITHIN

Silos are a source of resistance from within the company. To be successful with the fundamental strategic change to a coproduction orientation within your company, you must have a well thought out plan to overcome this resistance. This plan must encompass:

- What you are going to do
- Why you are doing it
- How you are doing it
- The resources needed to do it
- The commitment and understanding of who is doing it
- A realistic time frame for when things will be done

You can break down silos by mandating a cross-functional team for not only the implementation, but also the decision making. People will have a vested interested in maintaining the status quo. This is an organizational reality. Like anything, the status quo has some good points and some bad. Therefore, ensuring that your team knows the direction you are heading and that you have a plan for mitigating resistance is an important part of your planning process.

The triggers of resistance are many. Some departments will be asked to give dollars to this initiative, thus decreasing their operating budget. Some will be decreasing their number of people for some time frame, giving up on the prestige and power that comes from having a large contingent of employees. Some may be eliminated from the organization as this process succeeds.

As a person who is committed to enhancing the coproduction experience your company offers customers, you must be strong and committed, or you will fail. The failure of this type of initiative has significant risk. Do not allow the "loyal opposition" to triumph. They must know that resistance is futile!

## BY DESIGN, NOT BY DEFAULT

A central message in this book is that successful coproduction experiences come about by design, and not by default. Our two core ideas, the Coproduction Experience Model and Coproduction Experience Process, are tools that you and your team must use to not only design coproduction experiences, but also effectively communicate with each other and the rest of the company. These tools enable you to clearly articulate the aim, purpose, and process of initiatives that bring about change to the customer's experiences.

Consistently, we find that organizations make decisions and allocate inadequate resources, spending too little time planning or looking at issues from a multidimensional view. For example, the CEO might only consult marketing and sales to design a promotional strategy, but forget to include other portions of the organization: finance, technology, customer service, and so on. This, of course, is one of the artifacts of silos.

*By design* means that leaders of the coproduction revolution must take a multidimensional view of the company. This involves establishing cross-functional work teams internal to the organization, and integrating customer information and experiences into the design process. Furthermore, these cross-functional teams must truly understand the customer experience. It is our opinion that many company executives don't have a clue what it is like to be a customer of their own company. They have a belief that they understand what the customer goes through, but it is more often wrong than right.

In by design decision making, executives realize that they have an obligation to clearly define what needs to be done internal to the company. They must be able to articulate why the coproduction experiences initiative needs to be done in the company. They need to have a strong tactical plan on how they are going to execute, as well as having the appropriate resources ready (people, time, and money). This tactical plan also includes specifications for who is doing what and the schedule for implementation.

## BUILD FROM A BASELINE

You should know by now that your company already has numerous coproduction experiences in place. Understanding where you are is the first step in deciding how you will get to where you want to be. It is an important first step. As we have discussed, you must be sure that you have truly discovered where your company is and what your customers are experiencing.

Aside from your own baselines, competitors offer parallel baselines that drive the design of enhanced coproduction experiences as part of competitive differentiation. For example, McDonald's became an industry leader by using the Henry Ford model of hamburger making: you get it the way we make it. Customers were involved in very little besides selecting what they wanted from the menu. This is a baseline. When Burger King came on the scene, they exploited this limited coproduction experience into a point of differentiation. They offered customization of the product, enabling customers to "have it your way."

Customer abilities are, in some regards, a baseline. However, the abilities of your customer are changing. Technology, alternative distribution models, enhanced expectations, and greater expertise are putting you and your company into a *must do something* scenario. We know that by understanding and utilizing our tools and methods, you can and will be successful at designing and implementing coproduction experiences.

As you discover what your baseline coproduction experiences are, you will have a lens or a viewpoint as to how to better service, prepare, train, and condition your customer. Remember that the customer wants to be able to do business with your organization in the most effective manner possible. They do not want to be frustrated and they want to be successful.

## OPPORTUNITIES ARE EVERYWHERE

So how do you spot opportunities for enhanced coproduction experiences? The touchpoints that we discussed in Chapter 6 are important starting points as you begin the process of assessment. Your organization has spent years building these touchpoints (and will build more in the future). It is your job to travel these touchpoints as your customers do, looking through the same lens that they have. What's it like to prepare your products for use? How do customers react to the signage and cues in a service environment? How do customers respond to your employees? And most importantly, how much effort must customers exert to achieve their goals? In other words, how easy are you to do business with?

As you investigate these touchpoints, think about the different roles do-it-yourself customers may play in a coproduction experience. When people hear the words "do-it-yourself," they tend to think about one or two types of customers (the first two in the list below). However, do-it-yourself customers come in five different flavors. Look at your touchpoints through the eyes of as many of these do-it-yourself customers as you can:

1. **Transactionals** are those who like to perform everyday transactions themselves. They use self checkout at the grocery store, eat at the buffet, and book travel online.

2. **Traditionals** are what we typically think of as do-it yourselfers in terms of home improvement, gardening, financial management, auto repair, and so on. These are the people who frequent Home Depot, Smith & Hawken, Charles Schwab, and Kragen Auto Parts.

3. **Conventionals** acquire tangible self-contained products that are enablers for doing things themselves. For example, a Viking stove facilitates the do-it-yourself task of gourmet cooking. A snowblower enables one to clear the snow from the driveway.

4. **Intentionals** engage in do-it-yourself experiences to customize goods and services to their specification. Think Build-A-Bear® Workshops and Nike iD.com online design center.

5. **Radicals** take do-it-yourself to new extremes. Like the gentleman who re-wrote the operating system for his Lego® Mindstorms robot.

Even if you think the touchpoints you have are simple, they can always be improved. One of our clients distributes a line of nutritional supplements through health care professionals. This company had a seemingly simple, five-step process that customers needed to navigate before the company allowed customers to buy products. As we watched our client navigate through their own process, it was immediately obvious that the process had a high PITA score. In discussions with the team responsible for this process, we discovered that the process evolved from the need to "qualify" serious customers (resellers) and eliminate end users from buying products directly from the company.

The experience of our client playing "transactional customer" lit a light bulb of inspiration—the process needed to be streamlined! Ninety days later, our client unveiled the new process. The results were immediate. Revenues increased over 25 percent in the year following the change. Spurred by this success, the company continued with a complete review of every customer touchpoint. Each touchpoint was evaluated and assigned a nuisance score. It became an initiative to make every touchpoint an easier process for all types of customer roles. The company soon discovered that most of the hoops customers needed to jump through had been established to gain control of the process, which was an admirable intention. However, over time these operations-driven decisions had a devastating effect on the customer experience.

What are you doing? Why are you doing it? How are you doing it? Who is doing it? When is it done? These are the essentials in understanding at each touchpoint the nature of the customer experience. The frequent reality is that design expectations are not met with actual performance. This is caused most often by the fact that many of your customer touchpoints were created to support some internal control function. Accounting needed it, or marketing wanted it, or the first manager just plain did it that way the first time (which is why everyone in the company does it that way now). "That's the way we do it here," is a common response to our queries (to which we always retort, "Why?"). As you assess the customer suggestion box or actually talk with customers about how they accomplish tasks with your company, patterns emerge, processes unfold, and inconsistencies are discovered.

When you look at your customer touchpoints as they do, you may realize that your original idea has not become the reality for your customers. Keep in mind that what you are now doing is trying to determine ways that can enable your customers to do more and have a better experience with your company.

## TRANSFER CONTROL

The decision to transfer some portion of the process to the customer creates a bit of trepidation in most companies. Customers will also experience some trepidation as they learn new skills necessary for working with your company. We often see companies that assume a much higher level of customer sophistication. This can lead to performance gaps. Don't ask your customers to do too much all at once. Shape their behavior over time. Enable them to be successful in the very first experience. You only have one chance to make a good first impression.

You can speed the process of transferring control by leveraging crossover skills (these are skills learned in one context—ATMs—transferring to other contexts—self-checkout). If this is possible in your context, it will help guide you in the amount of work you can shift to customers. For example, many stores provide self-checkout lines—which are building customer skills as we speak. If you are going to implement a similar coproduction process, don't assume that it will work out of the box. Be aware that your context will have its own unique quirks and issues that others will not. Make sure you thoroughly test the process with pilot groups. Track their progress from first time usage to mastery. Determine if you can make the process more effective. Understand that a learning curve exists on both sides of the equation. Be patient and attentive.

Throughout all of this, don't lose sight of your employees. There is an emphasis on the company's part to make the process as painless and as frustration free as possible for the customer. We applaud those efforts. Yet be careful not to forget to put the same effort to benefit the employees. They are the ones who provide the last line of support in making the coproduction experience really work.

Now that customers have taken control of a part of the process, you can begin to expand. What else do they want to do? What more do you want them to learn and control? In a doctor's office it is very commonplace to witness patients filling out forms for the doctor's internal database—a simple coproduction experience. When the form is complete, a receptionist then enters this same information into the computer. Two people are doing the same process, one external and one internal. Would it not be reasonable to provide computers in the waiting room where new patients can enter their own information and save it to the doctor's patient database?

Of course, this enhancement of the coproduction experience might be only a short-term solution. The task could shift even more into the customers' domain, in which they fill out the forms online before even showing up at the doctor's office. Or perhaps the need for this manual data entry task will disappear. Patients might adopt a special card that contains their medical history. Upon arrival at the clinic, they swipe the card and the information is transferred to the doctor's database.

Finding the right tasks and designing the right experiences to ensure customer success is a guaranteed way to not only create customer lifetime value, but attract even more customers.

## SUPPORT CUSTOMER SOPHISTICATION

The evolution of the do-it-yourself customer is becoming a revolution. As companies realize the many benefits of codesign, cocreation, and coproduction as viable, long-term equity builders, the transference of tasks to the customer will become more widespread.

The sophisticated customer of today will become the standard for the rest of the customers that do business with you in the future. We are confident that the coproduction revolution is grounded in the reality that your customers want to save time, understand technology, have greater control, and personalize products to their own unique situations. Loyalty will be won by those companies, organizations, and institutions that have a good quality product with a low PITA score. Being easier to do business with is a competitive advantage you must enhance as your company moves into its next phase of growth.

The integration of technology as a competitive advantage is a foregone conclusion. Our early examples of pay-at-the-pump gas stations, self-service checkouts, ATMs, and online services are guideposts for what we believe the future will hold. Yet there are many initiatives that you can undertake to increase customer involvement that are not based on technology. They include the improvement of processes that already exist in your company such that you can transfer tasks embedded in those processes to your customers. For example, grocery stores already had a checkout system. The only difference in the new paradigm is that the customer (who has been observing the checkout process on each visit to the store for years) is now the labor component of the equation. In this shift of work, one cashier now handles four checkout locations. This is an obvious ROI that any accounting curmudgeon can get their calculators around.

Today, we are conditioning the customers of tomorrow to be more self-sufficient, self-reliant, and technically savvy. Fortunately, we are also serving the previous generations' understanding of customer service and their expectations of the experience.

The older generation uses web-based services to get a portion of the information necessary to accomplish certain goals that they have: shopping ideas, health care issues, driving directions, email, and a small number of other items. However, when they have a serious issue, they pick up the phone and call. That is how they have been trained.

The younger generation is more adept at using web-based technologies to solve issues independently. Some companies, such as NameSecure, have already transitioned to web-based service in total, not even including a telephone number on their website. These actions frustrate the older generation, while perhaps endearing themselves to the next generation.

Customer service solutions for the next generation of customers will undoubtedly be more dependent on very sophisticated customers. These types of customers will drive companies to a coproduction model if they want to serve this next generation. So what can you do to support this sophistication? Consider the following.

## Honor the Customer's Time

If you are going to get customers to do something, make sure you honor their time. A simple example illustrates this. An innovation in customer service via the telephone is to have customers enter their account number, four digits of their Social Security number, or other relevant and "important" data that the service person will need to process the transaction. Of course, of the 20 or so companies that we called, 85 percent had no tie between the phone system and the customer service rep's computer, so all the information that you painstakingly provided is not utilized and you get to do it again. If you need to be transferred you will continue to repeat this process with each new person you speak with. This process does not honor the time of the customer and only serves to escalate the dissatisfaction with your organization. And, no, the customer should not be expected to understand the lack of integration between your internal departments.

## Honor the Customer's Commitment

The customer who complains about poor service, policies, or technological failures often is looked upon as a pariah. Sometimes these customers are just disgruntled, never-able-to-please people, but in our experience these kinds of people are few and far between. Most often we find that customers have a vested interest in the improvement of your organization to deal with the problem they have brought to your attention. They could have left and done business somewhere else. The customer is trying (albeit sometimes not very effectively) to be a coproducer in solving an issue. Listen to them and when appropriate make a change to improve the overall process.

We will caution you that there are always exceptions to every rule. We believe that you should establish an exception process to handle these and not try to recreate a working, effective process to handle the exceptions.

## Increase the Customer's Satisfaction

The lifetime value of customers varies from industry to industry and from organization to organization. What does not change is the customer's expectation of having a satisfying experience. You may argue that when going to the dentist no one has any expectation of a satisfying experience; just a less painful one. We might have agreed with this perception years ago, but today even the dentist has to be focused on coproduction experiences. The point of fact is that the customer takes an active role in the prevention of tooth decay by brushing every day, flossing, using mouthwash, and eating the right foods.

Satisfaction from the view of the customer is an important incentive in our model. The customer being asked or trained or expected to do more work becomes even more intent on having a satisfying experience. When using the self-checkout system at a local grocer, we observed that experienced customers had higher expectations of speed, convenience, and control.

Providing the correct instruction, knowledge, and tools to ensure that the customer can do what is expected is critical to the success of creating the co-production experience. If you expect to increase customer satisfaction, it is of paramount importance to ensure that incentives you are using are the right ones. Remember, customers are learning a new behavior and will adapt at a speed of their choosing, not yours.

When an airline put in place incentives to attract customers to its website reservation system, they had expected an immediate reduction in the number of telephone representatives. They ran television and radio ads touting their online prowess and the wonderful rewards that you would receive. After a 30-day time frame, the executives sat down to determine the success of the campaign and were disappointed to learn that they had to hire additional telephone representatives. The numbers also showed a huge increase in numbers of online visits and reservations done via the Internet.

A more detailed review also showed that two additional variables needed to be included in their assessment. The first was the abandonment rate on the website by customers prior to confirming the reservation. The second was that almost 30 percent of all the telephone calls received were to answer questions regarding frustrating online experiences (read complaints) of how to make a reservation. Could the employees answer the questions or provide help? You guessed it. No training or instructions were given to company customer service reps on how to make an online reservation. This is yet another example of a disconnect in the customer experience.

For some, time is an important value. For others, it is control or hands-on service. Regardless of individual needs and desires, your organization must be able to respond with the best coproduction experience. Is it your responsibility to create this? You bet it is and it is your responsibility to consistently create this experience so that your customer will trust you.

## FINAL THOUGHTS

The pleasure that a customer receives from your goods and services is directly proportional to the expected lifetime value that you will receive from that customer. Investing in the customer experience includes a calculation to determine the return on investment. In reality, the company that is able to transfer work to the customer, reducing its cost and increasing customer satisfaction with the experience, is in a good position to grow. Those companies that are either unwilling or unable to increase the customers' commitment are in for a rude awakening.

The customer of today is smarter, more technology savvy, and better prepared to be a part of the process. There will always be business models and customers that want the company to do all the work, of course, but we believe that these companies will mostly be in the high-end service sector.

As an executive within an organization that is looking at the implementation of initiatives to transfer work to the customers, it is imperative that you keep your employees focused on the correct initiative. However, please keep in mind that this is still delegation, not abdication. The difference is important to keep in mind. For example, many companies have perfected the *go get 'em, tiger* approach to training. They hire individuals, do the appropriate legal paperwork to get them in the system, then pat them on the back (or push them) with the direction of *go get 'em, tiger*, hoping that through the ever popular Darwinian method of training, a few good employees develop. Otherwise, they have to hire again and go through the whole PITA paperwork process again and again.

While this may have some humor, in reality many companies adopt the *go get 'em, tiger* approach to customer retention strategies. The mentality is, "We got you to buy the product, now *go get 'em, tiger* and perform." This all occurs with little to no real knowledge of the difficulties that customers have. In one instance, we discovered a company that tracked all the 800-number customer support calls that came in, dually noted the causes of the problem, and then made hiring decisions based on the call volume and type of call. No information ever made it to the product manager to address the customer issues and prevent them. The statistics were used to justify increases in that operational budget (silo) and not to improve the customer experience.

Organizational structures often create customer issues that need not exist. As the salesperson promises, the accounting department denies, and the operations people get to do the work twice, customers look on with wonder— the wonder of why they ever thought of doing business with you in the first place.

You, as the champion for your customers, can avoid these pitfalls and succeed. The key things to remember are to identify the issues, understand the causal effects, and then improve the process. By using the Coproduction Experience Model of vision, access, incentive, and expertise, you will have the initial framework to bring your company up to speed, involve the right departments and executives, and ultimately free up budget dollars to execute initiatives that improve your company's coproduction experiences.

# NOTES

## Preface

1. Temkin, Bruce D. (2005), Self-Service Shift Requires Improved Usability, January 13, Source: Forrester Research, Inc., http://www.forrester.com/Research/Document/Excerpt/0,7211,36253,00.html. Accessed February 3, 2005.

2. See Day, George S., John Deighton, Das Narayandas, Evert Gummesson, Shelby D. Hunt, C. K. Prahalad, Roland T. Rust and Steven M. Shugan (2004), "Invited Commentaries on 'Evolving to a New Dominant Logic for Marketing,'" *Journal of Marketing*, 68(January), 18–27; Heskett, James L., W. Earl Sasser and Leonard A. Schlessinger (2003), *The Value-Profit Chain: Treat Employees Like Customers and Customers Like Employees*, New York: Free Press; Prahalad, C. K. and Venkatram Ramaswamy (2000), "Co-opting Customer Competence," *Harvard Business Review*, 78(January), 79–90; Vargo, Stephen L. and Robert F. Lusch (2004), "Evolving to a New Dominant Logic for Marketing," *Journal of Marketing*, 68(January), 1–17; Zeithaml, Valarie A., Mary Jo Bitner and Dwayne D. Gremler (2006). *Services Marketing: Integrating Customer Focus Across the Firm*, 4th Edition. New York: McGraw-Hill.

## Chapter 1

1. Prahalad, C. K. (2004), "The Cocreation of Value," *Journal of Marketing*, 68(1), 23.

2. Schlosser, Julie (2004), "Cashing In on the New World of Me," *Fortune*, December 13, 244–250.

3. See Kiviat, Barbara (2004), "May I Help You?" *Time*, September 6, 164(10); Speer, Jack (2005), "A Former CEO Glimpses Airlines' Future," NPR Morning Edition 02/03/05, http://www.npr.org/templates/story/story.php?storyId=4475981. Accessed February 3, 2005.

4. Alpert, Andrew and Jill Auyer (2004), "The 1988–2000 Employment Projections: How Accurate Were They?" Washington, D.C.: Office of Occupational Statistics and Employment Projections, Bureau of Labor Statistics.

5. Bureau of Transportation Statistics (2004), "Pocket Guide to Transportation," January, Washington, D.C.

6. Bateson, J. E. G. (1985), "Self Service Consumer: An Exploratory Study," *Journal of Retailing*, 61(Fall), 49–76.

7. Boone, Christopher and Kelly A. Matthews (2003), "Self Check-out Systems: Defining Retailers as Leaders of the Pack," IDC Whitepaper commissioned by NCR Corporation, June.

8. See Kontzer, Tony (2004), "Verizon Bets on Self Service," *Information Week*, January 28, 49; myKB (2002), "ROI of Self Service," http://knowledgebase.mykb.com/Article_1B19F.aspx. Accessed February 5, 2005; Rayport, Jeffrey R. and

Bernard J. Jaworski, "Best Face Forward," *Harvard Business Review*, 82(December), 47–58; Rich, Laura (2004), "Self Service: Help Yourself," CIO Insight. http://www.cioinsight.com/article2/0,1397,1610171,00.asp. Accessed February 5, 2005.

9. Rich, Laura (2004), "Self Service: Help Yourself," CIO Insight, http://www. cioinsight.com/article2/0,1397,1610171,00.asp. Accessed February 5, 2005.

10. Davis, Bob (1983), "Hundreds of Coleco's Adams Are Returned as Defective: Firm Blames User Manuals," *The Wall Street Journal*, November 20, 4.

11. Majmudar, Nishad H. (2004), "Defibrillator Training Proves Useful," *The Wall Street Journal*, Thursday, August 12, D3.

12. Hansen, U. and T. Hennig (1996), "Wie competent sind Ihre Kunden? [How competent are your customers?]," *absatzwirtschaft*, 39(October, special issue), 160–166.

13. See Bowen, David E. (1986), "Managing Customers as Human Resources in Service Organizations," *Human Resource Management,* 25(3), 371–383; Bowers, Michael R., Charles L. Martin and Alan Luker (1990), "Trading Places: Employees as Customers, Customers as Employees," *Journal of Services Marketing*, 4(Spring), 55–69; Mills, Peter, K. and J. H. Morris (1986), "Clients as 'Partial' Employees: Role Development in Client Participation," *Academy of Management Review*, 11(4), 726–735.

14. McWilliams, Gary (2004), "Analyzing Customers, Best Buy Decides Not All Are Welcome," *The Wall Street Journal*, November 8, A1, A8.

## Chapter 2

1. Jewell, Mark (2005), "Dunkin' Donuts Evolves From No-Frills to Espresso and WiFi," *Reno Gazette Journal*, February 6, 3E–4E.

## Chapter 3

1. See Bell-Gredler, Margaret E. (1986), *Learning and Instruction: Theory into Practice,* New York: Macmillan; Nord, Walter R. and J. Paul Peter (1980), "A Behavior Modification Perspective on Marketing," *Journal of Marketing*, 44(Spring), 36–47; Peter, J. Paul and Walter R. Nord (1982), "A Clarification and Extension of Operant Conditioning Principles in Marketing," *Journal of Marketing*, 46(Summer), 102–107; Rothschild, Michael L. and William C. Gadis (1981), "Behavioral Learning Theory: Its Relevance to Marketing and Promotions," *Journal of Marketing*, 45(Spring), 70–78.

2. Bandura, Albert (1977), *Social Learning Theory,* Englewood Cliffs, NJ: Prentice-Hall.

3. Bloom, Benjamin, et al. (1956), *Taxonomy of Educational Objectives, Book 1: Cognitive Domain,* New York: Longman.

4. Gagne, Robert M. (1985), *The Conditions of Learning,* Chicago: Holt/Rinehart/Winston.

5. Cialdini, Robert B. (1993), *Influence: The Psychology of Persuasion,* New York: Quill.

6. Gilbert, Thomas F. (1996), *Human Competence: Engineering Worthy Performance,* Washington, D.C.: International Society for Performance Improvement.

7. Norman, Donald A. (1988), *The Psychology of Everyday Things,* New York: Basic Books.

8. Bettman, James R. (1979), *An Information Processing Theory of Consumer Choice,* Reading, MA: Addison-Wesley.

9. Van Houwelinger, Jeannet H. and W. Fred Van Raaij (1989), "The Effect of Goal Setting and Daily Electronic Feedback on In-Home Energy Use," *Journal of Consumer Research,* 16(June), 98–105.

10. Meuter, Matthew L., Amy L. Ostrom, Robert I. Roundtree and Mary Jo Bitner (2000), "Self-Service Technologies: Understanding Customer Satisfaction with Technology-Based Service Encounters," *Journal of Marketing,* 64(July), 50–64.

11. Mavis, Brian E. and Bertram E. Stoffelmayr (1994), "Multidimensional evaluation of monetary incentive strategies for weight control," *Psychological Record,* 44(Spring), 239–252.

12. Mittal, Vikas and Mohanbir S. Sawhney (2001), "Learning and Using Electronic Information Products and Services: A Field Study," *Journal of Interactive Marketing,* 15(1), 2–12.

## Chapter 4

1. Johnson, Robert (2004), "Towards a Better Understanding of Service Excellence," *Managing Service Quality,* 14(2/3), 129–133.

2. See Ross, Gary (2004), "CDW Announces IDC White Paper Offering Best Practices for I.T. Purchasing Decisions," *PR Newswire,* February 25; Neder, Maria (2003), "Tyco Electronics Names Arrow Electronics Distributor of the Year," *PR Newswire,* 2003; CUNA (2003), "Discovery Conference emphasizes CU opportunities & partnerships," *Credit Union Magazine,* 69(8), 57–58.

3. See Warren, Audrey (2004), "Frequent Flyers Line Up To Bypass Extra Searches," *The Wall Street Journal,* July 21, D9; Reed Baker, Matthew (2004), "Welcome to the Fast Track," *Forbes,* 173(FYI Spring), 66–67.

4. Bell, Chip and Ron Zemke (1992), *Managing Knock Your Socks Off Service,* New York: Amacom.

5. Wood, Robert E. (1986), "Task Complexity: Definition of the Construct," *Organizational Behavior and Human Decision Processes,* 37(1), 60–82.

6. IBM Corporation (2004), User Engineering: Measures, http://www 306.ibm.com/ibm/easy/eou_ext.nsf/publish/2023. Accessed August 10, 2004.

7. See Zaltman, Gerald (2003). How Customers Think. Cambridge, MA: Harvard Business School Press; Useem, Jerry (2004), "Gerald Zaltman Can Read Your Mind," *Fortune,* January 20, http://www.fortune.com/fortune/subs/article/ 0,15114,405574,00.html. Accessed August 10, 2004; Schlosser, Julie (2005), "Scanning for Dollars," *Fortune,* January 10, 151(1).

8. Ellison, Sarah and Eric Bellman (2005), "Clean Water, No Profit," *The Wall Street Journal,* February 23, B1–B2.

9. Reichheld, Frederick F. (2003), "The One Number You Need To Grow," *Harvard Business Review,* 18(December), 46–54.

## Chapter 5

1. Bandura, Albert and Daniel Cervone (1983), "Self-Evaluative and Self-Efficacy Mechanisms Governing the Motivational Effects of Goal Systems," *Journal of Personality and Social Psychology*, 45(5), 1017–1028.

2. Spiegelman, Rande (2004), "How Much Should You Save For Retirement? Play The Percentages," Charles Schwab & Co., Inc., http://www.schwab.com/SchwabNOW/navigation/mainFrameSet/0,4528,866,00.html?dest=siretirement&orig=retirement&ebmk=acquisition. Accessed August 23, 2004.

3. Mikkelson, Barbara and David P. Mikkelson (2002), "Alka-Seltzer dramatically" increased their sales by instructing consumers to use two tablets instead of one, http://www.snopes.com/business/genius/alka-seltzer.asp. Accessed August 23, 2004.

4. See Zeithaml, Valarie A., Leonard L. Berry and A. Parasuraman (1991), "Understanding Customer Expectations of Service," *Sloan Business Review*, 32(Spring), 39–49; Zeithaml, Valarie A., Leonard L. Berry and A. Parasuraman (1993), "The Nature and Determinants of Customer Expectations of Service," *Journal of the Academy of Marketing Science*, 21(1), 1–12; Santos, Jessica and Jonathan Boote (2003), "A Theoretical Exploration and Model of Consumer Expectations, Post-Purchase Affective States, and Affective Behavior," *Journal of Consumer Behavior*, 3(2), 142–156.

5. Fidelity Investments (2004), "Retirement Planning Tools," http://personal.fidelity.com/planning/retirement/retiree/content/triageContent.shtml.cvsr. Accessed August 24, 2004.

6. OnStar Corporation (2004), "What is OnStar?" http://www.onstar.com/us_english/jsp/whatisonstar/idont_whatisonstar.jsp. Accessed August 25, 2004.

7. This section is derived from the work of Miller, George A., Eugene Galanter and Karl H. Pribram (1986), *Plans and the Structure of Behavior*, New York: Adams-Bannister-Cox.

8. Nielsen, Jakob (1993), *Usability Engineering*, San Francisco: Morgan-Kaufman.

## Chapter 6

1. See Greenberg, Paul A. (2001), "Nasty Return Policies Damage E-Shopper Relationships," *TechNewsWorld*, April 24, http://www.technewsworld.com/story/9179.html. Accessed September 9, 2004; Gap, Inc. (2004), Returns and Exchanges, http://www.gap.com/asp/cs_returns_ex.asp?wdid=0. Accessed September 9, 2004; Fry's Electronics, Inc. (2004), Returns, http://shop1.outpost.com/template/help/index/FE30/Service3/Assistance/Left_Topics/A6ReturningPurchases/#08. Accessed September 9, 2004.

2. Mager, Robert F. and Peter Pipe (1984), *Analyzing Performance Problems*, Belmont, CA: Lake Publishing.

3. Macromedia, Inc. (2005), "Macromedia Customer Participation Program," http://www.macromedia.com/macromedia/usability/. Accessed February 24, 2005; People Track, Inc. (2005), "Customer Participation," http://www.people-trak.com/pt/services/index.cfm?fuseaction=participation. Accessed February 24, 2005.

4. Nadler, Paul (2002), "Using the phone to tweak your overdraft policy," *American Banker*, 167(198), 7.

5. Sander, Ernest (2004), "The 'Soup Nazi' Expands," *The Wall Street Journal*, September 10, B1, B3.

6. Nussbaum, Bruce (2004), "The Power of Design," *Business Week*, May 17, 96.

7. Mage, Gene C. (2003), "Seal Up Seams in Service Delivery," *Health Care Registration: The Newsletter for Health Care Registration Professionals*, 13(Dec), 1–5.

8. Lunsford, J. Lynn (2004), "No Movie, No Frequent Flyer Plan—And No Gravity, Either," *The Wall Street Journal*, September 14, B1, B8.

9. U.S. Small Business Administration (2002), ADA Guide for Small Business, http://www.usdoj.gov/crt/ada/smbustxt.htm. Accessed September 14, 2004.

10. Florian, Ellen, Doris Burke and Jenney Mero (2004), "The Money Machines," *Fortune*, July 26, 150(2), 100–105.

11. Kiviat, Barbara (2004), "May You Help You?" *Time*, September 6, 164(10), 101.

12. IDEO, Inc. (2003), "Customer-driven Service for McDonalds," http://www.ideo.com/portfolio/re.asp?x=50175. Accessed September 14, 2004.

13. All, Ann (2001), "Getting Along on ADA?" ATM Marketplace.com, http://www.atmmarketplace.com/news_story.htm?i=10412. Accessed September 14, 2004.

14. Ramstad, Evan (2004), "Hong Kong's Electronic-Money Card Is a Hit," *The Wall Street Journal*, February 19, B3.

15. Bulkeley, William M. (2004), "Cash, Credit—or Prints?" *The Wall Street Journal*. October 10, B1, B4.

16. Norman, Donald A. (no date), "Interaction Design for Automobile Interiors." http://www.jnd.org/dn.mss/InteractDsgnAutos.html. Accessed September 15, 2004.

17. Nussbaum, Bruce (2004), "The Best Product Designs of the Year," *BusinessWeek*, July 5, http://www.businessweek.com/magazine/content/04_27/b3890601.htm. Accessed September 15, 2004.

18. Fleming, Malcolm and W. Howard Levie (1978), *Instructional Message Design*, Englewood Cliffs, NJ: Educational Technology Publications.

19. Gobé, Marc (2001), *Emotional Branding*, New York: Allworth Press.

20. See Martin, G. Neal (1999), "Smell: Can We Use It to Manipulate Behavior," Lecture Notes. http://www.mdx.ac.uk/www/psychology/staff/nmartin/rsa/rsa.html. Accessed September 17, 2004; Naik, Gautam (2004), "The Smell of Success Isn't Always Sweet for Paul Knight," *The Wall Street Journal*, October 11, A1, A15.

**Chapter 7**

1. Silverman, Steve (no date), "The Pudding Guy," *Useless Information*, http://home.nycap.rr.com/useless/pudding/. Accessed November 15, 2004.

2. Saranow, Jennifer (2004), "Check It Out: Incentives to Pay Bills Online," *The Wall Street Journal*, December 8, D2.

3. Cambell, Anne (2004), "Teens Kicked Off Paradise for Smoking," *CruiseMates*, http://www.cruisemates.com/articles/humop/smoking.cfm. Accessed November 16, 2004.

4. CruiseReports (2003), "Up In Smoke," *CruiseLog November 2003*, http://www.cruise-reports.com/DailyLog/NewsArchive/November2003/DailyLog.htm. Accessed November 16, 2004.

5. Fram, Eugene H. and Michael S. McCarthy (1999), "The True Price of Penalties," *Marketing Management*, Fall, 49–56.

6. Saranow, Jennifer (2004), "The Puncture Wound I Got for Christmas; Theft Prevention Behind Rise in Hard-to-Open Packaging; World's Worst Paper Cut," *The Wall Street Journal*, December 30, D1.

7. Swinyard, William R. (2003), "The Effect of Salesperson Mood, Shopper Behavior and Store Type on Customer Service," *Journal of Retailing and Consumer Services*, 10(2003), 323–333.

8. Machalaba, Daniel (2003), "Trucker Rewards Customers for Good Behavior," *The Wall Street Journal*, September 9, B4.

9. Dowling, Grahame R. and Mark Uncles (1997), "Do Loyalty Programs Really Work?" *Sloan Management Review*, Summer, 71–82.

10. Abu-Shalback Zid, Linda (2004), "Loyalty Doesn't Always Pay," *Marketing Management*, 13(May/June), 4.

11. Fram, Eugene H. and Michael S. McCarthy (1999), "The True Price of Penalties," *Marketing Management*, Fall, 49–56.

12. Woo, Ka-shing and Henry K.Y. Fock (2004), "Retaining and Divesting Customers: An Exploratory Study of Right Customers, 'At Risk' Right Customers, and Wrong Customers," *Journal of Services Marketing*, 18(3), 187–197.

13. Ibid.

## Chapter 8

1. Alba, Joseph W. and J. Wesley Hutchinson (1987), "Dimensions of Consumer Expertise," *Journal of Consumer Research*, 13(March), 411–454.

2. Mittal, Vikas and Mohanbir S. Sawhney (2001), "Learning and Using Electronic Information Products and Services: A Field Study," *Journal of Interactive Marketing*, 15(Winter), 2–12. Graphic © 2001 *Journal of Interactive Marketing*. Reprinted with permission of John Wiley & Sons, Inc.

3. Hennig-Thurau, Thorsten, Peter C. Honebein and Benoit Aubert (2005), "Unlocking Product Value Through Customer Education," *American Marketing Association Winter 2005 Educator's Conference*.

4. Johnson, Eric J., Steven Bellman and Gerald S. Lohse (2003), "Cognitive Lock-in and the Power Law of Practice," *Journal of Marketing*, 67(April), 62–75.

5. Build-A-Bear Workshops, Inc., http://www.buildabear.com. Accessed January 15, 2005.

6. Corporate University Xchange (2001), *Creating Smarter Customers*, New York: Corporate University Xchange.

7. Honebein, Peter C. (1997), *Strategies for Effective Customer Education*, Chicago: NTC Books.

8. Hewlett Packard (2005), "Available Certifications," http://h10017.www1.hp.com/certification/americas/avail_certifications.html. Accessed February 24, 2005.

9. Roush, Chris (1999), *Inside Home Depot: How One Company Revolutionized an Industry Through the Relentless Pursuit of Growth*, New York: McGraw-Hill Professional.

10. Wood, Robert E. (1986), "Task Complexity: Definition of the Construct," *Organizational Behavior and Human Decision Processes*, 37(1), 60–82.

11. Honebein, Peter C. (2004), "Should Products Be Complex?" *American Marketing Association Winter 2004 Educator's Conference Proceedings*, 15(1), 321.

12. Burton, Dawn (2002), "Consumer Education and Service Quality: Conceptual Issues and Practical Implications," *Journal of Services Marketing*, 16(2), 125–142.

13. Hennig-Thurau, Thorsten (2000), "Relationship Quality and Customer Retention Through Strategic Communication of Customer Skills," *Journal of Marketing Management*, 16, 55–79.

14. Personal interview with Steve Hufford, Executive Vice President of Sales and Business Development, Proficient Systems, Inc., March 18, 2005; see also www.proficient.com.

15. Saranow, Jennifer (2004), "Show, Don't Tell," *The Wall Street Journal*, March 22, R9.

## Chapter 9

1. Herriott, Scott R. (1997), "Communication Channels in Markets: A Definition and Conceptualization," *Journal of Marketing Communications*, 3, 139–149.

2. Khemsurov, Monica (2004), "Sexing Up Victoria's Secret," *CNN Money*, http://money.cnn.com/2004/04/08/technology/business2_victoria/. Accessed July 14, 2004.

3. Donnelly, Jr., Jim (1999), "Beware of Negative Customer Expectations," *Bank Marketing*, 31(August), 60.

4. Morton's Restaurant Group (2004). Frequent Questions, http://www.mortons.com/website/index.html. Accessed July 12, 2004.

5. Parasuraman, A., Leonard L. Berry and Valarie A. Zeithaml (1991), "Refinement and Reassessment of the SERVQUAL Scale," *Journal of Retailing*, 67(Winter), 420–450.

6. Stringer, Kortney (2004), "If At First You Do Succeed..." *The Wall Street Journal*, July 12, R4.

7. See CNN/Money (2004), "Stewart Convicted On All Charges," *CNN/Money*, http://money.cnn.com/2004/03/05/news/companies/martha_verdict/. Accessed July 14, 2004; also, http://www.marthatalks.com/

8. Maher, Kris (2004), "The Jungle: Focus On Recruitment, Pay and Getting Ahead," *The Wall Street Journal*, July 13, B6.

9. Wasserman, Todd (2003), "Dell Warns Shoppers away from Retailers," *Adweek*, 44(46), 8.

10. Staff (1994), "Why Comparisons Work," *Adweek Western Edition*, 44(7).

11. Ortego, Joseph J. (1998), "A Disparaging Word," *Marketing Management*, Winter, 53–56.

12. Fletcher, David (2004), "Advertising Through Word-of-Mouth," *Brand Strategy*, June, 38–39.

13. Abu-Shalback Zid, Linda (2004), "Money Where Your Mouth Is," *Marketing Management*, 13(March/April), 7.

14. Hennig-Thurau, Thorsten, Kevin P. Gwinner, Gianfranco Walsh, Dwayne D. Gremler (2004), "Electronic Word-of-Mouth via Consumer Opinion Platforms: What Motivates Consumers to Articulate Themselves on the Internet?" *Journal of Interactive Marketing*, 18(1), 38–53.

15. See Bor, Robert, Morris Russell, Justin Parker and Linda Papadopoulos (no date), "Managing Disruptive Passengers: A Survey of the World's Airlines," http://www.skyrage.org/PDF/ACADEMIC/RBor.pdf. Accessed July 19, 2004; Schwab, William P. (2001), "Air Rage: Screaming for International Uniformity," http://www.skyrage.org/PDF/ACADEMIC/BSchwab.pdf. Accessed July 19th, 2004; Staff (2002), "Firefighter Fined E600 for Air Rage," *The Irish Times*, December 27, 6; Mcveigh, Karen (2003), "Jet Crews' Anger as Branson Kisses and Makes Up with Air Rage Star," *The Scotsman*, February 7, 5.

16. Chen, John S. (2004), "A Message From John Chen on Sybase's Statement of Values and Business Ethics," http://www.sybase.com/detail?id=1018482. Accessed July 19, 2004.

17. Dellande, Stephanie, Mary C. Gilly and John L. Graham (2004), "Gaining Compliance and Losing Weight: The Role of the Services Provider in Health Care Services," *Journal of Marketing*, 68(July), 78–91.

18. Bateson, John (2002), "Are Your Customers Good Enough For Your Service Business?" *Academy of Management Executive*, 16(4), 110–120.

19. Harley Davidson, Inc. (2004), "H.O.G.®," http://www.harley-davidson.com/ex/hog/template.asp?locale=en_US&bmLocale=en_US&fnc=hog. Accessed July 19, 2004.

# BIBLIOGRAPHY

Abu-Shalback Zid, Linda (2004), "Loyalty Doesn't Always Pay," *Marketing Management*, 13(May/June), 4.

Alba, Joseph W. and J. Wesley Hutchinson (1987), "Dimensions of Consumer Expertise," *Journal of Consumer Research*, 13 (March), 411–454.

All, Ann (2001), "Getting Along on ADA," ATM Marketplace.com, http://www.atmmarketplace.com/news_story.htm?i=10412. Accessed September 14, 2004.

Alpert, Andrew and Jill Auyer (2004), "The 1988-2000 Employment Projections: How Accurate Were They?" Washington, D.C.: Office of Occupational Statistics and Employment Projections, Bureau of Labor Statistics.

Bandura, Albert (1977), *Social Learning Theory*, Englewood Cliffs, NJ: Prentice-Hall.

Bandura, Albert and Daniel Cervone (1983), "Self-Evaluative and Self-Efficacy Mechanisms Governing the Motivational Effects of Goal Systems," *Journal of Personality and Social Psychology*, 45(5), 1017–1028.

Bateson, John (2002), "Are Your Customers Good Enough For Your Service Business?" *Academy of Management Executive*, 16(4), 110–120.

Bateson, J. E. G. (1985), "Self Service Consumer: An Exploratory Study," *Journal of Retailing*, 61(Fall), 49–76.

Bell, Chip and Ron Zemke (1992), *Managing Knock Your Socks Off Service*, New York: Amacom.

Bell-Gredler, Margaret E. (1986). *Learning and Instruction: Theory into Practice*, New York: Macmillan.

Bettman, James R. (1979), *An Information Processing Theory of Consumer Choice*, Reading, MA: Addison-Wesley.

Blanchard, Kenneth and Sheldon M. Bowles (1993), *Raving Fans*, New York: William Morrow.

Bloom, Benjamin, et al. (1956). *Taxonomy of Educational Objectives, Book 1: Cognitive Domain*, New York: Longman.

Boone, Christopher and Kelly A. Matthews (2003), "Self Check-out Systems: Defining Retailers as Leaders of the Pack," IDC Whitepaper commissioned by NCR Corporation, June.

Bor, Robert, Morris Russell, Justin Parker and Linda Papadopoulos (no date), "Managing Disruptive Passengers: A Survey of the World's Airlines." http://www.skyrage.org/PDF/ACADEMIC/RBor.pdf. Accessed July 19, 2004.

Bowen, David E. (1986), "Managing Customers as Human Resources in Service Organizations," *Human Resource Management*, 25(3), 371–383.

Bowers, Michael R., Charles L. Martin and Alan Luker (1990), "Trading Places: Employees as Customers, Customers as Employees," *Journal of Services Marketing*, 4(Spring), 55–69.

Build-A-Bear Workshops, Inc., http://www.buildabear.com/default.aspx. Accessed January 15, 2005.

Bulkeley, William M. (2004), "Cash, Credit—or Prints?" *The Wall Street Journal*. October 10, B1, B4.

Bureau of Transportation Statistics (2004), "Pocket Guide to Transportation." January, Washington, D.C.

Burton, Dawn (2002), "Consumer Education and Service Quality: Conceptual Issues and Practical Implications," *Journal of Services Marketing*, 16(2), 125–142.

Cambell, Anne (2004), "Teens Kicked Off Paradise for Smoking," *CruiseMates*, http://www.cruisemates.com/articles/humop/smoking.cfm. Accessed November 16, 2004.

Carnival Cruise Lines (2004), "What is the Non-Smoking Policy on the Paradise?" Frequently Asked Questions, http://www.carnival.com/CMS/FAQs/Paradise_Non_Smoking_ Policy.aspx. Accessed November 16, 2004.

Chen, John S. (2004), "A Message From John Chen on Sybase's Statement of Values and Business Ethics," http://www.sybase.com/detail?id=1018482. Accessed July 19, 2004.

Cialdini, Robert B. (1993), *Influence: The Psychology of Persuasion*, New York: Quill.

CNN/Money (2004), "Stewart Convicted on All Charges," *CNN/Money*, http://money.cnn.com/2004/03/05/news/companies/martha_verdict/. Accessed July 14, 2004.

Corporate University Xchange (2001), *Creating Smarter Customers*, New York: Corporate University Xchange.

CruiseReports (2003), "Up In Smoke," *CruiseLog November 2003*, http://www.cruise-reports.com/DailyLog/NewsArchive/November2003/DailyLog.htm. Accessed November 16, 2004.

CUNA (2003), "Discovery Conference emphasizes CU opportunities & partnerships," *Credit Union Magazine*, 69(8), 57–58.

Davis, Bob (1983), "Hundreds of Coleco's Adams Are Returned as Defective: Firm Blames User Manuals," *The Wall Street Journal*, November 20, 4.

Day, George S., John Deighton, Das Narayandas, Evert Gummesson, Shelby D. Hunt, C.K. Prahalad, Roland T. Rust and Steven M. Shugan (2004), "Invited Commentaries on 'Evolving to a New Dominant Logic for Marketing,'" *Journal of Marketing*, 68(January), 18–27.

Dellande, Stephanie, Mary C. Gilly and John L. Graham (2004), "Gaining Compliance and Losing Weight: The Role of the Services Provider in Health Care Services," *Journal of Marketing*, 68(July), 78–91.

Deterline, William A. (1992), "Feedback Systems," in H. Stolovich and E. Keeps (Eds.), *Handbook of Human Performance Technology*, Washington, D.C.: International Society for Performance and Instruction.

Donnelly, Jr., Jim (1999), "Beware of Negative Customer Expectations," *Bank Marketing*, 31(August), 60.

Dowling, Grahame R. and Mark Uncles (1997), "Do Loyalty Programs Really Work?" *Sloan Management Review*, Summer, 71–82.

Ellison, Sarah and Eric Bellman (2005), "Clean Water, No Profit," *The Wall Street Journal*, February 23, B1–B2.

Fidelity Investments (2004), "Retirement Planning Tools," http://personal.fidelity. com/planning/retirement/retiree/content/triageContent.shtml.cvsr. Accessed August 24, 2004.

Fleming, Malcolm and W. Howard Levie (1978), *Instructional Message Design*, Englewood Cliffs, NJ: Educational Technology Publications.

Fletcher, David (2004), "Advertising Through Word-of-Mouth," *Brand Strategy*, June, 38–39.

Florian, Ellen, Doris Burke and Jenney Mero (2004), "The Money Machines," *Fortune*, July 26, 150(2), 100–105.

Fournies, Ferdinand F. (1988), *Why Employees Don't Do What They're Supposed to Do And What To Do About It*, New York: Liberty Hall Press.

Fram, Eugene H. and Michael S. McCarthy (1999), "The True Price of Penalties," *Marketing Management*, Fall, 49–56.

Fry's Electronics, Inc. (2004), Returns, http://shop1.outpost.com/template/help/ index/FE30/Service3/Assistance/Left_Topics/A6ReturningPurchases/#08. Accessed September 9, 2004.

Gagne, Robert M. (1985), *The Conditions of Learning*, Chicago: Holt/Rinehart/ Winston.

Gap, Inc. (2004), Returns and Exchanges, http://www.gap.com/asp/cs_returns_ ex.asp?wdid=0. Accessed September 9, 2004.

Gilbert, Thomas F. (1996), *Human Competence: Engineering Worthy Performance*, Washington, D.C.: International Society for Performance Improvement.

Gobé, Marc (2001), *Emotional Branding*, New York: Allworth Press.

Greenberg, Paul A. (2001), "Nasty Return Policies Damage E-Shopper Relationships," *TechNewsWorld*, April 24, http://www.technewsworld.com/ story/9179.html. Accessed September 9, 2004.

Hansen, U. and T. Hennig (1996), "Wie competent sind Ihre Kunden? [How competent are your customers?]," *absatzwirtschaft*, 39 (October, special issue), 160–166.

Harley-Davidson, Inc. (2004), "H.O.G.®," http://www.harley-davidson.com/ ex/hog/template.asp?locale=en_US&bmLocale=en_US&fnc=hog. Accessed July 19, 2004.

Hennig-Thurau, Thorsten (2000), "Relationship Quality and Customer Retention Through Strategic Communication of Customer Skills," *Journal of Marketing Management*, 16, 55–79.

Hennig-Thurau, Thorsten, Kevin P. Gwinner, Gianfranco Walsh, Dwayne D. Gremler (2004), "Electronic Word-of-Mouth via Consumer Opinion Platforms: What Motivates Consumers to Articulate Themselves on the Internet?" *Journal of Interactive Marketing*, 18(1), 38–53.

Hennig-Thurau, Thorsten, Peter C. Honebein and Benoit Aubert (2005), "Unlocking Product Value Through Customer Education," *American Marketing Association Winter 2005 Educator's Conference*.

Herriott, Scott R. (1997), "Communication Channels in Markets: A Definition and Conceptualization," *Journal of Marketing Communications*, 3, 139–149.

Heskett, James L., W. Earl Sasser and Leonard A. Schlessinger (2003), *The Value-Profit Chain: Treat Employees Like Customers and Customers Like Employee*, New York: Free Press.

Hewlett Packard (2005), "Available Certifications," http://h10017.www1.hp.com/certification/americas/avail_certifications.html. Accessed February 24, 2005.

Honebein, Peter C. (2004), "Should Products Be Complex?" *American Marketing Association Winter 2004 Educator's Conference Proceedings*, 15(1), 321.

Honebein, Peter C. (1997). *Strategies for Effective Customer Education*. Chicago: NTC Books.

IBM Corporation (2004), User Engineering: Measures, http://www-306.ibm.com/ibm/easy/eou_ext.nsf/publish/2023. Accessed August 10, 2004.

IDEO, Inc. (2003), "Customer-driven Service for McDonalds," http://www.ideo com/portfolio/re.asp?x=50175. Accessed September 14, 2004.

Jewell, Mark (2005), "Dunkin' Donuts Evolves From No-Frills to Espresso and WiFi," *Reno Gazette Journal*, February 6, 3E–4E.

Johnson, Eric J., Steven Bellman and Gerald S. Lohse (2003), "Cognitive Lock-in and the Power Law of Practice," *Journal of Marketing*, 67(April), 62–75.

Johnson, Robert (2004), "Towards a Better Understanding of Service Excellence," *Managing Service Quality*, 14(2/3), 129–133.

Khemsurov, Monica (2004), "Sexing Up Victoria's Secret," *CNN Money*, http://money.cnn.com/2004/04/08/technology/business2_victoria/. Accessed July 14, 2004.

Kiviat, Barbara (2004), "May I Help You?" *Time*, September 6, 164(10).

Kontzer, Tony (2004), "Verizon Bets on Self Service," *Information Week*, January 28, 49.

Locke, Edwin A. (1986), *Generalizing from Laboratory to Field Settings: Research Findings From Industrial-Organizational Psychology, Organizational Behavior, and Human Resources Management*, Lexington, MA: Lexington Books.

Locke, Edwin A., Lise M. Saari, Karyll N. Shaw and Gary P. Latham (1981), "Goal Setting and Task Performance: 1969-1980," *Psychological Bulletin*, 90(1), 125–152.

Lunsford, J. Lynn (2004), "No Movie, No Frequent Flyer Plan—And No Gravity, Either," *The Wall Street Journal*, September 14, B1, B8.

Machalaba, Daniel (2003), "Trucker Rewards Customers for Good Behavior," *The Wall Street Journal*, September 9, B4.

Macromedia, Inc. (2005). "Macromedia Customer Participation Program," http://www.macromedia.com/macromedia/usability/. Accessed February 24, 2005.

Mage, Gene C. (2003), "Seal Up Seams In Service Delivery," *Health Care Registration: The Newsletter for Health Care Registration Professionals*, 13(Dec), 1–5.

Mager, Robert F. and Peter Pipe (1984), *Analyzing Performance Problems*, Belmont, CA: Lake Publishing.

Maher, Kris (2004), "The Jungle: Focus on Recruitment, Pay, and Getting Ahead," *The Wall Street Journal*, July 13, B6.

Majmudar, Nishad H. (2004), "Defibrillator Training Proves Useful," *The Wall Street Journal*, August 12, D3.

Martin, G. Neal (1999), "Smell: Can We Use It to Manipulate Behavior," Lecture Notes, http://www.mdx.ac.uk/www/psychology/staff/nmartin/rsa/rsa.html. Accessed September 17, 2004.

Mavis, Brian E. and Bertram E. Stoffelmayr (1994), "Multidimensional evaluation of monetary incentive strategies for weight control," *Psychological Record*, 44(Spring), 239–252.

Mcveigh, Karen (2003), "Jet Crews' Anger as Branson Kisses and Makes Up with Air Rage Star," *The Scotsman*, February 7, 5.

McWilliams, Gary (2004), "Analyzing Customers, Best Buy Decides Not All Are Welcome," *The Wall Street Journal*, November 8, A1, A8.

Meuter, Matthew L., Amy L. Ostrom, Robert I. Roundtree and Mary Jo Bitner (2000), "Self-Service Technologies: Understanding Customer Satisfaction with Technology-Based Service Encounters," *Journal of Marketing*, 64(July), 50–64.

Microsoft Corporation (1999), *Microsoft Windows User Experience*, Redmond, WA: Microsoft Press.

Mikkelson, Barbara and David P. Mikkelson (2002), Alka-Seltzer dramatically increased their sales by instructing consumers to use two tablets instead of one, http://www.snopes.com/business/genius/alka-seltzer.asp. Accessed August 23, 2004.

Miller, George A., Eugene Galanter and Karl H. Pribram (1986), *Plans and the Structure of Behavior*, New York: Adams-Bannister-Cox.

Mills, Peter, K. and J. H. Morris (1986), "Clients as 'Partial' Employees: Role Development in Client Participation," *Academy of Management Review*, 11(4), 726–735.

Mittal, Vikas and Mohanbir S. Sawhney (2001), "Learning and Using Electronic Information Products and Services: A Field Study," *Journal of Interactive Marketing*, 15 (1), 2–12.

Morton's Restaurant Group (2004), Frequent Questions, http://www.mortons.com/website/index.html. Accessed July 12, 2004.

myKB (2002), "ROI of Self Service," http://knowledgebase.mykb.com/Article_1B19F.aspx. Accessed February 5, 2005.

Nadler, Paul (2002), "Using the phone to tweak your overdraft policy," *American Banker*, 167(198), 7.

Naik, Gautam (2004), "The Smell of Success Isn't Always Sweet for Paul Knight," *The Wall Street Journal*, October 11, A1, A15.

Neder, Maria (2003), "Tyco Electronics Names Arrow Electronics Distributor of the Year," *PR Newswire*, May 14, 2003.

Newell, Allen and Herbert A. Simon (1972), *Human Problem Solving*, Englewood Cliffs, NJ: Prentice-Hall.

Nielsen, Jakob (1993), *Usability Engineering*, San Francisco: Morgan-Kaufman.

Nord, Walter R. and J. Paul Peter (1980), "A Behavior Modification Perspective on Marketing," *Journal of Marketing*, 44(Spring), 36–47.

Norman, Donald A. (no date), "Interaction Design for Automobile Interiors," http://www.jnd.org/dn.mss/InteractDsgnAutos.html. Accessed September 15, 2004.

Norman, Donald A. (1988), *The Psychology of Everyday Things*, New York: Basic Books.

Nussbaum, Bruce (2004), "The Power of Design," *Business Week*, May 17, 96.

Nussbaum, Bruce (2004), "The Best New Product Designs of the Year," *BusinessWeek*, July 5, http://www.businessweek.com/magazine/content/04_27/b3890601.htm. Accessed September 15, 2004.

OnStar Corporation (2004). What is OnStar? http://www.onstar.com/us_english/ jsp/whatisonstar/idont_whatisonstar.jsp. Accessed August 25, 2004.

Ortego, Joseph J. (1998), "A Disparaging Word," *Marketing Management*, Winter, 53–56.

Parasuraman, A., Leonard L. Berry and Valarie A. Zeithaml (1991), "Refinement and Reassessment of the SERVQUAL Scale," *Journal of Retailing*, 67(Winter), 420-450.

People Track, Inc. (2005), "Customer Participation," http://www.people-trak.com/pt/services/index.cfm?fuseaction=participation. Accessed February 24, 2005.

Pervin, Lawrence A. (1989), *Goal Concepts in Personality and Social Psychology*, Hillsdale, NJ: Lawrence Erlbaum & Associates.

Peter, J. Paul and Walter R. Nord (1982), "A Clarification and Extension of Operant Conditioning Principles in Marketing," *Journal of Marketing*, 46(Summer), 102–107.

Prahalad, C.K. (2004), "The Cocreation of Value," *Journal of Marketing*, 68(1), 23.

Prahalad, C.K. and Venkatram Ramaswamy (2000), "Co-opting Customer Competence," *Harvard Business Review*, 78(January), 79–90.

Ramstad, Evan (2004), "Hong Kong's Electronic-Money Card Is a Hit," *The Wall Street Journal*, February 19, B3.

Rayport, Jeffrey R. and Bernard J. Jaworski, "Best Face Forward," *Harvard Business Review*, 82(December), 47–58.

Reed Baker, Matthew (2004), "Welcome to the Fast Track," *Forbes*, 173 (FYI Spring), 66–67.

Reichheld, Frederick F. (2003), "The One Number You Need to Grow," *Harvard Business Review*, 18(December), 46–54.

Rich, Laura (2004), "Self Service: Help Yourself," CIO Insight, http://www.cioinsight.com/article2/0,1397,1610171,00.asp. Accessed February 5, 2005.

Ross, Gary (2004), "CDW Announces IDC White Paper Offering Best Practices for I.T. Purchasing Decisions," *PR Newswire*, February 25.

Rothschild, Michael L. and William C. Gadis (1981), "Behavioral Learning Theory: Its Relevance to Marketing and Promotions," *Journal of Marketing*, 45(Spring), 70–78.

Roush, Chris (1999). *Inside Home Depot: How One Company Revolutionized an Industry Through the Relentless Pursuit of Growth*, New York: McGraw-Hill Professional.

Sander, Ernest (2004), "The 'Soup Nazi' Expands," *The Wall Street Journal*, September 10, B1, B3.

Santos, Jessica and Jonathan Boote (2003), "A Theoretical Exploration and Model of Consumer Expectations, Post-Purchase Affective States, and Affective Behavior," *Journal of Consumer Behavior*, 3(2), 142–156.

Saranow, Jennifer (2004), "Show, Don't Tell," *The Wall Street Journal*, March 22, R9.

Saranow, Jennifer (2004), "Check It Out: Incentives to Pay Bills Online," *The Wall Street Journal*, December 8, D2.

Saranow, Jennifer (2004), "The Puncture Wound I Got for Christmas; Theft Prevention Behind Rise in Hard-to-Open Packaging; World's Worst Paper Cut," *The Wall Street Journal*, December 30, D1.

Schlosser, Julie (2005), "Scanning for Dollars," *Fortune*, January 10, 60.

Schlosser, Julie (2004), "Cashing In on the New World of Me," *Fortune*, December 13, 244–250.

Schmitt, Bernd (2003), *Customer Experience Management: A Revolutionary Approach To Connecting with Your Customers*, New York: Wiley.

Schwab, William P. (2001), "Air Rage: Screaming for International Uniformity," http://www.skyrage.org/PDF/ACADEMIC/BSchwab.pdf. Accessed July 19, 2004.

Silverman, Steve (no date), "The Pudding Guy," *Useless Information*. http://home.nycap.rr.com/useless/pudding/index.html. Accessed May 20, 2005.

Sloane, Martin (no date), "The Infamous Texas Toothpaste Testers," *Martin Sloane's Classic Columns*, http://www.siteforsavings.com/content_mas/colclasic.htm#interesting%20letters. Accessed November 16, 2004.

Speer, Jack (2005), "A Former CEO Glimpses Airlines' Future," NPR *Morning Edition* February 3, http://www.npr.org/templates/story/story.php?storyId=4475981. Accessed February 3, 2005.

Spiegelman, Rande (2004), "How Much Should You Save For Retirement? Play The Percentages," Charles Schwab & Co., Inc., http://www.schwab.com/SchwabNOW/navigation/mainFrameSet/0,4528,866,00.html?dest=siretirement&orig=retirement&ebmk=acquisition. Accessed August 23, 2004.

Staff (2002), "Firefighter Fined E600 for Air Rage," *The Irish Times*, December 27, 6.

Staff (1994), "Why Comparisons Work," *Adweek Western Edition*, 44(7).

Stringer, Kortney (2004), "If At First You Do Succeed..." *The Wall Street Journal*, July 12, R4.

Suchman, Lucy A. (1987). *Plans and Situated Actions*. Cambridge: Cambridge University Press.

Swinyard, William R. (2003), "The Effect of Salesperson Mood, Shopper Behavior, and Store Type on Customer Service," *Journal of Retailing and Consumer Services*, 10(2003), 323–333.

Temkin, Bruce D. (2005), Self-Service Shift Requires Improved Usability, Forrester Research, Inc., January 13, http://www.forrester.com/Research/Document/Excerpt/0,7211,36253,00.html. Accessed February 3, 2005.

Tolsky, Ben (no date). The Soup Nazi Headquarters, http://users.aol.com/rynocub/soupnazi.htm. Accessed September 26, 2004.

U.S. Small Business Administration (2002). ADA Guide for Small Business. http://www.usdoj.gov/crt/ada/smbustxt.htm. Accessed September 14, 2004.

Useem, Jerry (2003), "Gerald Zaltman Can Read Your Mind," *Fortune*, January 20, http://www.fortune.com/fortune/subs/article/0,15114,405574,00.html. Accessed August 10, 2004.

Van Houwelinger, Jeannet H. and W. Fred Van Raaij (1989), "The Effect of Goal Setting and Daily Electronic Feedback on In-Home Energy Use," *Journal of Consumer Research*, 16(June), 98–105.

Vargo, Stephen L. and Robert F. Lusch (2004), "Evolving to a New Dominant Logic for Marketing," *Journal of Marketing*, 68 (January), 1–17.

Warren, Audrey (2004), "Frequent Flyers Line Up to Bypass Extra Searches," *The Wall Street Journal*, July 21, D9.

Wasserman, Todd (2003), "Dell Warns Shoppers away from Retailers," *Adweek*, 44(46), 8.

Woo, Ka-shing and Henry K.Y. Fock (2004), "Retaining and Divesting Customers: An Exploratory Study of Right Customers, 'At Risk' Right Customers, and Wrong Customers," *Journal of Services Marketing*, 18(3), 187–197.

Wood, Robert E. (1986), "Task Complexity: Definition of the Construct," *Organizational Behavior and Human Decision Processes*, 37(1), 60–82.

Zaltman, Gerald (2003), *How Customers Think*, Cambridge, MA: Harvard Business School Press.

Zeithaml, Valarie A., Leonard L. Berry and A. Parasuraman (1991), "Understanding Customer Expectations of Service," *Sloan Business Review*, 32(Spring), 39–49.

Zeithaml, Valarie A., Leonard L. Berry and A. Parasuraman (1993), "The Nature and Determinants of Customer Expectations of Service," *Journal of the Academy of Marketing Science*, 21(1), 1–12.

Zeithaml, Valarie A., Mary Jo Bitner and Dwayne D. Gremler (2006). *Services Marketing: Integrating Customer Focus Across the Firm*, 4th Edition. New York: McGraw-Hill.

Zid, Linda Abu-Shalback (2004), "Money Where Your Mouth Is," *Marketing Management*, 13(March/April), 7.

# INDEX

*Note*: Page numbers in *italic* type refer to figures or tables.

government, 213–214
Green, Gloria, 68

# H
handoffs, 125–126
Hansen, Ursula, 12
Harley Owner's Group (HOG), 220–221
Healthy Choice, 145
Hennig-Thurau, Thorsten, 12
Hewlett-Packard, 177–178, 192
hidden value, 55–83
 causes of problems, 76–78, 77
 identifying problems, 61–71
 model of, 60
 understanding problems, 71, 71–78
 unlocking, 10–13, 78–82
 value mapping to discover, 56–61
Hilton Hotels, 129
Hoch, Stephen J., 94
*Hog Tales*, 221
Home Depot, 4, 14, 17, 100, 103, 129,
 178–179, 184–185, 194, 219
home improvement support tools, 194
home inspectors, 209
*Human Competence*, 46
Huxley, Aldous, 20

# I
IBM, 218
ideal expectations, 97–99
iDrive, 133
image consultants, 209
incentive(s), 142–168, *see also* rewards for
 customers
 behavioral engineering model, 46
 cautions, 145–146
 conditioning and, 39
 consumer study involving, 52
 Coproduction Experience Model,
  21–22, 23
 need for, 146–154
 negative reinforcement and, 143–145,
  161–162
 positive reinforcement and, 143–146,
  148–149, 152–160
 punishment and, 143–145, 162–167
 scenarios, 147
 strategy, 144
 tactics for improving, 26

*Influence: The Psychology of Persuasion*, 43
information
 access enhanced by, 135–137
 behavioral engineering model, 46
 chunking, 124
 sources of controllable, 198–215
information processing, consumer choice
 and, 48–49
initial success factor, 172–173, 173
instruments, in behavioral engineering
 model, 46
Intel, 89–90
interface design, 132–135
internal feedback, 106–107
interviews, for customer feedback, 75
Interwoven, 203
intolerable expectations, 104
iPOD MINI, 133
Irshad, Mohamed, 78

# J
Jevons, W. Stanley, 55
Johnson, Robert, 68

# K
Kelleher, Herb, 15
knowledge
 behavioral engineering model, 46
 content-oriented, 171–172, 172
 process-oriented, 171–172, 172
 user-centered design, 47
knowledge of results, 106, *see also*
 feedback
Kroger, 129

# L
labor costs, 7
Ladies of Harley, 221
laggard, 18
Lake Tahoe ski resort, 148, 152
Lands' End, 117
Lanham Act, 210–211
law, communication consistency and,
 215–217
law enforcement, 207
learning domains, 43
learning, sources of customer, 198–215
Lemmon, Jack, 45
Levie, Howard, 136

# BE PART OF OUR NEXT BOOK

We would like to invite you to become a cocreator, codesigner, and coproducer of our next book. For this first book, we collected hundreds of stories from people like you about customer performance in various coproduction experiences. As part of our ongoing research, we want to collect a thousand more stories. You can help.

We are looking for stories that describe how companies help (or don't help) customers perform. If you decide to participate in this activity, the stories you tell should reflect your personal experience as:

- A customer
- An employee working with customers
- Your observation of another customer

Stories should be at least 200 words in length and include appropriate facts about location, situation, specific behaviors, and outcomes. See the stories we've included in this book or on our website for examples.

Submit your stories one of two ways:

- By a form on our website: www.doityourselfcustomers.com
- By email: stories@doityourselfcustomers.com

Submissions become the property of the authors.

## About TEXERE

**Texere**, a progressive and authoritative voice in business publishing, brings to the global business community the expertise and insights of leading thinkers. Our books educate, enlighten, and entertain, and provide an intersection where our authors and our readers share cutting edge ideas, practices, and innovative solutions. Texere seeks to cultivate, enhance, and disseminate information that illuminates the global business landscape.

www.thomson.com/learning/texere

## About the typeface

This book was set in 10.5/14pt Bembo. Bembo was cut by Francesco Griffo for the Venitian printer Aldus Manutius to publish in 1495 *De Aetna* by Cardinal Pietro Bembo. Stanley Morison supervised the design of Bembo for the Monotype Corporation in 1929. The Bembo is a readable and classical typeface because of its well-proportioned letterforms, functional serifs, and lack of peculiarities.

## Library of Congress Cataloging-in-Publication Data

Honebein, Peter C., 1963-
    Creating do-it-yourself customers : how great customer experiences build great companies / Peter C. Honebein and Roy F. Cammarano.
    p. cm.
    Includes bibliographical references and index.
    1. Consumer education. 2. Customer relations. I. Cammarano, Roy F. II. Title.

TX335.H5525 2005
640'.73—dc22

2005019734